"If you are at all interested in making a film of your own, this book is where it's at. If you are not interested in making a film of your own, read it purely for the ~~~~~~~~~e, straight-shooting fun of finding out how guys like Gaspard, Newton and 'nd some valuable time that might be better spent on food, d~~~~~~~~ kick over food, drink and sex any day if it mea~

— George Romero (Director, Ni~ ~~~ Day of the Dead, Land of the Dead)

"Fine book, clear, precise and infinitely pr~ ~~~~spard and Newton tell you how to do it from A to Z. The only thing they leave out is the blood, sweat and upon occasion tears of joy — that's where you come in."
— Tom DiCillo (Director/Writer, Living in Oblivion)

"This terrific little book explains how to make every penny count on the often arduous journey from script to screen."
— John Carpenter (Director, Halloween, Starman, Escape from New York)

"All the writer needs is a blank page to start a screenplay. But if you want to direct, get Digital Filmmaking 101. It will lead you step by step into the new age of movies."
— Amy Holden Jones (Writer, Mystic Pizza, Indecent Proposal, Beethoven)

"Whether your budget is in the millions, the thousands, or pocket change, the lessons in this book will help you get your cinematic vision on-screen. It's like a film school education between two covers."
— Bob Clark (Director, A Christmas Story, Porky's, Black Christmas, Murder by Decree)

"Almost everything I had to learn the hard way can be found in this book. Save yourself the heartache and read it before you make your first film."
— John McNaughton (Director, Wild Things, Mad Dog and Glory, Henry: Portrait of a Serial Killer)

"The pragmatically brilliant authors of this tome prove that, with the current digital revolution, there is quite literally no excuse for not making your film. They remove many of the fears and anxieties of those first steps of filmmaking, and unravel the mysteries that seem so daunting to most potential directors and producers. Follow their instructions, and you could find the perfect cure for the procrastination that has haunted your burgeoning career."
— Evan Shapiro (Executive Vice President and General Manager, Independent Film Channel)

"Gentle readers, heed my words: Before you pick up a camera, pick up this book! Full of practical advice from two guys who've been there, Digital Filmmaking 101 breaks down the daunting filmmaking process into manageable steps. Every aspiring filmmaker — and quite a few seasoned ones — can benefit from Newton and Gaspard's hard-earned lessons."
— Peter Rudy (Co-writer/Co-director, No Sleep 'til Madison)

"Digital Filmmaking 101 takes the mystery out of filmmaking. If you have a good story and the tenacity and resourcefulness to see it through to the screen, this book will connect the dots to help you finish the project — and it encourages you to experience the fun of film-making as well. If you want to become an indie filmmaker, this is a book you should read."
— Barbara Morgan (Executive Director, Austin Film Festival)

"Most first-time filmmakers suffer the same mistakes over and over again. I wish a magic Filmmaking Fairy would slip this book under their pillow the night after they first utter the words, 'I want to make a movie.' Then again, they could just buy it."
— Richard Schenkman (Director, The Pompatus of Love, Went to Coney Island on a Mission from God... Be Back by Five)

"Dale and John's book gives filmmakers the critical tools to make their film. It's a great guide for beginners and experienced filmmakers alike. So many filmmakers skip the planning process and their films suffer because of it. This book makes the planning process easy and can only improve the filmmaking."
— Jason Carney (Festival Director, Phoenix Film Festival)

"At a time when technique and planning seem to have been erased from most filmmakers' agendas, this book is critical. It may actually save both producers and audiences precious dollars and keep them from unneeded angst. Before you DYI, do yourself a favor and read this book!"
— Rajendra Roy (Artistic Director, Hamptons International Film Festival)

"If you are even thinking about making a movie — get this book. Gaspard and Newton's comprehensive insight into all aspects of independent film production, given in their best-buddy-like manner, make it an invaluable source of inspiration and vital information for filmmakers at all levels of the craft. Don't load your camcorder without reading *Digital Filmmaking 101* — this is inspiration at its best!"
— Mark Bosko (Author, *The Complete Independent Movie Marketing Handbook*)

"Great fun to read and packed with valuable information learned by actually doing what they're talking about. They cover everything from the initial dream to legal considerations to production phases to self-distribution options, with the enthusiasm of friends hoping to encourage fellow independent filmmakers on minimal budgets."
— Christopher P. Jacobs (University of North Dakota film instructor, and producer-director of five no-budget digital features)

"*Digital Filmmaking 101* isn't for everyone, just anyone who wants to make the most of the incredible opportunities shooting digital affords every independent filmmaker on the planet. Dale Newton and John Gaspard have explained the technical and artistic aspects of digital in such non-technical, user-friendly terms, this book is bound to shorten your learning curve and economic outlay no matter how practiced a filmmaker you are. Very highly recommended."
— Jeffrey M. Freedman (Consulting Producer/Writer, *Vivaldi*)

"This book gives you everything you need to know about creating a low-budget film. This is all you need to have (besides a camera and a dream) to get your movie made."
— Matthew Terry (Screenwriter/teacher/columnist for *www.hollywoodlitsales.com*)

"Strong, smart, funny advice for independent filmmakers from people who've gone through the process more than once — and lived to tell about it."
— Peter Tolan (Co-creator, *Rescue Me* and *The Job*; Screenwriter, *Analyze This*, *Just Like Heaven*, *My Fellow Americans*)

"These guys don't seem to have missed a thing when it comes to how to make a digital movie for peanuts. It's a helpful and funny guide for beginners and professionals alike."
— Jonathan Demme (Academy Award–winning Director of *The Silence of the Lambs*)

"Gaspard and Newton are the undisputed champs of straight talk when it comes to moviemaking."
— Timothy Rhys (Publisher and Editor, *MovieMaker* Magazine & *MovieMaker.com*

"Simply put, this is the best book on digital moviemaking I've yet read."
— *Screentalk* Magazine

"Cheap is cool. John Gaspard and Dale Newton have compiled a great primer and check-list on modern micro-budget filmmaking. Getting into the game, or getting back in, this is the book to have."
— Whit Stillman (Director/Writer, *Metropolitan*, *The Last Days of Disco*, *Barcelona*)

DIGITAL FILMMAKING 101

AN ESSENTIAL GUIDE
TO PRODUCING LOW-BUDGET MOVIES

SECOND EDITION

DALE NEWTON & JOHN GASPARD

Published by Michael Wiese Productions
3940 Laurel Canyon Blvd. #1111
Studio City, CA 91604
tel. 818.379.8799
fax 818.986.3408
mw@mwp.com
www.mwp.com

Cover Design: MWP
Book Layout: Gina Mansfield Design
Editor: Paul Norlen

Printed by McNaughton & Gunn, Inc., Saline, Michigan
Manufactured in the United States of America

© 2007 Dale Newton & John Gaspard

Library of Congress Cataloging-in-Publication Data

Newton, Dale, 1957-
> Digital filmmaking 101 : an essential guide to producing low-budget
movies
>/ Dale Newton & John Gaspard. -- 2nd ed.
>   p. cm.
> Includes bibliographical references.
  ISBN-10 1932907238
  ISBN-13 9781932907230
> 1. Motion pictures--Production and direction. 2. Digital video. I.
>Gaspard, John, 1958- II. Title.
> PN1995.9.P7N47 2007
> 791.4302'33--dc22
>   2006036459

Table of Contents

Acknowledgments

We always knew that filmmaking was a collaborative art, but we had no idea that a crowd was required to write a book as well. There are many people to thank for their help and support in putting this book together. Since we're big supporters of the alphabet, we'll do this in that order:

Randy Adamsick, Robin Alper, Bruce V. Assardo, James Babcock, Soodabeh Babcock, Jeff Baustert, William Bayer, Tom Belanger, Daniel J. Berks, Michael Brillantes, Jeff Butcher, Julie Chang, Ruth Charny, Al Cohn, Patrick Coyle, Daniel Curran, Wade Danielson, Michael de Avila, Victoria Eide, Heidi Ehalt, Beth Gilleland, Richard Glatzer, Trent Harris, Walter Hart, Julie Hartley, Jess Hill, Jay Horan, Jennifer Howe, Rachel Katz, Janusz Kaminski, Sean King, Ted King, Seth Kittay, Marc Kramer, Michael Paul Levin, Tom Lieberman, Steve Lustgarten, Jane Minton (IFP North), Steve Molton, Peter Moore, Eric Mueller, Nicola Muoio, Liza Nagle, Jerry Nelson, Roger Nygard, Andrew Peterson, Daniel Polsfuss, Dave Reynolds, Tim Rhys (*MovieMaker* Magazine), Deb Rose, Richard Seres, Donna Smith, Nelle Stokes, Eric Tretbar, Mark Tusk, Thomas Vitale, Cynthia Widlund, and Amelia Oriani (for her excellent poof reading).

Special thanks to Kathy, Jenny, and Holly for their infinite patience, Amy Gaspard for her continued support, and to all the actors and crews who have made our movies possible.

Introduction

Now you've done it.

You opened this book because you want to make a movie... if only you knew how... if only you had enough money. Well, your life just got complicated because we wrote this book to tell you how to make your feature-length movie a reality and how to do it on an ultra-low budget.

You hold in your hand a guide to making your dream come true. Now what do you do?

It's up to you, but let us tell you about the path we chose that led us to writing this book about digital moviemaking. It might help you decide.

The two earlier versions of this book, *Persistence of Vision: An Impractical Guide to Producing a Feature Film for Under $30,000* and the re-named *Digital Filmmaking 101: An Essential Guide to Producing Low-Budget Movies*, passed along everything we learned from doing three independent low-budget feature movies.

The movies were *Resident Alien, Beyond Bob*, and *Grown Men* — a science-fiction comedy romance, a romantic-comedy ghost story, and a comic-drama about what it means to be a grown man. Of course, there were trials and tribulations in making them, as well as some of the best fun we've had in our lives.

We love film. We're products of the home-movie boom in the 1950s. Well, actually byproducts, because, in the true spirit of independent filmmakers, we each started filmmaking using 8mm cameras that were castoffs from our uncles. There's nothing like the excitement of looking at the film after it comes back from the processor or splicing together a scene out of your shots or realizing you're part of a 100-year chain linking back to the Lumière brothers' first movies. Like most filmmakers, between films we also tried out film's electronic cousin, videotape. We even found jobs working with video. But our first love was always film.

Poster art for Beyond Bob, Resident Alien, *and* Grown Men.

It's a measure of the magnitude of the digital-film revolution that when we were planning to embark on our third feature film, *Grown Men*, it quickly became clear that we would shoot it on digital video. We also realized that we might never shoot film again, at least not when we were putting up the budget.

There had been signs for a half-dozen years that a revolution was in the making. The advent of low-cost non-linear editing systems and inexpensive high-quality formats like Hi8mm and S-VHS were changing how filmmakers edited and how documentary filmmakers shot. When digital-video formats entered the arena with broadcast quality and price tags that were within the reach of filmmakers' personal finances, the revolution burst onto the streets. The movie products from these new tools have proven good enough to be transferred to film stock for theater presentation and good enough for cable television and home video, which are the most common distribution routes for low-budget, independent movies.

Now, far be it from us to suggest film is dead. It's a well-loved format that is deeply imbedded in our perceptions of what cinematic storytelling is, and it's survived virtually unchanged for over 100 years. As moviegoers, when we see the look of a film, we've been visually trained to settle back and fall into the story being told. Film's not going away anytime soon, but on the other hand, independent filmmaking won't ever be the same again. Digital moviemaking further loosens the budget shackles on movie production, and lightweight, moderately priced, flexible equipment creates new opportunities for those of us working on the fringes of the movie world.

Also, the Internet and the continual invention of new ways to communicate on it promise to revolutionize the second half of the moviemaking process — getting your movie to an audience. The gates of distribution in theaters have long been guarded by the large corporations that run the Hollywood movie machine. Only a small percentage of little movies were ever granted permission to pass into wide distribution. Using the Internet, many independent filmmakers have now found ways to circumvent the Hollywood system and are delivering their movies directly to consumers.

All of these changes have turned the two of us into digital moviemakers. The quality of the format and its low cost fit our possible audiences and our budgets. And this book tells you everything we've learned about making digital movies.

As we write this book, digital moviemaking means shooting on one of the digital videotape formats, but undoubtedly other developments won't be far behind.

What we won't be talking about are shooting and editing on motion-picture film. So if that's your plan, get a copy of the earlier film edition of this book. If a digital movie is your goal, don't worry that you're missing good stuff from that earlier book. In this digital edition, we've kept the parts that are universal to movie storytelling and the parts that tell you how to turn the chaos of a movie production into an actual finished movie. And for this second edition, we've also included fresh examples, updated information, and new insights on digital-movie production.

The one disadvantage to the fast pace of change in digital production is that this book started to be outdated the moment we typed this sentence. The technology is changing faster than software developers change Porsches. Then again, every book on digital filmmaking is going to be behind the times before it reaches the bookstore shelf. But if you're an independent moviemaker (the polite way of saying "mostly impoverished moviemaker"), that's not all bad. Outdated technology is cheap, and it still does the job. And, even though the technology changes, the techniques for doing a professional-looking movie on a shoestring budget apply whether you're making it on digital videotape or the latest and greatest technology.

These techniques served us well. We used them when we shot our first two feature films in four weekends each. *Resident Alien* was described as "the best low-budget independent project ever to come out of the area" by a big-city newspaper critic in Minnesota, which was high praise given the large number of independent films done in the metropolitan area where we live. *Beyond Bob* received a bronze award at an international film festival up against other films with budgets close to a million dollars. Studio executives and distributors who saw the films guessed that they had casts from New York or Los Angeles and had budgets in the million-dollar range. In truth, the casts were all from the talented pool of actors in our area, and our budgets were 30 times less than guessed.

Our techniques put all of your tiny budget up on the screen where it helps to tell your story. With our first digital feature, *Grown Men*, we used these methods along with new digital techniques that saved us a bundle in production and postproduction costs, so we could dedicate our efforts to getting a great story on the screen, rather than to raising funds and searching for deals on lab work.

If digital video had been available, we could have shot a half-dozen feature films for the cost of our first two 16mm movies. Because independent movies are financially risky, it's important to keep your budget low to reduce the financial stress of the production, letting you spend more time doing what you love — making your movie.

Now that we've told you what this book will do, let's take a moment to cover what it won't do. This book won't spend a lot of time on movie history and theory. There are lots of good books on those topics, some listed in our bibliography. We're here to help you get your project finished, so expect nuts-and-bolts, down-to-brass-tacks, practical advice on how to take your movie from a nagging idea in a corner of your brain to the glowing screen in front of your audience. The new digital-video tools can do great things, but owning a hammer doesn't mean you know how to build a house. We'll tell you what you need to know in order to put these new tools to use creating a professional-quality production.

But that doesn't mean it will be easy. Some people will tell you that making your own movie is impossible. We've heard that, and so have lots of other moviemakers. What makes independent movies happen is a fierce persistence of vision — a complete unwillingness to give up even when all signs and reason say you should. Be sure you have a bunch of this persistence stored up in the closet, in the attic, and under the basement steps before you start. You'll need all that you can get your hands on.

Besides a little bit of money and a lot of persistence, you'll need a strong vision and some creativity. If you've got these ingredients, we'll be happy to be your guides in putting them all together into a movie.

We realize that the readers of this book may have a wide range of experience and knowledge, so we've tried to balance our presentation so we don't talk down to people who've done a lot of film and video work and so we don't confuse those just starting out. Undoubtedly, we'll fail sometimes. So if you find yourself at any point patronized or perplexed, please accept our apologies in advance.

Well, have you decided to take a shot at that dream of making your own feature-length movie? If so, hop on board for a wild ride.

Chapter 1

The Dream ~ *Taking a Leap*

Everything we're about to tell you is wrong.

Really?

Well, no. Not really.

However, a healthy dose of skepticism will help sustain you on the long journey that lies before you. The process of making a digital feature requires breaking lots of rules. Sometimes all the rules. Even the rules we've laid out in this book.

However, if nothing else, the rules in this book can act as a good starting point and touchstone for you to return to as you make your way through the preproduction, production, and postproduction processes.

And how, you impatiently ask, do you start on this amazing, frustrating, and often exhilarating journey?

With a dream.

≈ ● ≈

They used to call moviemaking a "silver addiction," referring to the old days when silver salts were used to create film stocks. Although you won't need film stock to make your movie, you will need that addiction. And it better be a strong one. It has to be, because often the dream of making your movie is all that carries you over the long days/weeks/months/years that it takes to go from idea to screen.

Since you're reading this book, odds are that you already have at least the beginnings of a dream. You have:

- A story you're dying to tell,
- A character you'd love to see developed, or
- An idea or issue you're burning to explore.

The next step is to look at that dream with a cold, realistic eye: Is it a reasonable dream? Can you produce it with few resources?

While there's certainly no absolute answer, there is a ballpark that you should at least try to play in if you're going to work at this level. For example, is your story idea a historical costume drama, involving large crowd scenes and multiple, historically-accurate locations? If so, then keep dreaming. Or is your idea a small, contemporary dramatic (romance, comedy, suspense, horror, farce, mystery, melodrama, science-fiction) story that can take place in just a few locations with a handful of characters? Great. Now you're in the ballpark.

Once you've defined your dream, you're ready to take the next important step. Start telling people that you're going to make a movie. It doesn't matter where. At a cocktail party, after church, on a bus, or at the water cooler. It also doesn't really matter who. Your parents. Your significant other. Your co-workers. Your dentist.

It only matters that you say it out loud. "I'm going to make a movie."

Why do you have to say it out loud to someone else? Two reasons. The first is that, since this is a statement most people aren't used to hearing, you're bound to get some interesting responses. Responses along the lines of, "What's it about?" "Where are you getting the money?" and the best of all, "Great. Can I help?"

While all these questions are valid and important, it's the last one that you're really listening for, because once you've got the dream, the next step is to get other people excited about it. You need other people excited about your project because there's virtually no way you can do it all alone.

The second reason you should begin telling people that you're going to make a movie — saying it often and out loud — is because it takes your dream and begins to make it real. Just saying it isn't going to make it happen, of course, but it does put your pride on the line. You're more likely to push forward if your friends start asking, "Whatever happened to that movie thing you were going to do?"

It also makes the idea more concrete, and it raises other questions that you have to start thinking about. When will you start shooting? Where will the equipment come from? How will you fund it? Who's going to be in it? When is it going to be done? How are you going to edit it?

The following chapters will provide you with the means to answer those questions. But nobody's going to ask the questions until you make the statement... out loud.

"I'm going to make a movie." (Congratulations. You've just taken the first step.)

$$\approx \bullet \approx$$

Making a feature-length movie, even for someone who's done it before, is a daunting process. For someone who's never done it, it can be downright overwhelming. Take solace that it isn't one long process, but is instead a series of discrete and attainable steps. Each step leads logically to the next.

You also don't have to navigate these unfamiliar waters without charts. Others have done this before, or at least something similar. The model for making a digital feature is very similar to making any type of feature-length project, whether it's a low-budget Roger Corman–style masterpiece or a mega-mondo-budget Hollywood spectacular.

Reading this book and others on writing, producing, and selling movies can provide valuable background. Taking classes can be good preparation on specific parts of the process. Working on other people's movies (regardless of the budget) can be an education in itself on what to do and what not to do.

One of the best sources of information we've found is people who have made a feature before, whether on film or digitally. They're generally more than happy to talk to you. They'll mention a few pitfalls to watch out for, recommend some cast and crew people, suggest who else to turn to for free advice, and maybe even volunteer to help. At least, that's been our experience.

If there's one thing we learned, it's that dreams are contagious, and you should try to infect as many people as possible with yours. You have a long, challenging journey ahead, and you'll need their help if you're going to start — not to mention finish — a digital movie.

Regardless of the length of your journey, there is a destination — the moment when the finished movie is projected in front of an audience. And at this moment you can see the fruits of your labor — your dream — come to life. The audience laughs. They cry. They gasp. They applaud.

And your dream has become reality.

Chapter 2

The Script ~ *If It Ain't on the Page...*

Analogy #1: Just as the basement is the foundation for your house, so too is the screenplay the foundation for your movie. A strong foundation makes for a stronger house and a stronger movie. However, unlike your basement, you can't fill up your screenplay with extra stuff you're not using. There's just no room in your digital movie, in your shooting schedule, or in your budget.

Analogy #2: Your screenplay is your road map. It tells you, your cast, and your crew where you're headed and how you're going to get there. Without a good road map, you might make it to your destination but not before wasting a lot of time and money, two commodities that are in short supply.

A dramatic feature-length movie is only as good as its screenplay and rarely any better. While this is certainly common knowledge, you'd be amazed at the number of filmmakers (and we're not just pointing fingers at Hollywood here; independents are just as guilty) who dive into production with a screenplay that simply isn't ready to be shot.

Therefore, be prepared to spend a lot of time on your script. It's a difficult process, but you'll be happier about it in the end, and the results will show in your finished production. Making a good movie out of a bad script is not unlike the proverbial silk purse and sow's ear. It's simply not going to happen.

The Basics

While this chapter isn't intended to provide you with an exhaustive course in screenwriting, it will give you the basics you need to construct a script that can be shot on your ultra-low budget.

(For further reading on the finer points of screenwriting, along with sample formats, please refer to the appendix. There are a number of excellent books out there on screenwriting; however, remember the words of screenwriter William Goldman, "Nobody knows anything." For every absolute rule someone states about screenwriting, you can always find several examples of successful features that have broken that rule. The appendix also lists where you can buy or download screenplays of existing movies, which can be an excellent educational resource.)

Story

As an independent moviemaker with no budget to speak of, story is your friend, your biggest asset, and your secret weapon. The reality of making movies on this scale is that you're not going to impress a distributor or festival planner with your big-name stars (unless you're married to one), your exotic locations (unless you live in one), or your stunning crowd scenes (unless you have a stunningly large family). You simply don't have the bucks for them.

That leaves you with story, the one place where you can compete head-to-head with the Hollywood big kids. You can have a better story in your $8,000 digital movie than there is in some $100 million box-office bomb starring the latest rock star/actor in a remake of some baby-boomer Saturday-morning cartoon.

Story is your best selling point. If the story is great, shortcomings in lighting, videography, sound, set design, and so on will be forgotten as the viewer is drawn into the narrative. Consider the early films of D. W. Griffith or Charlie Chaplin. No sound, only natural light, black and white, static camera shots. Yet they are still powerful, entertaining, and remembered today because they presented engaging characters in interesting stories.

The Three-Act Structure

We're big fans of the three-act structure: Act One (known as The Beginning), in which you establish characters' motivation and set the scene, which leads to an inciting moment, catharsis, crisis, or conflict that requires the main character to make a decision about what he or she wants to do.

Act Two (also known as The Middle), in which the main character faces challenges and obstacles to carrying out that decision, leading to a "scene of recognition" in which the character reaffirms his or her commitment to the decision.

Act Three (you guessed it, The End), in which the story reaches its climax, and the main character succeeds or fails to achieve what he or she wants.

Of course, this isn't the only way to structure a screenplay, but it's tried and true, and 90% of the successful and well-loved movies follow this pattern.

There are, of course, exceptions to the rule. Quentin Tarantino took the classic three-act structure and turned it on its ear with *Pulp Fiction*, which contained a three-act structure, but ordered them as Act One, Act Three and then Act Two.

Christopher Nolan put his own spin on those three acts, structuring his film *Memento* so that we see the story's conclusion at the beginning of the film and then work our way backwards so that the beginning of the story occurs at the end.

If you have in mind a bold, innovative, stunning new screenplay structure, go for it. It just might be your ticket. If you haven't been struck by a bolt of inspired genius, then stick to the proven, audience-tested structure.

Writing for a Tiny Budget

While the traditional three-act screenplay structure can apply to any movie, there are special considerations that you must be aware of in crafting your ultra-low-budget feature script. And we do recommend writing the script specifically for a tiny budget. It's easier to make your limitations invisible if you aren't imposing them on a bigger-budget story. With that in mind, here are some of the building blocks for your screenplay:

Creating Unique Characters

Any respectable movie needs interesting characters that the audience cares about. This is doubly important to your project. Unique, unusual, remarkably-true-to-life, or endearing characters will help you attract an audience, which in turn will help attract attention to your movie. But of more immediate concern, juicy roles will draw the high-quality actors you need. This is a case of one strong asset attracting another. Actors live by their resumes, so the better the role, the more good people who will be auditioning.

Director/writer Dylan Kidd used that as his guiding principal in writing his low-budget classic, *Roger Dodger*: Create a strong character, and a great actor will want to do it, regardless of the budget. Confident that he had a great main character in Roger, Kidd spotted actor Campbell Scott in a café, asked him to read the script, and the rest is history.

Along this same line of thought, give good lines to all the characters, even the waitress in the walk-on role. Speaking parts are the currency of an actor's resume. Since you can't pay them much — or any — money, give them something useful, a good scene for their reel.

The late Jim Varney did a whole series of silly *Ernest* movies on the strength of a character he created in a popular car ad. Jeff Goldblum virtually launched his career with "I forgot my mantra" in Woody Allen's *Annie Hall*. And Bronson Pinchot leveraged a short scene as Serge in *Beverly Hills Cop* into a hit TV series.

Bottom line: Give all your actors something interesting to play.

Mystery

A bit of uncertainty can really help propel your story forward. As the saying goes, "Don't spill your popcorn in the lobby," which simply means don't tell the audience everything at once. Let the story be revealed. Make the audience want to see the next scene to learn the truth about a character, to see how a scheme unfolds, to find out what that crazy person was building. A little mystery can go a long way towards preventing your story from slowing down. But — and this is a big but — make sure the answers are worth the wait.

Twists

Keep your audience engaged in the story by turning the plot direction on its ear occasionally. (The heroine in peril was actually married to the villain! The priest is the blackmailer! The dog can talk!) If they are concentrating on the story, they're less likely to notice that you couldn't afford a room at the Ritz for that romantic scene and are instead shooting in your parents' attractively-paneled basement rec room.

Dramatic Tension

Don't forget to create conflict between your characters. Who are you most likely to watch, the couple on the corner quietly holding hands or the ones with the flailing arms who are shouting at each other? Make use of that rarely-admitted-to human instinct, voyeurism. This is an easy point to forget, but the fact is that if your characters agree on everything, you don't have much dramatic tension. And without dramatic tension, you won't have much of a movie.

Building Drama or Comedy

Many of the strongest movies set the stage for their climax in the first act, sometimes even in the first moment of the story. Usually this means that some essential characteristic or life experience of the protagonist is presented early in the narrative. This aspect of the person then becomes a pivotal challenge for the character as the story's climax unfolds, causing the story's ending to resonate back to the beginning.

An example is *The Truman Show*. In the early scenes of the film, Jim Carrey's character can't leave his island home for a job assignment because he has a life-long fear of water after the childhood experience of seeing his father fall from a boat in a storm and drown. At the story's climax, the character must face his deepest fear and sail a boat in a raging storm in order to achieve his goal. Way cool; do this if you can (and we don't mean sail a boat in a storm).

Testing Your Story

Test your stories on your friends — the ones who will tell you if it stinks. If you don't have any friends who are that honest, find people you don't know well. If your story wins them over, it's good. The point is, make sure you have a tale that people want to be told because, at its heart, moviemaking is storytelling.

You can also get actors to read your script in a public reading — basically readers' theater — or join a writing group and read it to other writers. You'll get feedback, and even better, it will turn your wince detectors up to full sensitivity. It's like having a new friend over to your house for the first time: You find yourself cringing at every bit of peeling paint and every stain in the carpet as you look at your house through another person's eyes. Reading the script aloud will do the same for your story. You'll know where it drags or where it becomes implausible because you'll wince. Keep track of where that happens and fix those spots.

≈ • ≈

These are the things you need for a successful screenplay. Next we've got the list of things you can't have if you want to finish your ultra-low-budget movie.

Cash constraints can be gratifying to overcome, and we think they bring out the true creativity of a production team. If you can just throw money at a problem, you tend to take the first solution that comes to mind, usually the one that's been done a dozen times before. If you have to come up with a novel solution to your problem, you've usually added a new creative element to your movie. A tight budget can squeeze those creative juices out of you. So here's a list of constraints to inspire your best ideas.

Number of Characters

Limit yourself to three main characters, or barring that, don't include more than three main characters all together in a scene or have them all interacting at the same time. For instance, if you have a party scene, break up the conversations into subgroups of three or less. Why? You don't have time and money to do more.

Equipment rentals mean every minute you spend in production is like having dollars slip through a hole in your pocket. Your cast and crew will be giving up real pay to essentially work free for you, and inevitably their neglected spouse, a bill-wielding landlord, an unexpected illness, their waning interest, or real work will cause them to leave your production. The longer you shoot, the more likely you'll lose key people. And the number of main characters in your movie directly affects your production time and production costs.

Here's how it works out. Your fiscal and temporal resources (money and time) will only allow for a three-to-one (3:1) or four-to-one (4:1) shooting ratio. A 3:1 ratio means you can shoot only three minutes of tape for each finished minute of your movie.

For example, let's say you're shooting the climactic scene where Rhett walks out on Scarlett (apparently you've ignored everything we've said about historical costume dramas and crowd scenes). With a 3:1 shooting ratio, this gives you just enough tape to shoot the scene in a master shot showing both of them and then to shoot two other takes with different camera setups for a close-up of Rhett and a close-up of Scarlett. That's 3:1, with no margin for error.

If Rhett screws up and says "Give a hoot" in the master shot, you can do a second take — which would move you up to a 4:1 ratio for this scene and force you to shoot some later scene in a 2:1 ratio to compensate — or you can make sure that you get him to say "Give a damn" in the close-up. Most of the time you'll try to work in a 3:1 or 2:1 ratio to save time and tape for that tricky shot that's going to need a 5:1 ratio.

So what's shooting ratio got to do with the number of main characters in your script? Let's add Ashley to the scene with Rhett and Scarlett, and you'll quickly realize that you're into a 4:1 shooting ratio — a master shot and three close-ups (Ashley, Rhett, Scarlett). And that assumes there are no mistakes that require a retake. The more group scenes like this in your script, the more your expenses for tape and equipment will rise and the more your production schedule will stretch out.

Here are the numbers. We find that each camera move for a new setup consumes about 15 minutes to adjust camera, lights, focus, and whatnot. With an extra setup for each of the 20 to 25 scenes you need to shoot a day, that adds up to about five hours of lost production per day. Over four weekends of shooting, that's almost two more weekends spent on extra setups (emphasis on the word "spent" because it comes out of your wallet).

"But what about retakes from the same camera setup?" you plead. "It doesn't take much time and the extra tape costs will be cheap."

Not necessarily so. While the tape costs won't be much, the time still adds up if this is your standard operating procedure.

A location also can be made to look completely different to create a new mood for a different scene. You can change lighting, add props and furniture, change characters, or completely change the interactions between the characters. All of these will reinvigorate the scene, and the audience will scarcely give a thought to whether they've seen this location before.

You can also pick a bland setting and redress it to serve as more than one location. If you could afford a sound stage and set pieces (which you can't, so forget it!), this is how you'd shoot all of your interiors for the same reason Hollywood productions do: to save the costs and time of moving cast, crew, and equipment. You can find a location that can serve the same purpose for you.

For example, in *Resident Alien*, we shot in Dale's living room and workroom for one afternoon. We spent the morning shooting in his backyard, so the whole day really counted as one location. With the use of office partitions, desk, computer, file cabinet, chairs, and careful camera angles, we transformed the neutral-colored walls of the living room into a welfare office. Not three feet away, again using a few selected decorations and pieces of furniture, we created the interior of a North Dakota farm house.

Another 12 feet away in a workroom with unfinished gypsum-board walls, we moved a few appliances, propped up a few more pieces of gypsum board for additional walls, and — voila! — we had a motel laundry room in central Minnesota. Four hundred miles of travel in less than two dozen feet of distance. And no one has ever suspected when seeing the finished film. So if you're planning to repaint the living room, pick something nondescript.

You may have noticed that we've mainly referred to interior locations. That's because your script should primarily take place indoors, unless you live somewhere where the weather is reliable. (We don't.) On your fast-paced schedule, you need as much control as possible, so limit the outdoor dialogue scenes and try to locate them near an indoor location you can switch to in case of typhoon, blizzard, tornado, or other acts of God.

To compensate for shooting most scenes as interiors, you can add a large number of establishing shots to your script that won't need dialogue or extra lighting. (You won't have to rent a lighting kit. If you own or borrow the camera, then these shots become virtually free.) You can even have your actors in the shots as long as there isn't dialogue. This second-unit shooting is cheap and can be done as time permits.

We shot the first ten minutes of *Beyond Bob* — which were essentially silent exteriors — as second-unit work over the course of three months after principal photography was completed. So, if you want other interesting locations, just write them as simple establishing shots in your script. We've even used miniatures of building signs and other exteriors to get the look of a bigger-budget movie.

Remember, every time you introduce a new location, think of where else you can use it in your story.

Write What You Own

Another point you can never forget while writing the script is that you have no money! Nada! Zippo! All of your money is going for equipment, tape stock, and food for the cast and crew. So don't write in any props or locations that you don't own, can't beg or borrow, or can't sneak into long enough to get your shot.

Forget about that old truism, "Write what you know." You need to write what you own. Robert Rodriguez took that dictum to new heights when he based the script for his breakout movie, *El Mariachi*, on those items he knew he could get for free: "A pit bull, a motorcycle, two bars, a ranch, and a turtle."

Clearly, expensive set dressings are not going to be your strong suit. They're simply too time-consuming and expensive. However, you can enliven your scenes by using unique props and costumes.

On *Grown Men*, one story segment was set in the apartment of a character who flits between artistic pursuits. Taking advantage of this character trait, we borrowed an artist's warehouse workspace to create an interesting setting. And because the building was something of an artist's colony, we were able to borrow many distinct (and large) pieces of art, simply by walking down the hall and knocking on doors. Props worth thousands of dollars can be just a phone call away.

Also look around where you live. It may be old hat to you, but unless you live in Los Angeles or New York, it's a unique regional location for the rest of the world. What is mundane to you may never have been seen by most audiences. In his offbeat film *Plan 10 from Outer Space*, filmmaker Trent Harris used local Mormon statuary in his hometown of Salt Lake City as truly memorable settings for several of the movie's scenes.

This is one of the biggest reasons we're fans of regional moviemaking; 90% of the films released look like the terrain within 100 miles of Los Angeles. There are thousands of interesting settings, urban and rural, that are rarities on the screen. So when you think of locations for your scenes, pick settings that are unique to your neck of the woods. What is an expensive location shoot for Paramount is a cheap backyard set for you. Your neighborhood can add hundreds of thousands of dollars of visual impact to your movie for next to nothing. This kind of thinking will have distributors guessing you spent a million bucks on your digital feature.

Sometimes what you *don't* have can be turned to your advantage. When Kevin Smith made *Clerks*, he had complete access to the convenience store that served as his primary location.

The one drawback was that he only had use of the location at night, and his story took place during the day. Not having the budget for lights to create the illusion of sunlight, he took this disadvantage and made it his character's problem. Dante, the beleaguered store clerk, arrives at work to find that someone has jammed gum in the lock that secures the metal shutters over the front window of the store. As a result, he can't get the shutters opened.

This is just one of the many problems that plague Dante throughout the day. Smith took a problem and turned it to his advantage as part of his story.

Night vs. Day & Big vs. Small
Here's a simple mathematical equation: Lights = money. As you will have limited money for your production, it follows that you will have limited lighting. How does this affect the scripting process? Let us illuminate.

The first requirement is to not write scenes set in large locations that must be lit artificially. Now if you're reading carefully, you see that this doesn't prevent you from using large locations. You can use the Grand Canyon during the day; thanks to the sun, you don't have to rent lights to do it. Trey Parker used this concept on his first film, *Cannibal: The Musical*, using the splendor of the Colorado Rockies as the backdrop for his story. The settings were magnificent; the lighting costs were nil.

Night shots seem like a cheap idea, but they actually may require a lot of money — that is, light — to make them visible on tape. Again, if you're reading carefully, you'll notice we said "may require." If you limit the size of the area you are trying to light, the simple lighting kit you can afford (four 1000-watt lamps) will be more than adequate. We even simulated a blinding UFO landing using this lighting kit by limiting the area we were lighting.

We were also able to shoot under-exposed shots during the magic hour, just after sunset but before dark, to simulate night. We could see headlights on vehicles and details in the dark trees and cars without using any artificial lights.

So, the lesson here is to write scenes requiring artificial lighting only for small locations or small parts of large locations. For large locations, keep in mind that they must be shot in daylight, during magic hour (this will have to be a short sequence that can be accomplished in less than an hour), or as miniatures that you can afford to light.

Surely, you are thinking, these are enough shackles to place on one project. Dream on.

Other Constraints

These are only the budgetary constraints you must suffer through. They'll seem easy once your project is facing the list of "artistic" requirements from most potential distributors. Most of these requirements are so lowbrow (more blood, more girls, more blood, more bikinis, more blood, more sex, more nudity, and did we mention more blood?) that we were glad we didn't pander to them.

Make a movie that's your vision, a movie of which you can be proud. When you face the inevitable rejections, you can sleep nights if you've followed your dream. It's hard to justify risking your hard-earned savings and thousands of hours of your personal time just to make a return on your investment. If you're only in this for the money, there are better investments that are a lot less work.

Just because most of this advice from distributors is fecal doesn't mean there aren't some valuable points.

The best piece of advice we've heard is to get your story moving in the first five minutes. *Resident Alien* doesn't kick into gear until about 15 minutes in. This is a long time without the aid of a well-known star or stunning visuals. We've been fortunate that most people are willing to wait for the good stuff that follows. However, attention spans are short in the world of distribution and increasingly so among audiences, so it's important that your story hits the ground running.

This is why we rewrote the opening of *Beyond Bob* to show Bob's tragic (yet oddly comic) death in a hang-gliding accident. It's a fast, fun opening that grabs the audience's attention and keeps it while we set up the story and the other characters over the next 20 minutes.

You need to make sure something intriguing, startling, or dramatic happens in the first five minutes to draw them into the story. And then you darn well better use the next 85 minutes to build on that opening. Ideally, the viewers will be so captivated by your story that they'll never get to think about it being an ultra-low-budget movie again until it's all over. By that point, they won't care if you had a big-name star or a Riviera locale.

Finding the Write Stuff

So what do you do if you're not a screenwriter but you have everything else it takes to make a movie? Obviously you need to find a screenwriter, which really won't be that difficult. The tough part will be finding the *right* screenwriter.

As with every other crew and cast position you'll need to fill, we recommend that you opt for excitement about the project and a positive attitude over experience. Not that we're knocking experience. Experience is great... when you can afford it. The main problem with experience is that by the time someone becomes really proficient at something — like writing, editing, photography, whatever — they often expect to receive a paycheck that is commensurate with their skills. And who can blame them? You can't, but you can't afford them, either.

The people you're looking for are the ones who are really excited about the project and who appear to have the basic skills necessary to get them through their tasks. In our case, it was often people who had experience in movie production, but usually one or two steps down from the position they were taking on our project.

For example, a production assistant becomes a production manager; a boom operator becomes a lead sound person; or an assistant editor becomes an editor. These are people who want to move up but who haven't really had the opportunity. That is, until your digital movie came along.

The same will probably be true of your screenwriter. Odds are you aren't going to get a working, professional, card-carrying Writers Guild member to write your script for you. First, because you can't afford them, and second, because as union members, they can't work on your decidedly non-union project.

So how do you find this budding William Goldman? Well, if you followed our earlier advice (tell people that you're making a feature), you may have already heard from a couple writers. Word travels fast, and the word about feature-length movies seems to travel at supersonic speeds. (We even had someone call us from New York to inquire about the possibility of being an extra in one of our productions. In Minnesota. Trust us, word travels fast.)

However, if writers haven't started seeking you out, there are a number of ways to beat them out of the bushes. Here are a few:

- Many colleges and universities offer scriptwriting and playwriting courses. Call the professors at a school near you, and see if they can recommend any of their students. You may even get the professor interested.

- If you have a chapter of the Independent Feature Project nearby (see the appendix), check with them about putting an announcement in their newsletter or on their bulletin board (cork, voice mail, or computer). In the announcement, specify what you're looking for ("an ultra-low-budget script") as well as what you're not looking for (for example, "no slasher, horror, or exploitation" if that's your plan). This will save you and the respondents a lot of time.

- If your city or state has a film office, talk to the people there. We've provided contact information in the appendix. Generally, film boards are in the business of bringing big-buck movies into your area, but most of them also do their best to help out local folks interested in movie work. At the very least, they'll have a directory of local production talent, which will come in very handy later on. Odds are, they'll even know who the up-and-coming screenwriters in your area are and will help put you in touch with them.

- If all else fails, you can place an ad in one of the Hollywood trade papers — *Variety* or the *Hollywood Reporter* — or with one of the on-line services that cater to budding screenwriters. However, we'd recommend that this be your avenue of last resort for a few key reasons. First, it costs money to place an ad, and you don't have any money to spare. Certainly not to be placing ads. Second, you will be inundated with scripts. Your mailbox will be stuffed. Boxes of scripts will land on your doorstep. Your answering machine will explode from overuse. Your home will be swallowed by paper. Your body will never be found. Perhaps we exaggerate, but not by much. And, finally, 99.99% of these scripts will not be written for your budget level. And cramming a million-dollar (or 20 million-dollar) script into an $8,000 budget is not a pretty sight. Picture Orson Welles in a Speedo.

If you feel you must take this approach, be sure to specify "ultra-low-budget" in your ad. This will tell the reader two things: Don't bother sending big-budget scripts (they will anyway), and don't plan on getting paid. Also specify what you do or don't want, such as "no horror," "no period pieces," and so on. We've put the addresses and websites for these trade papers in the appendix. Contact them for information on ad rates (and don't get mad when we say we told you so).

Once you've found your screenwriter, you need to settle on your story. He or she may have a story or script that can be adapted to your budget. If so, great. Or you may need to outline the parameters and let the writer go off and stew on it for a while. Most writers like a challenge, and writing for an $8,000 movie certainly qualifies.

Of course, you may already have a story that you'd like the writer to adapt. This is a fine approach, with a couple caveats:

If it's a story you made up, you're in great shape because that means you own the rights to it. You can do whatever you want with it.

If it's a story that's in the public domain, you're also in good shape. Public domain means that the author is dead and has been for a good long time. As such, no one person owns the rights to the material, but it is now owned by the public. Shakespeare is a good example of a writer whose work is in the public domain. Stephen King is not.

However, with writers who are dead but not nearly as dead as Shakespeare, it's often tricky to figure out what's in the public domain and what isn't. If it's older than a hundred years, you might be okay, but you'll want to check with the Library of Congress on the copyright to make sure.

If the story you're interested in adapting isn't in the public domain, you're going to have to get the rights from the author, and that's going to cost you money. Probably. For example, if you've got your eye on a Dan Brown or John Grisham story, forget it. These guys are out of your league. But if the story is by a less well-known author, you may be able to work something out. Regional writers are — not so surprisingly — great resources for regional stories and may be interested in seeing their work transferred to the big (or semi-big) screen.

As with everyone you bring on board, you'll need to establish a contract with your writer so it's clear who owns what rights and what is expected of you and what is expected of the writer.

One final housekeeping note: Whether you write the script yourself or contract with someone else to write your script, be sure that you copyright the material and the writer registers it with the Writers Guild of America.

Technically, anything original that you write is copyrighted the moment you write it. However, it is a good idea to go through the simple copyright procedures when your script is finished. To copyright your script, you need the Form PA from the Library of Congress. You can handle it on-line at *www.copyright.gov*. As of this writing, it costs $30 to register a copyright.

You should also register your script with the Writers Guild of America. This registration doesn't take the place of copyrighting, but it does provide you with an additional level of security should there be any question as to the ownership of your script. You can register the script on-line at *www.wga.org*, or mail them an unbound copy of your script. The registration fee is $20 (for non-members). Their address is in the appendix.

≈ • ≈

Part of the creative challenge for the screenwriter of an ultra-low-budget movie is how to turn every penny into screen image. The right script for your digital movie is literally worth hundreds of thousands of dollars in apparent value for the finished production, so it's not a creative challenge to take lightly or to do quickly.

As you — or your new best friend, your screenwriter — shape your script, think of what it costs to do everything, and then think of how you can reuse that expense several more times to get maximum screen value for it.

Remember, your screenplay is the support structure for the rest of this project. Build this foundation with the strongest material you can find; it's got to carry a heavy load.

Chapter 3

The Budget ~ *and How to Budge It*

Figuring out how to shoot a 90-minute digital movie for $8,000 is a lot like losing your job and finding out you can live on $100 a month. All those things that were essentials suddenly become luxuries you have to do without. You sleep on your best friend's couch. You dine at the grocery store on the days they have free food samples. You accept and even ask for handouts and favors. You distill your existence down to bare necessities. To succeed within this budget, you will have to discover how to make a movie using only the barest of necessities.

Making an ultra-low-budget digital movie may give you freedom and let you keep your integrity, but you've got to swallow a lot of pride and inhibitions along the way and discard many of your preconceived notions of moviemaking. More than once as we planned and shot our movies, we found ourselves following the model of the silent films of the 1910s. There were few rules about how to make a film back then, and most movies were done on shoestring budgets. They didn't have years of "standard practices" to constrain them.

To create your budget and your production, you have to throw off nearly 100 years of accumulated ideas about moviemaking. You don't need dressing rooms for the stars. You don't need most "standard" crew positions. You don't need a day to shoot one scene. You don't need that lighting truck or camera dolly. You don't need to follow the "rules." Once you've broken free of these mental shackles, you'll find developing your budget is a lot easier.

It's best to start your budget by including only items that would prevent you from starting and completing your movie:

Essentials
- Script
- DV camcorder, batteries, zoom lens, tripod
- Tape stock
- Cast (unless your movie is about inanimate objects)
- Very abbreviated crew
- Good food and drinks for cast and crew (to prevent mutiny)
- Editing equipment (a computer-based, non-linear system)
- Music score
- Recording-studio time for music recording
- Recording of sound effects, foley, and dialogue looping
- Final master tape output

Once you start adding up the numbers, you'll be appalled to see that these items will chew up most of your budget, and any moviemaking experience you have will be screaming that you've left out a bunch of important stuff. We know. This is where you apply your creativity. You start looking at the list and figuring out what you can get for free, borrow, defer, or get for a discount rate. Once you've done this (don't panic; we'll give you some more help on this), there's even less money to spend on the almost-essentials.

While the list of essentials included the items you need in order to make a salable feature-length movie, the list of almost-essentials is governed by the unique aspects of your project. You may be able to do without some of the items on this list.

Almost-Essentials
- Lighting equipment (if you can shoot in natural light, you can get away with just light-control devices such as bounce cards, scrims, and reflectors)
- Shotgun mike, wind screen, and boom pole (to record dialogue cleanly)
- Token payments to cast and crew
- Video dubs (for postproduction sound work)
- Titles (do-it-yourself ones)
- Digital camera to shoot publicity photos
- Publicity photos, publicity packets

- Photocopying for scripts, maps to locations, cast-and-crew phone lists, etc.
- Preview DVDs for reporters, distributors, and film festivals
- Postage for publicity and preview DVD mailings

If you still have a few pennies left after including all the essentials and almost-essentials, then you can move onto the luxuries:

Luxuries

- Wardrobe rentals or purchases
- Makeup
- Models and miniatures
- Vehicle rental
- Location rental
- Camera dolly
- A small-name actor or personality for a cameo role
- Festival entry fees
- Film market entry fees

You'll notice that a lot of Hollywood essentials don't appear in this list of luxuries. No big-name stars, no exotic locations, no sound stage, no insurance, no gala premiere, no stock footage, and no cute little chair with the director's name on it. Your movie doesn't have the cash or time for these non-essentials. So readjust your perspective, and move on.

The budget for our first digital feature was a hybrid consisting of a standard budget and a lengthy list of freebies from friends, relatives, and businesses we know through our day jobs in audiovisual production. These cost savings let us rent specialty equipment and extend the shooting schedule to ten weekends. This longer schedule worked because the movie was essentially five different stories.

Also, because we had set up a nonprofit organization to do movie productions (finally acknowledging the truth in ten years of financial ledgers), we were also able to have our director, producer, actors, crew, and writers work as volunteers.

This was great for us, but it won't work for you unless you do a non-profit production and have budget-cutting business connections. So we've created a realistic, no-frills, no-freebies budget for producing your digital movie, based on current costs for rentals and purchases. The good news is that digital-video equipment keeps getting better and cheaper (causing more perfectly usable "obsolete" equipment to go on the bargain table), so you'll have even more options for cutting budget costs in the future. You can also purchase used gear to trim your budget even more.

This budget presumes you're a for-profit enterprise, so it includes four possible ways to handle paying your cast and crew: deferred payments with signing fees, wages, stipends, and unpaid work contributed by company owners.

Deferred payments — in the event that you make profits — are for staff positions that can be independent contractors. With them there is a signing fee of a small amount of cash. Minimum wages are included for cast and crew positions that must be employees according to federal Internal Revenue Service rulings. Minimum wage currently averages about $6.00 per hour with social security, unemployment compensation, and worker's compensation insurance and varies by state. Cash stipends are an alternative to wages if you choose to have cast and crew be interns instead of employees. Then they just receive a token cash payment. Unpaid work contributed by company owners is an option if you are organized as a limited liability company, and each person on the cast and crew is one of the owners. Instead of payment, they own a share of the production and any profits from it.

Though we've included the wage figures, you'll see that you can't stay within an $8,000 budget if you pay them. The business chapter will give you more detailed ideas on how to avoid these wage costs, but they are included here to give the full budget picture. Here's how you'll spend that extra $8,000 you have rolled up in the corner of your sock drawer.

The Budget

ITEM	CAST AND CREW	CASH
	DEFERRED [D]	
	SIGNING FEE [F]	
	WAGES [W]	
	STIPEND [S]	
Screenplay and rights	$4,000[D], 0[F]	
Producer	4,000[D], 0[F]	
Director	4,000[D], 0[F]	
Lead Actors		
3 Actors	2,592[W], 60[S]	
($864 x 3[W], $20 x 3[S])		
Supporting Actors		
4 Actors	1,728[W], 80[S]	
($432 x 4[W], $20 x 4[S])		
Day Players		
5 Bit Parts	360[W], 25[S]	
($72 x 5[W], $5 x 5[S])		
5 Walk-ons	120[W], 25[S]	
($24 x 5[W], $5 x 5[S])		
Extras	0	
Crew, Equipment and Supplies		
Unit Production Manager/	1,248[W], 20[S]	
Script Supervisor		
Production Assistant	768[W], 20[S]	
Art Director	500[D], 5[F,S]	
Set-Construction Coordinator	120[W], 10[S]	
Set-construction materials		100

ITEM	CAST AND CREW	CASH
Model Builder	500[D], 5[F,S]	
Model-building materials		50
Wardrobe Supervisor	120[W], 10[S]	
Wardrobe rentals/cleaning		0
Makeup-and-Hair Supervisor	204[W], 10[S]	
Lighting Gaffer/	768[W], 20[S]	
Boom-Mike Operator		
Light (rental and purchase)		845
Lighting supplies (purchase)		91
Director of Photography/	1,032[W], 30[S]	
Videographer		
3-CCD digital-video camcorder,		
UV filter, battery, and charger		1800
(purchase)		
2 camera batteries (purchase)		180
Fluid-head tripod (purchase)		395
Scene slate		0
Sound Recordist	768[W], 20[S]	
Sound mixer (rental)		105
Microphone, boom pole, windscreen,		
batteries, cable, headphones (purchase)		510
Vehicles (on-camera and production)		0
Meals on location		500
Locations		0
10 DV 60-min. tapes		30
Digital still camera		110
Productions stills (4 CDs for storage)		4
Storage vault rental		0
Video, Sound, and Music Editor	3,000[D], 20[F,S]	
Non-linear edit system and		
backup hard drive (purchase)		1,500
Video-editing software (purchase)		450
Still-image editing software (purchase)		80
Software to create film look		0

ITEM	CAST AND CREW	CASH
10 VHS Video dubs for audio work		10
Composer/Music Supervisor/Songwriter		
(synchronization rights)	3,000[D], 5[F,S]	
Singer (synchronization rights)	30[W], 5[S]	
4 Session Musicians		
($30 x 4[W], 5 x 4[S])	120[W], 20[S]	
2 Back-up Vocalists		
($30 x 2[W], 5 x 2[S])	60[W], 10[S]	
Music recording studio (rental)		250
1 CD music master		10
Sound effects, foley, dialogue looping		0
Titles		0
Sneak Preview		0
DV deck for final output (rental)		220
VHS record/DVD playback deck (purchase)		80
4 full-size DV tape (120 min.)		64
20 DVD-R discs single-side 4.7Gb		20
preview DVDs		
15 sets of publicity packets and		15
photos on CD		
Publicity-packet writing		0
Photocopying 18 scripts		100
Miscellaneous photocopying		40
Postage for publicity packets CDs		
and preview DVDs		40
Cast and Crew Costs		
Total deferred salaries	19,000[D]	
Total signing fees with	35[F]	
deferred salaries		
Total wages	10,038[W]	
Total stipends	400[S]	
Equipment and supplies costs		
Total equipment and supplies		$7,599

Based on the cost above, here are four possible budgets for your feature-length movie, depending on whether your production is for profit or nonprofit and depending on the employment status you choose for your cast and crew.

Four Budget Options

1. Production with employees and independent contractors

Total cash costs	**17,672**
(equipment, supplies, employee wages, independent contractor signing fees)	
Total deferred costs	**19,000**

2. Production with interns and independent contractors

Total cash costs	**7,999**
(equipment, supplies, intern stipends)	
Total deferred costs	**12,000**
(screenplay, producer, director only)	

4. Production with Limited Liability Company owners

Total cash costs	**7,599**
(equipment, supplies, all cast and crew are company owners)	

4. Nonprofit production with volunteers

Total cash costs	**7,599**
(equipment, supplies, all cast and crew are free volunteers)	

If you have priced out any of the services or products listed in this budget, you're probably saying, "Impossible! There's got to be a trick." Yes, lots of them.

Pinching the Pennies (Until Abraham Yells)

There are several basic principles to use when whittling down your budget: You have more time than money. Use what you already own. Make it, or borrow it. Use other people's waste or surplus. Dicker for everything you have to buy. Use crew with their own equipment. Rent equipment when business is slow.

Because you're going to spend a lot of money renting and purchasing budget items, we'll start with some general thoughts about these activities.

This budget assumes that you are shooting your production over four weekends, the times when no one else is renting the equipment. Most rental houses will give you an entire weekend for the cost of one or one-and-a-half days' rental; you can get the most out of that rate by picking up the equipment late on Friday afternoon so you can shoot some night shots that evening.

You may be able to get better rental deals if you ask for a bid on the whole package you want to rent for four weekends. You might get an even better deal if you use their favorite four-letter word, CASH. Some rental houses have cash flow problems while they wait 90 days for their invoices to be paid. They may trim your bill to put some cash in the till. Sending out a formal bid form will make them think you're getting bids from their competitors even if you're not. However, it's a good idea to get multiple bids. No matter what the rental or purchase price, plead poverty and ask for a deal. A painful wince at the price and saying "We're on a really tight budget. Can you do any better?" will get you an almost-automatic 5% to 10% discount at all but the most hard-hearted businesses. And from there, you can bargain for better. You've got to keep pushing for more and more or, in this case, less and less.

If you can be very flexible and if you're feeling really lucky, make a deal to rent the equipment dirt cheap if no one else rents it for the weekend. When you offer this, be sure you're talking to the owner, who is going to recognize extra income. The sales people don't necessarily care if they rent anything or not. They're not paying the overhead. Odds are that most of the equipment sits idle on the weekend, so this is a pretty safe rental deal, and one the owner is likely to consider. Remember, only suckers pay list price.

Because of the low cost of much of the equipment in the digital video format, you don't necessarily have to deal with rental houses. Many professionals own their own equipment and will rent it to you for prices well below the going rates. They have a lot of money tied up in their lights, sound gear, video camcorder, video deck, and tripod, and often it's gathering dust, not income. Before they rent to you, you'll have to demonstrate to them that you are conscientious and won't trash their $2,000 lighting kit. If they agree to rent it to you, be sure to get instructions from them on how to take care of and use their equipment. Then follow their instructions. You will soon be colleagues of these people, and you want only good things said about you. So don't burn any bridges.

You also might find that while you're arranging a rental, this professional becomes excited about your project. Since you're working weekends when these professionals usually aren't working, they may be willing to join your crew for the experience and the fun of working on a movie. A videographer friend of ours offered his services and his digital camcorder to shoot *Grown Men*. In the course of the production, he brought in other people who provided a top-of-the-line camcorder, audio gear, trucks full of lights, and even a Steadicam system with operator. Movies are infectious.

You also can get some equipment and supplies for lower prices from retailers outside the movie industry. For example, we bought photoflood bulbs for $1.70 from a wholesaler that sells all types of bulbs; photo-supply stores wanted $3.00 for the same bulb. Instead of renting a boom pole for $10 a weekend, consider buying an adjustable painter's pole for $15 at the hardware store. You'll have to modify the screw fitting (a three-dollar roll of duct tape will do this if you're not handy), and you'll save $25 for more essential supplies. Moviemaking gives you all kinds of opportunities to use your imagination.

Squeezing the Budget
Let's go point-by-point through this budget for a 90-minute digital movie.

Screenplay and Rights
This area is important in budget trimming for two reasons. The first we've already discussed in the chapter on designing the script. What you write in the script is going to affect what you have to include in the budget. Hopefully, you have a script that limits your expenses and showcases what you have at hand. But when you make your budget, keep in mind that changing the script will change the budget. If you find yourself trapped in

a financial corner, you may need to revise the screenplay. This may be an affront artistically, but it's the kind of ruthless act that is needed to get a small story to the big screen. At least you get to do it and keep control. If other people were producing your story, they'd make changes, too—ones you probably wouldn't like. If there's no way out of a financial corner, write an escape route.

The other budget-slimming aspect of story and rights is limiting your cash payment for the script or have it donated free for a nonprofit production. As screenwriters, we can tell you this will be easy to do, especially with writers who haven't been produced. As we've said before, it would be great to pay all the people on your project what they are worth, and you will. Just not in cash. Your currency is experience and credentials, and for people new to the movie business, these rewards are worth almost as much as cash. Your screenwriter (who may be you) will be thrilled to see her or his words brought to life. Other than a deferred payment if there are profits, that will have to be enough.

Cast and Crew

In this budget, we included a bare-bones crew and a generic cast of three lead roles, four supporting roles, and ten bit parts and walk-on roles. Of course, you'll want to adjust this to match your cast, but keep in mind that it will be hard to shoot 12 pages of script a day if you have more than three main characters. If your list of cast and crew is much larger than the one in this budget, think about revising the script. There's only so much that you can do with an $8,000 budget.

When we did deferred payments for staff that qualified as independent contractors on our first two movies, we made sure there was a signing fee that gave those crew members just enough cash so that they didn't feel like it cost them money to work on our productions (basically, gas money). For ourselves, as director and producer, we took no money. Since we were financing the production, it would have meant paying ourselves.

For the staff who were independent contractors, the contract arrangements gave them a portion of any profits, but we made it clear that profits were a long shot, at best. We also arranged it so we, as producer and director, would share in profits only after everyone else did. This made it very clear to everyone that we weren't out to make a profit off their almost-volunteer labor. This helped create an atmosphere of camaraderie that was needed to get us through the tough spots.

Most of the cast and crew can't be independent contractors under federal rules, and minimum wage will not be a minimal amount. Paying these wages will more than double your production budget and your paperwork. If you decide to go this route, you may need to hire a payroll person or a payroll service because doing the required withholdings, payments, and form filing is a real job. One that you won't have much time for during your hectic four weekends of production. For these wage calculations, we assumed that four weekends of production add up to 128 hours (four hours on Friday evenings and 14 hours each for Saturdays and Sundays). Some jobs require many more hours and some require much less. Wage costs were assumed to be $6.00 per hour. Following is a quick list of the hours for the wage employees based on our production experience:

- *Lead actors* — 128 hours (4 weekends shooting) + 16 hours (rehearsal) = 144 hours each
- *Supporting actors* — 64 hours (2 weekends shooting) + 8 hours (rehearsal) = 72 hours each
- *Day Players* — 8 hours (1 day shooting) + 4 hours (rehearsal) = 12 hours each
- *Walk-ons* — 4 hours (1/2 shooting day)
- *Unit Production Manager* — 128 hours (4 weekends shooting) + 80 hours (preproduction) = 208 hours
- *Production Assistant* — 128 hours (4 weekends shooting)
- *Set-Construction Coordinator* — 20 hours (as needed)
- *Wardrobe Supervisor* — 20 hours (preproduction)
- *Makeup-and-Hair Supervisor* — 24 hour (2 hours each shooting day) + 10 hours (pre-production) = 34 hours
- *Lighting Gaffer/Boom-Mike Operator* — 128 hours (4 weekends shooting)
- *Director of Photography/Videography* — 128 hours (4 weekends shooting) + 20 hours (preproduction) + 24 hours (3 days of second-unit shooting) = 172 hours
- *Sound Recordist* — 128 hours (4 weekends shooting)

- *Singer* — 5 hours (studio recording session)
- *Session Musicians* — 5 hours (studio recording session)
- *Back-up Vocalists* — 5 hours (studio recording session)

If you decide to have your cast and crew be interns, the stipend you pay should be enough to give them bus fare or gas money. Beyond that they are getting a learning experience tuition-free.

We did *Grown Men* as a not-for-profit endeavor, so everyone volunteered their time. Total cast and crew costs, zero. We were careful to have cast and crew sign releases that gave all rights to their work to the non-profit organization. That way there would be no barriers to distributing the movie.

Just as we did, you will probably feel embarrassed that you can't offer real payment to these talented performers and technicians. However, don't underestimate the value of the experience and credentials you are offering. One of the most gratifying parts of producing your dream movie is that you can also help other people realize their dreams in the process.

For example, one of our lead actors was called by her actor friends in Los Angeles. They couldn't believe they'd made the trek to Hollywood and were still struggling to break into movies while she had stayed in the Midwest and had gotten the lead in a feature film. She went on to work on a larger feature film and a popular British TV series.

One of our unit production managers, who had been the assistant to John's agent prior to working with us on two films, now makes her living in Hollywood. She has worked on the Academy Awards and Emmy Awards programs for many years, the *America's Funniest Home Videos* television series, the World Cup final-game ceremony, the Super Bowl half-time show, and low-budget feature films, to name a few. She's a very talented person, and having two feature films on her resume didn't hurt when she was knocking on doors.

Several of our lead actors have gone on to perform lead and supporting roles in Hollywood low-budget films (meaning million-dollar budgets), larger films, and a prime-time television series.

Our composer, who had never done a movie's music score before doing two of our films, used a CD of those sound tracks as his ticket into USC's film-music program. Before he even graduated, he was writing

The Budget   35 scores for other movie productions, and he has gone on to score numerous Hollywood films.

We're not saying that their work with us paved the way. But it didn't hurt.

Of course, even the small money you'll be paying your crew will add up. It will add up to big money if you decide to have wage-earning employees. So keep your cast as small as the story allows and work with the absolute minimum crew size in order to reduce the cost of personnel. Also, a smaller crew can keep up with your fast production schedule. (Ironically, the more helpers you add to your crew, the slower it moves.)

You may have a story that calls for extras. A contraction and two words of advice: Don't pay them. Amazingly enough, even after a hundred years of moviemaking in this country, people are still thrilled to be in a movie, even a crowd scene. Just put their name in the credits. We had dozens of people who volunteered to skate for hours in the middle of the night on a Fourth of July weekend for *Beyond Bob*. It was far from glamorous, but only a handful went home before we finished our shots. For budget purposes, the one thing you have to remember about extras is that you can't afford to feed them, at least not much. You can provide lemonade and cookies, but that's it. So when you are preparing your shooting schedule, plan to have extras start right after a meal and to be finished with them before the next meal. It's crass, but necessary.

Finally, don't be discouraged that you can't afford a big-name star. You can afford lots of actors who may become stars. The pre-stardom films of Julia Roberts and Tom Hanks are making money for somebody. You might be able to get a celebrity from outside the entertainment field to do your movie as a lark. Bill Gates in a cameo as a computer repairman would be a hoot. A little creative thinking might find you a recognizable name without paying for a star.

Set Construction

Looking over our budget, you may be asking, "How the heck did they do set construction for just $100?" Our secret is, "We didn't build any." In truth, we did do some limited set construction on our movies. We just created a false wall to change the look of an existing interior. In the case of *Beyond Bob*, we divided a kitchen and sitting room into two separate rooms. We built a crude wood framework to support a couple of sheets of wood paneling that had come loose from our director of photography's basement wall. If you've ever seen a Hollywood set, the pressure is off. You can get away with murder. Even the crudest sets look 100 times better on tape.

If you have to do some set work, look for borrowed or discarded materials. Haunt the dumpsters at construction and demolition sites. (Yes, you will sink this low to get your movie done.) Commercial construction sites are the best because they often discard items that still look new, such as lumber, sheetrock, paneling, carpet, cabinets, bathroom fixtures, and electrical wiring. Much of this material still looks good enough to serve on a movie set. Routinely check dumpsters at businesses for your furniture needs. Tons of repairable furniture are thrown out every time the office staff decides it looks too old-fashioned. You can even find computers and other high tech–looking trash for those science-fiction projects. Dumpsters are a do-it-yourself set-building kit for low-buck moviemakers. Just add sheetrock screws. (Using screws and an electric drill, you can assemble and disassemble sets in minutes.)

A word of caution: When dumpster diving, be sure to wear good solid boots, heavy gloves, and even a dust mask. Watch out for hazardous items; this is garbage after all. A small step ladder can help avoid the embarrassment and danger of leaning too far into a dumpster.

Model Building

We only included a small amount for model-building materials. You can either do it yourself or find model makers through your local hobby store. Offer to pay for materials, and they'll go to town. This is their passion and getting money to do it will make their day. In our case, Dale did most of our model work using free salvaged materials. (Guess who had all the information on dumpster diving.) We'll talk more about models in the chapter on special effects, but for budgeting, you should know that live-action shots that are difficult to set up can sometimes be accomplished as miniatures, saving lots of time and money. This is how we once created and lit a night scene showing jets on the tarmac at an Air Force base, something we couldn't have afforded to do for real even if we had permission.

Wardrobe

You only need a fistful of dollars to get the wardrobe you'll require, especially if you've written a script that doesn't call for Halston designer gowns. There are several methods to pay little or nothing for your costumes. Use what you have, borrow, buy cheaply, make it, or rent it.

If you've written the script yourself, it will be easy to use what you have. You should have written in your old prom dress or that beekeeping hat Uncle Jim bequeathed to you. Also ask actors if they can provide their own costumes. If they are working actors or just the wild-and-wonderful people that actors usually are, they probably have a closet full of interesting clothing that fits them. The exotic dancer who performed the lead in one segment of *Grown Men* brought a selection of her professional wardrobe to a rehearsal at John's house, but not before mistakenly knocking at his neighbor's door and asking for John. We didn't need to arrange for any other costumes for this performer, and the resulting neighborhood gossip could be considered the first step in a word-of-mouth publicity campaign.

Borrowing opens up a world of attire to you. Friends and relatives of anyone connected to your project become sources of clothing, uniforms, and professional gear. We literally got the shirt off the back of Dale's minister, and most of the costumes in *Grown Men* came from the costumes of the actors and their friends. Think of it as thousands of dollars of wardrobe just out there for the begging.

You can even ask local stores and local designers to loan clothing in exchange for screen credit and any publicity that it will garner. We've found that independently owned stores get in the spirit of the project more than chain stores, which discourage most initiative and independent thought in their employees. You also can find fledgling designers, who are happy for the exposure, at technical colleges or by asking around at fabric stores and funky clothing shops. We got some unique costumes from an up-and-coming designer recommended by a sales person at a clothing boutique. Screen credit and any publicity that mentions the clothing designs can return the favor for the designer's career.

You can ask people working in a profession to borrow their special clothing and accessories, or you can approach suppliers of professional gear. It's called product placement, and Hollywood overdoes it daily. We got some name-brand roller skates (Oberhamers — we're still repaying the favor) this way for no cost, and they even let us keep them after the shoot. You can thank businesses by sending them a photo of their clothing or equipment being used in the movie. They can print it in their company newsletter or put it on the bulletin board..

Professional wardrobe used in Grown Men. *(Pictured, David Fields and Melissa Kashmark. Photo courtesy of Granite Productions, Unlimited.)*

If you are forced to spend actual money on some of your costumes or accessories, head to thrift shops, garage sales, and used-clothing stores. In most cases, costumes don't have to look brand new, and an imperfect fit can be made presenta-ble for your movie with safety pins, needle and thread, or even gaffer's tape. By doing a little hunting, you'll find that you can buy more than a pocket for pocket change. Before you go bargain hunting, strip off those preconceived costume ideas, and be open to finding surprising new concepts in the rag bin.

For technical and scientific costumes, consider disposable coveralls, gloves, footwear, and head gear from safety equipment suppliers. This dis-posable clothing is the real stuff, but it's meant to be cheap. We needed the science-nerd look for two characters in *Resident Alien*, and we got it by buying orange disposable coveralls for three dollars each. To this costume we added a 50-cent used belt, borrowed safety glasses, and inspired casting of nearly-identical bald guys, and, voila!, we had convincing techno-weenies for only $3.50 each.

Specialty costumes, like the alien space suits we used in *Resident Alien*, can be hard to find in friends' closets or at the neighborhood tuxedo shop. However, if there's a modicum of sewing talent handy, you can make specialty costumes. You can even do it without sewing talent. Our alien spacesuits were made from thrift-shop long underwear, foam rubber, contact adhesive, cardboard, and spray paint. Sure, the spray paint tends to rub off. Sure, the costumes deteriorate pretty quickly. Sure, the actors don't have a full range of movement. But the spacesuits lasted long enough to get the shots we needed, they cost less than $10, and they looked like hundreds of dollars on the screen.

You can rent costumes, but this is an avenue of last resort and only permissible when a particular costume is so critical to your project that you are willing to sacrifice other resources for it. Since a $50 costume rental is the price difference between a very good shotgun microphone and a pretty good microphone, ask yourself, "Am I willing to accept a lower-quality soundtrack for my movie?" This should tell you how important the costume is. Presuming you do need a costume badly enough to rent it, you'll need to get the best deal possible. Actual costume shops are probably too expensive unless you can get the owners to give you a deal in exchange for publicity and screen credit. Theater groups will sometimes loan their costumes for a reasonable fee. You can also try making arrangements with a local high-school or university drama program. We found that uniform and specialty-clothing shops sometimes would rent items they stock, but their prices were often high, and their willingness to strike deals was low.

Selecting your wardrobe may or may not require a wardrobe supervisor. If you have very limited costumes — such as two characters lost in the desert wearing just shorts and T-shirts — the director, producer, and production manager can select costumes. A more extensive and fashionable wardrobe benefits from the attention of someone with a flair for clothing. Even if you have a wardrobe supervisor, you don't need this person on the set, except to deliver the proper wardrobe to the location and maybe to stay around for repairs if there are delicate items being used. Otherwise the production manager can supervise wardrobe changes, which lets you have one less crew person to feed, move, and keep out of the way.

The time you spend getting good costumes will pay off in the finished movie. Costumes play an important part in creating the screen image of every single scene and the overall look of your movie. You can easily add $100,000 to your apparent budget on the screen by using these free methods to get a top-notch wardrobe.

Makeup and Hair

We've done one production with a makeup-and-hair supervisor and two without. Whether or not you need one on your set depends on the unique needs of your production. If you have a very small cast, simple hair and makeup that doesn't change, and experienced actors, the cast can do their own makeup and hair styling. If you have a larger cast or makeup and hair that need changing during the shooting day, you'll probably need this crew position. It is a comfort to the actors to have someone else watching these details, but you have to weigh it against adding another crew person who will slow down the march of your little rebel band of digital moviemakers.

The first thing you must do is discourage your makeup-and-hair supervisor from tweaking and primping the actors before every shot. When you're trying to shoot up to 100 shots each day, a minute to do makeup on each shot wastes 100 minute of production time. And the difference is rarely discernible in the end. Except for makeup effects (bruises, bags under the eyes, and fragile hair styles), makeup and hair can be spiffed up after lunch break, and that's good enough. On the finished movie frame, hair styles gone wild are more noticeable than lip blush wearing off, so concentrate on hair the most. This advice will insult makeup professionals, who do an important job well. But remember you're operating in subsistence moviemaking. Only the vital elements. You can only get 90% of what you want, and you have to be willing to sacrifice the other 10% in order to get your movie finished. Touching up hair and makeup definitely falls into the 10% category.

If you have professional actors or a professional makeup-and-hair person (or beautician or hair stylist with a dream), they likely can supply the makeup you need out of their basic makeup kit. Everyone on the production should be in the "My uncle's got a barn, and I've got footlights" mode, so ask if they can scrounge or donate the needed supplies. Only pay for what you have to, and definitely don't pay for a shopping spree at the cosmetic counter. It's okay to say you can't afford something. This will cause the makeup person or any crew member to use their creativity to find a solution. Our makeup supervisor scrounged a lot of the makeup for *Beyond Bob* from the set of a made-for-TV movie that shot in town. Their crew was routinely throwing out barely-used makeup supplies — another example of Hollywood waste and how to profit from it.

Also, don't make it a secret that you're throwing your personal resources into the project. This will encourage everyone on the crew and cast to add what they can, so you all can succeed.

Lighting and Lighting Supplies
You can't have enough lighting. That is to say, you can't have as much lighting as you want because you lack the necessary money and power (the electrical kind). You won't be working on a sound stage equipped with its own electrical substation, and you can't afford a portable generator, much less the truck and the time to pull it around. So accept the situation. Your power shortage actually works well with your money shortage. You couldn't afford to rent more lights even if you had more electricity. Fortunately, you can get by with a small, lightweight, not-too-expensive lighting kit because of the low-light capabilities of digital video cameras.

We've worked with a kit that includes four 1000-watt lights (called "1Ks") that can be flooded or spotted, such as Arriflex or Lowel DP lights. These same lights can be outfitted with 650-watt or 500-watt lamps if you find you're singeing the actors' eyebrows in tight locations. The kit contains barndoors for blocking the lights' spill, stands, and extra lamps. With tax and insurance this kit will cost about $175 a weekend. The total rental cost of this kit is more than $700. You can buy a kit of three Lowel DP lights plus a Lowel Totalight (a flood light), including tripods, barndoors, and other useful accessories for about $1200. If you are planning to do a second movie or if you can sell the kit for a reduced price to another moviemaker when you're done, it could be cheaper to buy a lighting kit.

In the budget, we've also added $110 for the purchase of two 1000-watt softlights for lighting larger locations, such as a small auditorium or an exterior night location. This is too cheap for professional video lights, but you can buy a professional construction light with a tripod and two 500-watt halogen lights for $30. If you add a 32-inch white photo umbrella to this light for $25, you have a very usable softlight. Make sure the photo umbrella is rated for exposure to 1000 watts of continuous light, such as the Westcott 2012 umbrella. (Otherwise, your production could include the "flaming umbrella" special effect.) Since you will own these lights, you can use them for a second-unit shot or a reshoot later. If you need to have a lot of lights for big scene, you can get 500-watt halogen work lights that sit on the floor for under $10 each. Better yet, since many people own them, borrow them. The light from them is harsh, but there's a lot of it for a low cost.

For outdoor daytime shooting, the only lighting equipment we used was a 38-inch silver-white Flexfill, which is a collapsible reflector. It's great for filling in harsh shadows. We also used it as a reflector on indoor settings. It will cost about $35 for four weekends with tax and insurance.

Now you may be tempted to skimp on other equipment and add more lights because your director of photography really wants some 5Ks. Forget it. Here's the mathematical reason: Most residential and commercial circuits are 15 amps or 20 amps. At 120 volts that means you have 1800 watts (15 amps x 120 volts = 1800 watts) or 2400 watts (20 amps x 120 volts = 2400 watts) of power available. Using more watts or continuously using up to the maximum wattage will cause fuses to blow or circuit breakers to trip. It's easy to see that a 15-amp circuit can only support one 1000-watt light reliably. A 20-amp circuit can handle two. Switching to 500-watt lamps in the lights will give you less light, but you can run three of them on a 15-amp circuit or four on a 20-amp circuit. In most locations, you'll be running a lot of extension cords just to get two circuits, so four lights will max out your power.

Our budget also includes some expendable lighting supplies: a $12 roll each of black, white and gray gaffer's tape (useful for taping everything from cables to the floor to troublesome clothes to the actors), six "practical" bulbs (150 to 200-watt tungsten bulbs that fit standard light fixtures for brighter light sources within a scene — beware of overheating the light and shade), four 20" x 24" sheets of daylight-correction gel to color the tungsten (incandescent) light to match sunlight (3202 Full Blue CTB from the Rosco company), four 20" x 24" sheets of 105 Roscolux tough spun (a fabric-like material similar to tissue paper but without the same flammability) to soften and reduce the intensity of the lights. With the daylight-correction gels, you will be able to match the color of the sunlight if you want to see out windows during your indoor scenes.

From our personal supplies, we scrounged other important lighting gear: wooden clothes pins to clamp gels and spun to the barndoors, aluminum foil to make flags for blocking light, leather gloves to avoid cooking hands when moving hot lights, extra 15-amp and 20-amp screw-in fuses, and three-prong to two-prong electric-plug adapters.

We also built some lighting gear. For locations that were hundreds of feet from the nearest power outlet, we built some 100-foot extension cords from 10-gauge copper cable used in home construction. They were wired to fiberglass electrical outlet boxes, which were nailed to squares of wood for stability. Use the cable that's intended for wet locations (type UF). You'll need heavier-gauge cables for longer runs (otherwise you'll overheat the cable, blow fuses, and not get enough power to the lights). As with all extension cords, protect them from damage and keep them off wet ground. These cables were not designed for use in the rain, but that's the least of your troubles because neither are your lights or camera equipment.

To weight down lights and other equipment, we made sandbags rather than rent them. We put a plastic bag three-quarters full of sand inside the cut-off legs of worn-out jeans and sewed the ends shut. This was better than spending $20 a weekend to rent them, and it made decisions on what to wear easier.

As with all the equipment rentals, you can get a substantial budget savings on lighting if your crew person owns the equipment you need. This allows you to limit your costs to replacing burned-out lamps and buying the gels and spun. This approach also gives you an efficient lighting person who knows and cares about the equipment.

Camera Equipment

After all our harping on how you can't afford this and that, you were probably surprised that we recommended buying a digital-video camcorder. Here's how it works out. To rent a small digital-video (DV) camcorder, such as a Sony DSR PD170, it will cost about $1,230 for four weekends. You'd need to rent a DV playback deck for a minimum of four separate days for $585 or buy a $400 consumer DV camcorder to select your takes and to digitize the footage into your non-linear edit system. That's at least $1,630, and you won't have a good second-unit camera available to do establishing and insert shots, to shoot miniatures or special effects or title elements, to record intermediate outputs from your non-linear editing system, to use for recording CD-quality sound effects and dialogue replacement, or to redigitize footage when the gremlins of the edit system attack.

If you spring for another $170 you can purchase a good-quality DV camcorder with a screw-on UV filter to protect the lens, two extra five-hour lithium-ion batteries, and a charger to keep empty batteries charging while you're shooting. The benefits of a second-unit camera, a playback-and-record deck for your edit system, and an audio recorder will be worth a lot more than $170. As an extra benefit, you may be able to rent out your camcorder to other moviemakers to recoup some of your costs.

In general, the camcorder needs to have three CCDs to capture a high-quality image. The sizes of these imaging chips range from 1/6" to 1/2", but the size doesn't matter much. Having three of them to separately capture red, green, and blue components of your images is the most important factor in creating a top-notch picture. That said, there are a few new camcorders that get high-quality results using one big imaging chip. Your camcorder also needs to have a zoom lens, zebra striping to show proper exposure, audio metering, time code, and manual controls for the focus, white balance, exposure, shutter speed, and audio level. It must have an IEEE1394 (also called FireWire and i.Link) DV-in and DV-out connection. Connectors for composite video and audio input and output are also important for bringing in audio elements and for outputting working copies to VHS tape. Though not essential, some of these cameras will also shoot small digital stills that can be used for publicity photos, especially on a website.

Prices on these DV camcorders keep dropping as their features improve, so you'll be able to get better and better camcorders for this amount of money in the future. Right now, the JVC GR-HD1 camcorder, which shoots in DV and HDV (high-definition video on a DV tape) formats, is available for under $1,800 and has all the essential features. It uses a one-megapixel CCD instead of three CCDs to capture high-quality images. The Sony DSR-PDX10, which shoots in DV and DVCAM, and the Panasonic AG-DVC30, which shoots in DV format, routinely have sale and rebate prices that put them within this budget. If you want to watch for rebates and spend another $300 dollars, you can buy the Panasonic AG-DVC60 (DV format, a mid-sized camcorder if size matters to you), the Sony DCR-VX2100 (DV format), the Canon GL-2 (DV format), and the Sony HVR-A1U (DV, DVCAM, and HDV format. It uses one three-megapixel image chip to produces the quality of three CCDs). All of these camcorders shoot in 4:3

normal and 16:9 widescreen formats. Each of these camcorders has different extra features, such as microphones, programmable controls, XLR microphone connectors, and night-shooting capabilities. Review their specifications for the one that will work best for the circumstances of your project. Don't pay extra to get features that aren't crucial to your movie. You'll need that money elsewhere.

We don't recommend a camcorder with a changeable lens because you'll be using a zoom lens for your videography. While prime lenses that are a single focal length do give better image clarity, a zoom lens speeds up your production, letting you reframe in seconds.

If your project needs a home-movie look or depends on narration and doesn't need high-quality sound, you might consider one of the DV camcorders with 3-CCDs that are in the $1,100 price range: the Panasonic PV-GS500 and the JVC GR-X5US. They both lack manual audio controls and zebra striping. The JVC lacks manual white balance, and the Panasonic lacks a headphone jack and only does regular 4:3 image format. However, they are the lowest cost 3-CCD camcorders available and might do the job for the right project.

Check around for which camcorders are new on the market (and how they have lowered the price of other camcorders) before you buy. Also look beyond your local video store. There are many companies selling nationally on the Internet who offer some great deals. It's fine to support the local businesses as long as they support your local moviemaking with a similar price break. Keep in mind that you may have to pay local sales tax if you buy equipment and supplies out of state. Factor in any tax and shipping costs before you decide where to buy any big-ticket item. Also beware that there are some unscrupulous Internet retailers selling this equipment for impossibly low prices. These are often scam operations that have many unhappy customers. Check reviews of companies on the Internet. Be sure to read the negative reviews because they will tell the true story of these scams, which routinely advertise in national publications. (Sometimes these companies flood the review sites with their own glowing reviews.) To help you out, in the appendix we've listed a few reputable retailers we know.

Be sure you buy an ultraviolet (UV) haze filter for your camcorder's lens. This filter is virtually clear glass and doesn't noticeably affect the image.

Digital Filmmaking 101 ~ Newton & Gaspard

Keep this cheap filter on your lens all the time. If something accidentally hits the camera lens, the filter will take the blow, not the expensive lens. Most camcorders include a neutral-density filter to cut down light levels in bright daylight. If your camcorder doesn't have one, you'll probably need to buy one for shooting scenes outdoors on sunny days.

There are lots of tempting features for digital-video camcorders, such as DVCAM, DVCPRO, HDV formats; interchangeable lenses; professional configuration of controls; XLR (three-pin) sound connectors; etc. These are all very nice, but none of them are essential to getting your movie done, and they can blow your budget if you try to buy or rent them. Now if someone wants to give these things to you, that's great. However, consider what it will do to other parts of your budget. We had a Digital Betacam camcorder loaned free to us for shooting *Grown Men*. This gave us stunning visual quality in a wide-screen format, but it wasn't really free. The tape costs were three times higher, and we had to transfer them to DV tapes in order to digitize them. Similarly, HDV format is tempting until you realize that you have to use a more expensive editing system that isn't as time-tested as DV. Be sure you really know what freebies will cost you in the end.

One advantage of the compact DV cameras is that they look much like the camcorders used by the parental paparazzi at kids' soccer games. Consequently, you can avoid dealing with curious passers-by and hassles about permits on public streets and other such nonsense. You can set up your shots, shoot, and disappear before anyone really notices you. One team of gutsy moviemakers shot the movie *Windhorse* about the modern-day struggles of Tibetans under Chinese military occupation. They used their small camcorder and silent hand signals to shoot street scenes in Tibet virtually under the noses of Chinese officials. (You may not want to risk permanent residence in a foreign prison on your first digital movie.)

To support your camera, you need a tripod with a fluid head. Fluid heads don't give you the jerky camera moves that friction heads do. We recommend you buy a tripod instead of renting one. A rental for four week-ends will cost about $245, and you still need a tripod for second-unit shots and establishing shot. A $75 lightweight consumer tripod with a fluid head is good enough for those second-unit shots that are just a stationary shot or a simple pan. For this rental and purchase, you will have spent $320. For

$395, you can own a very good Manfrotto tripod (model 351MVB2) with the 501 fluid head (model 3433) and ball-claw leveling. This quality tripod will be available for all your shooting. If you're thinking of renting out your camcorder, having a professional tripod with it might pay for itself pretty fast. However, if you really need to tighten up the budget, the rental option will save $75.

Don't bother renting a camera slate to mark the beginning of shots. Use a child's chalkboard or paper on a clipboard. Anything that you can write legible scene and take numbers on will do the job. A real slate looks cool, but on your production "cheap" is the ultimate cool.

Sound Equipment

There aren't many corners to cut on the sound-recording equipment you'll need. Even big-dollar features don't get a lot more elaborate than what you will be using. We're always amused to see major productions using the same sound-recording techniques we use.

Thanks to the CD-quality sound recorded by digital-video camcorders, you won't need to rent a tape recorder. But because of the compact sound controls on small DV camcorders and because you don't want the sound recordist breathing down the videographer's neck on every shot, you'll want to rent a small portable mixer to control the sound levels away from the camera.

While renting the mixer is a good deal, we recommend purchasing the microphone system. Rental costs for a microphone system for four weekends will be a little over $400. Buying an equivalent system will cost $494, and you'll own sound equipment to record replacement dialogue and sound effects later. If you buy a camcorder that has a detachable microphone that you can use later (Sony DSR-PDX10, Panasonic AG-DVC30, or Sony HVR-A1U), then you may want to rent the sound gear and save $94.

If you're renting, you'll want a Sennheiser MKH-416 (or an ME-66, ME-67, ME-80 or equivalent microphone). If you're buying, go for the Audio Technica AT897 short shotgun condenser microphone with a Rode SM3 universal shock mount ($270 as a package). The shock mount prevents the mike from picking up noise from the boom pole. This microphone will run for 1200 hours on an AA battery. If you can find a good package price with a shock mount, the Audio Technica AT815b long shotgun and AT835b shotgun are also good options. These microphones all come with foam windscreens, but you'll want a "zeppelin"-style windscreen with a furry cover to really cut wind noise on outdoor locations. The Lightwave EQ104 Equalizer windscreen will cost you $121, and you'll know it's worth every penny when you hear the clean outdoor sound it gives you. (Note that the AT815b microphone takes an EQ108 windscreen and the AT835b takes an EQ107.) If you rent a windscreen, get a zeppelin style that fits the rental microphone. You can save some money by only renting the zeppelin on the weekends you shoot outdoors.

As we mentioned earlier, you can substitutes a $15 collapsible painter's pole for the boom pole, but make sure it's light enough for your boom operator to hold overhead all day.

The last things you'll need are headphones for the mixer, a 20-foot and a 100-foot mike cable, and at least three sets of batteries for the mixer and for the microphone. A $30 AKG K-55 closed-back headphone will work great, and you can use it to keep from waking your significant-partner while you're being a picaresque moviemaker editing late into the night in your picturesque garret. Don't spend any extra money on headphones for the boom operator. We never used them. With a little advice from the sound recordist, our boom operator still knew where to point the mike. The two XLR (3-pin connectors) mike cables will cost about $58. If you have a boom operator, run the 100-foot cable from mike to mixer and the 20-foot cable from mixer to camcorder. Reverse the cable positions if the sound recordist is wearing headphones and operating the boom pole as ours did on *Grown Men*. Using just a sound recordist worked because it was rarely necessary to adjust sound levels during a take, and if the levels were set high enough to get the quiet sounds, louder sounds could be cut down by not aiming the shotgun microphone directly at the sound sources.

A word about using wireless microphones: Don't. It may seem like a great idea. You don't have to follow the actors with a microphone, and you can cut out the boom operator, saving a crew position. Unfortunately, these systems use tiny lavalier microphones that are more apt to sound tinny than other microphones. They are super-susceptible to sibilance, so they sometimes hiss on "S" sounds. (This last sentence would be a good test.) If your actors are going to move, lavaliers are going to pick up clothing noise, unintended body sounds, heartbeats, and the rubbing of skin or hair against the mike.. They are hard to hide and still get good sound. The radio-receiver units for these microphones sometimes pick up truckers' CBs and radio signals from the French underground. In short, they are not worth the trouble. There's a reason most big productions use shotgun mikes.

As with other equipment, you may find a person who personally owns a mixer and mikes. If so, try to rent cheaply from them or get them to join your crew and bring along their equipment.

Vehicles

We didn't budget anything for vehicles. We used what we had. John needed to buy a new used car shortly before we began shooting *Beyond Bob*, so he bought the kind of car we wanted the main character to drive. If you've done your scriptwriting well, you'll be using vehicles that are available to you free. If you need something exotic, try to find someone with a car compulsion who owns one. They are as excited by cars as you are about movies, so they are usually glad to drive theirs in the movie for you as long as it's not a crash scene. You may be able to talk a local car dealership into providing a vehicle, but beware if they start talking about insurance. You'll be buying a camcorder instead of insurance.

As for larger vehicles to haul equipment, you'll soon discover you don't need any. The equipment you can afford will fit in the trunks of cars.

Meals

Don't skimp on the quality of the food, just the price. We've included some sample menus in the appendix that don't require expensive ingredients, but are good, hot, substantial meals. You can buy the food in bulk to save costs and prepare it yourself to avoid the extra cost of prepared food. Fortunately, Dale's wife is a very good cook and a tolerant woman. She, along with her sisters and in-laws, prepared and served meals for the cast and crew on our first two productions. These days few people actually make meals from scratch, so even the simplest homemade meals taste like Mom's finest to them. For the cast and crew, these meals almost made up for the meager pay and long hours. Some cast members from our first film agreed to work on the second film only if Dale's wife was making the meals. Others said it was the best they'd eaten in years. Now, we didn't made gourmet meals. This was just standard fare prepared by human hands rather than extruded from vats in a factory. On *Grown Men*, our non-profit status was parlayed into free food from many local restaurants and grocery stores.

Basically the budget includes a snack for a Friday-evening shoot and three meals a day for the Saturday and Sunday shooting days. Six meals and a snack for about 20 people for $125. Or about 89 cents per person per meal. This may seem like a miracle, but it's not that hard to do if someone makes it.

The snack and breakfasts can be simpler, so you can save some money there to add a little to the lunch and dinner meals. Plan menus for your entire production ahead of time, so you can buy larger quantities of food at lower prices. For drinks, fruit-juice concentrates and generic-brand pop are cheapest (though we ultimately bought some name-brand pop because of crew complaints). For the non-perishable items (canned goods, chips, pop, coffee, tea, baking supplies), buy them as they go on sale during the months ahead of the production. Meats, cheeses, and fruit-juice concentrates can be bought on sale and frozen until needed. Frugal shopping, filling but inexpensive menus, and home cooking can make these meals a high point of your production and a low cost in your budget.

Locations

We found it pretty easy to get use of private locations for nothing. Most people are thrilled to see a movie in production, though they quickly learn that it is tedious, hard work, even on fast-paced productions like ours. It's fun for them to tell the neighbors about hosting the movie crew. If you live in a town where movie productions are common, you may run into more people asking for money to use their property. You can't afford it, and tell them so. They may relent. If they still want money, move on. Sometimes losing your first choice leads to a better, more interesting choice. At least, try to look at it that way because you lose a lot of first choices making a feature-length movie with no visible budget.

We found small towns to be very accommodating. They don't usually ask for permits to shoot in public areas, and we were even allowed to work on some residential streets after a casual conversation with the police chief and notifying the neighbors who might be inconvenienced. Friends, neighbors, and relatives are also good sources of locations, as are state and federal parks.

Be mindful of distances when you plan your production. You can't afford to put up your cast and crew overnight, and if you drive a long distance to a location, the rental dollars you spent on your equipment will be ticking away every minute you're on the road. Select sites that are near to your cast and crew and that can be clustered together on the production schedule. We're fortunate that where we live there are landscapes ranging from rocky cliffs to secluded woods to city skyscrapers to urban decay to suburbia to cows in the fields all within one hour's drive. If you look at your own hometown area with the eye of an outsider, you'll probably discover a great variety of unique settings for your movie as well.

We believe a cardinal rule of using locations is to be courteous and careful. Don't use things without asking. Take great pains not to damage anything. Clean up when you are finished. And be friendly to the owners and neighbors. When actors are waiting for their next scene, encourage them to chat with the natives. This is part of the thrill of having a movie crew shoot at your home, and it builds good will that allows you to come back for retakes if necessary. We think it is irresponsible of moviemakers to leave property owners unhappy. This poisons the waters for future productions and gives a bad name to all independent productions. To our knowledge, there aren't any locations that wouldn't welcome us back.

Tape Stock

After years of falling prices, mini-DV tapes seem to have settled out at a low of $3 for a 60-minute tape without a memory chip. In the appendix, we've listed some suppliers who generally have this price.

In order to figure out how much tape stock you actually need, count script pages. Each full page works out to one minute of screen time. You'll be amazed how accurate this is if you use standard script format (see example in the appendix), but be cautious of lines like "We see the Crimean War begin." This may require more than a few seconds of screen time.

Let's assume you have a perfect script... meaning 90 pages long, 90 minutes in length. Since your camera will use mini-DV cassettes and the 60-minute version is the best price; that's one-and-a-half tapes. You'll be shooting in a three-to-one ratio (3:1), meaning you'll shoot three minutes of tape for every minute of the finished movie. So at a 3:1 ratio, you'll use 270 minutes of tape (90 x 3 = 270) or four-and-a-half hours of tape or five tapes for production. By the same calculations, a 4:1 shooting ratio will require six tapes. You'll obviously need more tape if your script is longer. (If your script is longer than 100 minutes, it requires cutting to fit an $8,000 budget. Trust us; this surgery is much easier and cheaper to do now.)

We've thrown in another four mini-DV tapes in the budget to cover intermediate outputs from your edit system. Further down in the budget, ten VHS tapes are included for dubs to be used for music and sound work. Full-size DV 120-minute tapes are listed for the final output and backup copies. The 120-minute DV tapes will be extra expensive because most have a memory chip in the cassette. Panasonic's PAAYDV120EJ 120-minute tape is the lowest price at $16. For your 60-minute camera tapes, there are cheaper versions available without the memory chip. We like Sony's DVM-60PR as a well-built, reliable, mini-DV tape.

Digital Still Camera and Production Stills

You'll be sorry later when you do publicity, but you're going to be giving short shrift to still photos of your production. As the director and producer, we've taken photos during the shoots, but the results have been lackluster because we were busy helping with the movie magic when the interesting photo opportunities happened. We had thought of getting someone who wanted to take photos, but we were concerned about having another person to feed on the set and one more body to slow down a crew that needs to be lightning fast. We opted for one less person on two of our movies, knowing we'd regret it when it came time to assemble a publicity package, and we did.

On *Grown Men*, we did have a friend shoot some publicity photos on a couple selected days and got some nice shots. We recommend picking one day in your production schedule that promises to be photogenic and having a volunteer paparazzo tag along for the day. Another approach is to shoot your publicity stills later as staged shots. We did this to get poster shots for our movies. Digital photography has helped cut costs of publicity photos. If you or your photographer already own a digital camera, you can eliminate this $110 expense from the budget. A camera with at least three-megapixel resolution can cheaply shoot a good variety of photos that can be printed up to 5 x 7 inches in size. We've included four CDs in the budget for storing backup copies of all of your images.

Storage Vault Rental

When we shot on film, we felt the need to safely store our negatives and master soundtracks in a film vault. It costs about $100 a year. Since it doesn't cost us extra, we've stored our digital movie's master tapes there, too. However, we think you can skip this expense. Just take care to store your tapes safely. It's wise to store them in double plastic bags (in case of roof leaks or exploding water heaters) inside sturdy containers. Make sure the tapes are well away from magnetic fields, such as refrigerator magnets, electric motors, and coils of electrical cord. Steel drums buried in the back-yard are pretty secure if the Environmental Protection Agency doesn't dig them up for analysis.

For added protection, you can rent another DV camera or deck (unless you can borrow one) and shell out for enough extra tapes to make a copy of each original master tape. (Aren't lossless tape formats grand!) Then have this set of tapes stored at a different geographic location that is far enough away not to be struck by the same hurricane, lava flow, locust, or meteor impact that is going to nuke you and your master tapes. Don't forget to flip the record lock-out tab on the camera tapes the moment they come out of the camera to avoid artistic devastation resulting from clumsy fingers on the VCR controls.

Non-Linear Edit System

Along with digital-video camcorders, computer-based non-linear edit systems are responsible for rewriting the manual on how to do independent movies. They produce professional results, have all kinds of high-end professional features, and are no more expensive than buying a personal computer. You can own your editing system for less than it cost us to rent a 16mm flatbed editing table for our film, *Beyond Bob*. And we got a good deal at the time.

At this point in time, we're recommending the Macintosh Intel Core Duo iMac (or the previous iMac G5 with almost identical features) with 17-inch widescreen monitor, 1.83GHz speed, 160GB hard drive, 1GB RAM (random access memory), dual-layer 8X Superdrive (which burns and reads CDs and DVDs), and USB and FireWire ports. Add to this an external FireWire hard drive, 160 GB or more, to back up your files. It's equipped with plenty of hard-drive space, speed, and memory to cut your digital movie and mix it's soundtrack. There are more powerful Macintoshes and PCs that can do the same job, but not for so little money. The iMac will cost you $1,300, and the external hard drive is less than $200. Of course, by the time you read this, there will be faster computers available, which means you can get a better system for the same money, or you can buy this system cheaper and cut your budget even more. Either way, you win.

If you plan to use an older computer, make sure to buy an older (and cheaper) version of video-editing software that matches the capabilities of your specific computer. Don't worry about not having enough whiz-bang features. Editing software has exceeded the basic needs for editing a digital movie for several years, considering that the most common movie edit is a plain old cut.

If you're looking at PC-based systems, be sure they can successfully run video-editing software in the real world, not just in their carefully worded promotional brochures. It's best to see the system work or at least talk to someone using the same gear you're going to buy.

Assembling your own system is an option, but one that can be fraught with hazards because video demands a lot of a computer system. For example, hard drives must have a 3.6 MB-per-second *sustained* data rate for video editing. Lots of drives can meet this requirement for average rates (meaning they go faster and slower than this speed but average out to it), but they may not be able to sustain this rate (meaning they never run slower). Another difficult selection is a capture card to get your digital video into the edit system. They come in an ice-cream-shop variety of flavors, and not all will do the job for you. Before putting together your own editing system, get a complete list of specifications from a working system to use as your blueprint. We'd hate for you to spend a big chunk of your budget and end up with a high-tech space heater.

For those of you who want to limit your risks (as if producing an independent movie weren't risky!), buy an integrated video-editing system like the Macintosh G4, G5, and newer iMac models and PC systems specifically designed for video editing. Also, get as much hard-drive size and RAM as you can for the money available.

In order to complete your editing system, you'll attach your camcorder using a FireWire cable, and you'll use the audio and video outputs from your camcorder to connect to your own TV so you can check the quality of your images as you edit. (Or you can add a 13" color TV to your edit system for under $70 so that your long-suffering roommate can escape reality by watching reality-TV shows.)

Editing Software

While this iMac system comes with iMovie HD editing software, don't plan on editing with it. Unless your digital film is an ersatz home movie, iMovie won't have the controls and features you need to do a professional-looking and professional-sounding project. You'll need professional video-editing software to play with the big kids. For the $450 we've put in the budget, you'll have your choice of three professional options for Macintosh and Windows editing systems.

Apple's Final Cut Express HD at $300 operates only on Macintosh and has the essential features of its widely-used big sister Final Cut Pro HD. This software will work and play nicely with the iDVD software that's included with the iMac computer, so you'll be set for making your DVD previews with no additional equipment or software.

Avid Xpress DV at $495 list ($350 retail) will work with Macintosh and Windows computers and is the DV version of Avid Xpress Pro HD. It includes software to output mpeg2 files that can imported to iDVD or a Windows-based DVD program for making previews.

The third option is Sony's Vegas 6 + DVD production suite at $450 ($410 retail) for Windows-based PCs only. This program has features equivalent to the other two softwares and includes DVD production tools.

Of course, each of these softwares has slightly different features and sometime additional useful software, so review their specifications closely before deciding which one will work best for your movie.

If your money situation requires you to reduce this bare-bones budget, there is one almost-professional software option. Adobe's Premiere Elements at $99 is a light version of Premiere Pro, but unlike most low-cost software, it supports enough audio tracks to do a professional-quality sound track. This software is for Windows PCs only and includes DVD-making capabilities. However, it currently isn't rated for use with the professional camcorders (most likely to keep pros from buying it), so you should try it with your camcorder before buying.

Adobe Photoshop Elements is sometime bundled at a bargain price with Premiere Elements. That's good because we recommend Photoshop Elements for still-image editing. This powerful software is available for Macintosh and Windows computers, and it will help you prepare your publicity stills, create title elements, and even do some simple special effects.

Expect your editor to want the latest editing software and a real-time system that doesn't have to render transitions and effects (always more expensive—usually lots). Be ready to negotiate with and explain budget realities to whomever will be doing the editing. If that's you, don't let anyone hear you talking to yourself. They already think you're loony for making a feature-length movie, and you don't want to give them more evidence for the commitment hearing.

Film-Look Software
We didn't budget for software to create a "film" look for your digital movie even though there are some products available in the $150 range (such as DVFilm Maker from the DV Film company). You don't need this additional expense if you shoot your digital video to look as much like film as possible and then use the effects filters in your editing software to enhance the film look. We'll talk more about this in the production and postproduction chapters.

Video Dubs
You'll need dubs of your movie for your composer to write the music score, for actors to loop lines that were badly recorded, for timing sound effects not recorded on location, and for doing postproduction special-effects shots. While some of these needs can be met by making QuickTime files, VHS is still the most widely available playback format and a fast way to

record some of these working copies. Just record edited segments of your movie out to your DV camcorder, and then duplicate them on the VCR sitting under your TV. We've included a VHS recorder and DVD player in the budget in case you don't own them, but most likely you can save this $80 for something else.

Music Recording

Dramatic changes in audio-recording technology have led to the growth of home studios (more accurately, garage, basement, spare-bedroom, or attic studios) and ultra-low-budget music production. This means there are lots of composers who have their own recording capabilities, and you may be able to eliminate much of this budget item except for tape and CD supplies. If you get the final music soundtrack on a CD then you won't have to dig up any additional equipment to digitize it into your editing system. If your composer can't do the recording, then you have to start looking for the blue-light specials.

Start by thinking small and looking for special arrangements. We've recorded music tracks in the basement studio of a freelance audio engineer. The sound booth was tiny and the cheapest in town, and the results were as good as with a larger studio. It's the quality of the microphones and the recording and mixing equipment that are most important.

There's only enough money in this budget item for about five hours of studio time, though you may be able to arrange a lower rate by agreeing to work only when the studio has no other bookings. Either way, your composer isn't going to have weeks in the studio to complete your music tracks. She or he is going to have to record on the musical equivalent of your 3:1 shooting ratio, with very few takes of live performances. Any editing will need to be done on the video-editing system. Plenty of rehearsals before entering the studio will make this feasible.

When we needed to record an orchestra and a big band, our composer arranged for free use of the studio and recording equipment at a technical school for audio engineers and musicians. Good connections and lots of friends can help with these kinds of expensive items.

Sound Effects, Foley, Dialogue Looping

Thanks to the CD-quality sound on digital video, you can do the recording of any sound effects and foley (sounds for the actor's motions) and the "looping" of replacement dialogue using your camcorder. If you purchased your shotgun microphone, you're all set to go. If you have an on-camera microphone that can be removed, use an extension cable to get it away from any camera noise. While a sound booth at a recording studio will give you the best quality audio, you can get very usable results in a quiet room with blankets or drapes hung on the walls to quiet echoes. This makeshift sound booth also will work well for doing looping to replace poorly recorded dialogue. Your video-editing software has the basic capabilities to put all this audio together in a very good soundtrack. Sure you'll make compromises, but that's life in the ultra-low-budget lane, and 90% of your audience will never hear the compromises.

Titles

Thanks to the power of your video-editing software you can make titles that rival those of any feature film you've ever seen — at no added cost. Even animated ones are within your grasp.

Sneak Preview

A sneak preview is a good way to test how your movie will play to an audience, to see if its comedy, drama, suspense, or romance works the way you intended. Of course, there's no money to do this. So we have a free alternative. There are three ways we know to do this for nothing. Start by making a VHS cassette of your edited movie or burning a DVD. It doesn't have to be a perfect version to get some helpful audience feedback.

The first option is to loan the movie to people who are your intended audience, whose opinion you value, and whose candor you can count on. This probably won't be the most helpful feedback because most responses will be about how surprised these people are that you've been making a "real movie." Also you won't be in the room, which is one of the most helpful aspects of a sneak preview.

The second option is to invite a group of people (same credentials as above: intended audience, valued opinion, candor) to your home or any nicer place you can get for free. Make some popcorn, give them soft drinks, and show your movie. Many of the audience reactions will be "Wow, I didn't realize you were making a *movie* movie," but you may get a group dynamic going in the response. More important, you will be there to observe their real reactions and your own. Their reactions will tell when you really drew the audience into the story. If you don't see it, you probably didn't do it. Your reaction will be the "wince factor." When you find yourself cringing at an upcoming scene or special effect or line of dialogue or performance, it's probably one you should fix. Just like in script writing, you can convince yourself that the problem areas are not really problems, but the scales fall from you eyes when you sit down with a real audience. Use this unvarnished look at your movie to make it better.

The third option is to use your salesmanship or the kindness of friends to arrange for your movie to be projected free in a theater for an audience. This can be done from your VHS tape, your DVD, or from your mini-DV tapes with a quick tape change after the first 60 minutes. We were able to arrange for a sneak preview of *Beyond Bob* as a fundraiser for the local Independent Feature Project chapter. They arranged for the theater, the video projector, and publicity. They collected a small admission fee to add to their funds, and we got a preview audience. You can use some of your photocopying funds to make up short response sheets for the audience to fill out after the movie, but these comments were of less use than what we learned observing the audience and our own winces.

Final Output and Preview DVDs

When it comes time to get your finished movie out of your non-linear editor, you'll need to rent a DV record deck that can take a full-size DV tape that is 120 minutes long. (Your camcorder uses mini-DV tapes that are a maximum of 80 minutes long... a little short for your 90-minute movie.) You'll be making a DV master and a backup copy and then two more copies to be put away in a safe place. If your digital-video camcorder doesn't have "pass through" capabilities that send the edit system's signal from the FireWire connection to the audio and video outputs, then the rented DV deck will be your chance to make a handful of VHS copies of your entire movie for previews.

You'll also want to burn about 20 DVD previews of the movie using the iMac's Superdrive. If you're going to use Apple's iDVD for this purpose, you'll be happy you followed our advice to keep the movie to 90 minutes. The maximum length that iDVD will put on a disk is 90 minutes. To make a longer DVD, you're going to need to pay about $450 and invest a couple weeks in learning more advanced DVD software, such as Apple's DVD Studio Pro (if you've gone the PC route, Sonic Solutions' DVDit at $300 to $400 or Roxio's MyDVD at $70).

This would be a good time to make mini-DV copies of a few scenes to use for TV previews, such as talk shows or news interviews. You don't need the whole movie, just two or three good scenes. A couple VHS copies of the same scenes might be useful if you're being interviewed on cable-access shows or having to explain your movie to your grandmother.

Publicity Photos and Packets

For our publicity packets, we selected photos from the ones we'd shot on location. While not a sterling collection, they were interesting enough to get them published in more than a dozen newspapers and magazines. We recommend "modest but pithy" as the theme for publicity packets. Don't waste money on color glossy photos. Most publications can do everything necessary with a three-megapixel high-resolution digital photo in .jpg or .tif format. In fact, in the reporter's world of "I need it yesterday," they get positively giddy when you can e-mail them an image to use.

The Internet is your friend when it comes to publicity packets. As you move into the publicity mode, your non-linear editing system will become your Internet publicity machine. Use it to write a synopsis, cast list, and a feature article for the publicity packet. All of your written materials, your digital photos, and any logo can be e-mailed directly to entertainment reporters anywhere in the world or put on a Web site where they can find them... at no cost. You can even create some short QuickTime or AVI files showing brief segments of the movie to put on your website. We also recommend putting all of these publicity pieces on a CD that you can send with a cover letter to reporters and magazine writers. With so much spammy e-mail these days, a package in the mail is the postal equivalent of Christmas, and it often goes to the head of the line. Indicate in the publicity kits that preview copies of the movie are available, but save money and only send them out if a reporter is interested enough to request one.

Photocopying Scripts, Miscellaneous Photocopying

You'll need one full copy of the script for each main performer and supporting role, so you may be able to trim script copying costs if your cast is small. The bit players only need the pages they are in. You also need copies for the director, producer, unit production manager, director of photography, sound recordist, art director, wardrobe supervisor, makeup-and-hair supervisor, editor, and composer. Miscellaneous copying will include maps to locations, call sheets for the shooting days, release forms, shot-log sheets, and dozens of items that will crop up before, during, and after production. Some of these items can be sent by e-mail, but be sure people actually read them and print them out. A map on the home computer won't help a lost actor in a car find your location. Try to get a photocopying shop to do all of your copying free or for a reduced rate in exchange for being listed in the screen credits. Your local Independent Feature Project office may have a deal with a local photocopy shop; check with them for details.

Postage for Publicity and Preview DVDs

You'll want to send the publicity packets by first-class mail. Don't get sucked into the "send it express" or "fax it to me" syndrome. Planning ahead or waiting until the next printing deadline for a publication will eliminate these unnecessary costs. Everybody wants the material today so it can sit on their desk for two weeks until they get to it. First-class postage and a mailing envelope will cost about $1 per publicity packet (cover letter and CD), totaling $15 for 15 packets. Mailing out 20 preview DVDs to distributors and festivals will cost you another $20. Sometimes postal workers will use your precious CD or DVD as a stress-relief device, so put it between two pieces of cardboard for some extra protection.

Video-to-Film Transfer

You may notice that there's no line for a video-to-film transfer in the budget. Darn tootin' there isn't. Creating a motion-picture version of your project will more than double your production costs. Companies that can transfer your digital-video image to 16mm with mono soundtrack or 35mm film with stereo soundtrack have published prices ranging from about $150 to $300 per minute. Since most companies don't publish their prices, don't expect to find anything cheaper. A 35mm transfer costs about 50% more than a 16mm transfer. For this $13,500 to $27,000 (if you stay on the cheap side of town), you'll end up with an image negative and an optical-sound negative and one answer print of your movie. (Consider that it would cost $4,000 to $6,000 to buy a video projector powerful enough to show your digital movie in a small auditorium.)

Obviously, video-to-film transfer is not a cheap path to take, and you'll want to be quite sure it's necessary before you run down it. For any feature-length movie, there are two major routes of distribution, release on film or release on video (tape or DVD). Film releases are designed for big festivals that don't accept video (a dinosaur attitude that is almost extinct) and for showings in theaters. We chose to stay on video because movies as small as ours have a hard time even making it onto the screens at art-house theaters these days. Even movies from major studios go directly to home video without ever flickering onto a theater screen. We knew that any potential distributor would preview our movie on video and that it most likely would be distributed in the home-video market. If a distributor is really excited to do a theatrical release of your movie, the cost of the transfer to film can be built into the distribution deal. Whether you pay for it yourself or the distributor pays for it (which really means it will be taken out of your potential profits), get bids from several vendors before selecting someone to do a tape-to-film transfer. A little Internet research will give you loads of information about the best way to prepare your digital movie for transfer and about the merits and weaknesses of different transfer procedures.

As more theaters and major producers investigate projecting digital movies on movie theater screens, this topic will probably evaporate from your list of things to decide. So unless you're seriously committed to having your production end up on film stock, we recommend staying in the digital-video format and seeking your fortune there.

≈ • ≈

If you've done all the begging, finagling, dickering, and short cutting we recommend, you now have a budget of $8,000 or less. Congratulations. You've just taken one of the biggest steps towards making your feature-length movie a reality. You've set realistic expectations for the kind of digital movie it can be and created a plan for making it happen. You're on your way to a successful production. Savor the moment, and visualize what it will be like shooting your movie and seeing the story you love on the screen in front of an audience. Remember this vision of your goal well because it has got to last when the realities of funding, organizing, and launching your production come stomping into the room.

We hit those realities right away on our digital movie. We didn't have $8,000 lying around ready to use on the date we set for starting production. Our solution? Figure out how to shoot it for a lot less. Here's what you can do if you find yourself in this situation.

How to Shoot It for Less

If you throw out all the postproduction — that's everything after "Storage vault rental" in the budget except for photocopying — you'll get rid of close to half of your budget expenses, leaving your cash need at $4,820. You won't be able to do any editing, music-track or sound-effects work, titles, sneak preview, final output, or publicity. But you won't be ready to do any of that work until after you've finished shooting anyway. And once you've got your principal shooting done, you can set the postproduction schedule to match your ability to raise cash.

If this dollar amount is still an insurmountable mountain to climb, then shorten the mountain. Fire up your networking skills and start talking to people about the movie you want to shoot, especially people who own DV cameras. If you can get use of a camera and tripod for free (and possibly the videographer with it), you can shoot your movie for $2,445. If you can also get your lighting and sound equipment donated, your shooting budget will be $985. That's between $50 and $20 a week for a year. That's a part-time weekend job for a year or less. This is a hill you can climb if you really want to shoot your movie.

Of course, the Hydra of the remaining budget costs will rear its ugly heads at a later point, but you can lop them off one at a time if you're persistent… and you keep working weekends at the video store.

Chapter 4

The Business ~ *Ultra-Low Budget, Inc.*

When we first dreamed of making our movies, we never dreamed of becoming accountants. We never dreamed of becoming corporate officers or contract lawyers or corporate tax preparers.

To us, these weren't dreams. They were nightmares. That's not to impugn any of these professions; they're just not ones to which we aspired. But just as your dreams at night sometimes cast you in unusual roles, the dream of making your own feature-length movie may put you into some unexpected professions. We found ourselves pushed, pulled, and thrown into all of these jobs as we got into the business end of making movies.

Now if you're as passionate about making movies as we are, you're probably thinking about skipping this chapter and saying to yourself, "I don't want to be in business. I just want to make my movie." We said that too, but it didn't help. We still ended up in business, and you will too if you plan to have your feature shown somewhere other than your basement. This is one of the dark chapters of making movies, so you might as well come to terms with it because it's not going away.

Here's the bad news of this book for anyone in love with making movies. It's a business.

During the 17 years that we've spent producing our feature-length projects, at least ten years of that time has been drained away running a business. Sometimes it seems like producing and shooting movies is just a sidelight. But no matter how grisly it is, this work has to be done. Even gourmet cooks have pots to wash. And since you're going to be a gourmet cook working at a diner, you probably can't afford to have someone else do your dirty work.

Now we're not saying we've got the inside track on the business of business. It remains the one area we are least certain about. However, we avoided having any really scary discussions with tax collectors or other people's attorneys, so we make the bold presumption that we did okay.

Nevertheless, before we started our production of *Grown Men*, we switched business tracks. We incorporated an educational nonprofit organization to produce the movie. There were several considerations that led us to that decision. We were tired of doing corporate tax filings; we were not making profits as a business; we couldn't accept volunteers or donated services and materials as a for-profit business; and we acknowledged that we aren't very entrepreneurial by nature. So we've seen both sides of this fence, and there's some green grass in each place.

What follows is how we took care of business — both for profit and not for profit — but it comes with a warning: "Results may vary." The bad news is that almost every state has different rules related to business and non-profit issues. The Internal Revenue Service (IRS) has consistent rules, which may be interpreted differently by individual IRS personnel. The good news is that we work in Minnesota, which has some of the more stringent rules and most aggressive tax structures. (We're not complaining — both lead to an above-average quality of life.) This means that some issues we faced may not exist where you work.

The details of our experience aside, you can't ignore business issues without repercussions later. You will have to investigate to find the best solution for your personal situation under the current laws and tax structure. Our two approaches are just a few out of many strategies. There may be better options for you.

Trust us on this point. You'll be glad you took care of business issues when the distributor who wants your movie asks, "Are all the rights clear on this film?" It may be the difference between getting your movie distributed and not.

Business Decisions

There were four main factors that motivated the business choices we made:

1) Money: As always, we couldn't afford to spend any money that wouldn't show up on the screen somehow.

2) **Rights:** We wanted to produce movies that were ready to be sold as professional productions, meaning we clearly owned all rights to our productions and could sell them.

3) **Legal Liability:** We owned houses and cars that we didn't want to lose in a lawsuit.

4) **Tax Obligations:** We didn't want to spend the rest of our days in tax jail (where you can make license plates or produce movies that explain tax code).

Because these four factors are often joined at the hip, please excuse some repetition in our ramblings. It's important to know how each of these factors will affect other decisions you must make.

Money

If the point hasn't been made already, let us reiterate. Money and the lack of it are going to be the undercurrent that affects every decision you make. To complete a feature-length digital movie for a paltry $8,000, you can't spend a penny that isn't going to somehow improve the look or the sound of your movie. This means a big list of people you can't hire (but need) and things you can't buy or rent (but need).

Professional Help

At the business end of film production, lack of money primarily translates into not being able to afford lawyers, accountants, and tax preparers. This means you'll need free help to set up your business or nonprofit, develop contracts and releases, keep your books, and prepare tax statements. Since we didn't have friends who could do this work for us, we had no option. We learned to do it ourselves.

There are a number of how-to books and websites that are immensely helpful, everything from basic accounting to incorporating a business to starting a nonprofit to boilerplate examples of essential documents. We've listed ones we've used in the appendix, but don't let this list limit you. There are many fine works out there in your local library and on the

Internet. Keep in mind that most libraries can borrow from bigger or more specialized libraries if they don't have what you need. Library books and websites are resources that fit your budget.

We also asked other people who had done this before for their ideas, warnings, sample contracts, release forms, articles of incorporation, and such. We took a local class on incorporating a nonprofit organization. We learned that we could take the work of other people's expensive lawyers and tailor it to our needs. We also learned that being a lawyer doesn't mean you can write a good contract or release form or articles of organization. We've seen contracts and release forms with serious holes that could really hurt both parties. Personally, we believe that complex legal language creates more misunderstandings than it prevents. We feel that plain language makes it less likely that you'll have problems with contracts, release forms, and other written agreements. That's been our experience.

Lack of money will probably force you to do your own accounting, bookkeeping, and tax preparation, too. But they're not so bad when compared with being trampled by stampeding wildebeest. Truly, these tasks are the most boring, confusing, and terrifying work on a film production. And you'll need to do them even if you are operating as a nonprofit organization, though there are some shortcuts available. Do whatever you can to find someone who loves doing these jobs, and get them to take on the task. Dale, as producer, reluctantly took on these duties and learned basic corporate accounting and tax preparation in the trenches. Even if you hand over these duties, be sure to learn enough about the accounts to know where the money is going. (There are too many stories of accountants flying off to Rio... not that they don't deserve the break.)

If you're forced to do your own taxes, take heart. Surveys of professional tax preparers have shown extreme differences in the final tax returns they prepared. Just do your honest best, and hope the IRS treats you kindly.

As for the accounting, it's one of those mystic arts, but it is learnable. If you start with a basic accounting text the way we did and spend a few evenings studying it, you'll soon understand the basic principles of accounting... or you'll renew your efforts to find someone to do it for you. Many textbooks also include helpful examples of lists of accounts, general ledgers, ledger entries, and year-end reports, which are the basic tools of accounting. There are accounting computer programs that will do most of this work for you once you set up the accounts.

Insurance

Working on an $8,000 budget means your production will do without liability insurance, completion bonds, or errors-and-omission insurance unless you scrape up more money. There's only one of these that we would suggest you even consider, but you should know what they all are.

Liability Insurance: Liability insurance is the basic coverage that pays for damage or injury you cause, such as dropping an electrified klieg light into a hot tub full of bathers. Not having liability insurance has prevented us from using some locations, has caused us to pay out of pocket for some minor damage to buildings, and has caused us to lose more than a few minutes of sleep. The cost of this insurance will add a significant percentage to your tiny budget, but if you are planning to do especially risky work or are accident prone, it may be worth rounding up the extra greenbacks to pay for it. If you happen to work in the audio-visual field, you may already carry annual production insurance that you can apply to your digital movie, or you may be able to add a cheap rider to your existing policy. Unless you have one of these policies in your pocket ("Is that an insurance rider, or are you just glad to see me?"), you'll be on the high wire without the "good hands" to catch you. That's what we did. You just have to be very cautious, safety conscious, and careful with borrowed props, costumes, and locations. The one liability insurance we got was a low-cost damage option on our rental equipment. Given the cost to replace this equipment, it was worth doing.

Completion Bonds: Completion bonds are essentially insurance policies that will pay over-budget costs in order to guarantee investors that you will complete the production. Forget it. Anyone putting money into an $8,000 movie had better recognize that this is a long-shot proposition. There are a hundred minor things that can cripple a fringe production like yours, and only three things that will get it finished — the tenacity of your production troupe, good luck, and the kindness of strangers. And you're depending on all of these. You and everyone on your production are rolling the dice and gambling that your skills and creativity are going to win big. There are simply no guarantees, and any investors should recognize that they are betting on you, plain and simple.

Of course, you couldn't afford to get a completion bond anyway. Even if you tried, the completion-bond company would probably shriek with laughter. It's the equivalent of smoking unfiltered cigarettes, flying home-built jets, cliff diving… and then applying for life insurance. Completion-bond companies don't want to pay to finish your movie, so the only way they will give you a completion bond is if your production uses the safest, time-tested production procedures. Wrong universe! You're going to do something that is completely alien to completion-bond companies. You're going to break most of the rules to make something out of nothing. And that's only going to happen if you and your investors close your eyes really tightly and repeat "I believe. I believe. I BELIEVE!"

Errors-and-Omissions Insurance: Errors-and-omissions insurance is liability insurance that protects you in case you failed to get all the necessary rights and releases from performers, used copyrighted material without permission, included libelous material, didn't get location releases, infringed upon a famous title, or based your screenplay on someone else's published work. Simply put, it's insurance to protect against you — the producer — having not done your job.

There are three reasons we didn't bother with this insurance. First, we did our job right and got all the necessary rights and clearances. Second, no one will issue this insurance to you unless you have done your job right. ("Sure, we'll insure you against dying while deep-sea diving now that you've given up diving.") Third, this primarily protects the distributors, so let them pay for it if they're so nervous. If someone insists on errors-and-omissions insurance, give them copies of your paperwork, and make it part of the contract that they will pay for the insurance.

Employees

As a business, lack of bucks will prevent you from having employees, especially union ones. You can't afford employees because you have to pay them minimum wage — except for corporate officers, sole proprietors, partners, and members (owners) of limited liability companies, who can forego salary. If you were a union production, even at the union's low-budget rates, you'd have to pay union scale to cast and crew. That alone would use up all of your production money and more. So if you come from a long line of union activists, either give up this ultra-low-budget movie idea now, or steel yourself for some tense family reunions.

The employee issue is a real problem for low-budget independent productions these days. When we started making movies, we were able to have all crew members be independent contractors and defer their salaries to be paid out of any profits — if there were any. Everyone on our productions was okay with this arrangement because we were all doing it for the experience not the money. Well, it can't be done that way today. This was one big reason for us to start up a nonprofit organization to do productions as educational experiences. Here's what happened to independent contractors — the condensed version, as we understand it.

The federal Internal Revenue Service (IRS) audited the film-and-video industry's practices and found that most people — actors, crew, directors, producers, etc. — were hired as independent contractors who were responsible for paying their own income tax, social security withholdings, and such. The IRS also found that many of these taxes and withholdings weren't being paid. Then the IRS looked closely at the nature of these jobs and found that most of them met the statutory description of employees, not independent contractors. So today, only a few positions, such as director and producer, can qualify as independent contractors on a production. This may sound like arcane tax talk, but it significantly affects your production. If you have employees (actors and crew), you have to pay them minimum wage and maybe overtime if you manage to shoot more than 40 hours on a given weekend. (We did 32 hours.) You'll also have to withhold income tax and social security and pay for worker's compensation insurance. As you saw in the sample budget, this very quickly adds up to all of your production money being spent on salaries.

We've come up with six ways to deal with this issue on an ultra-low-budget movie. We've only used the last one, and of other four legal ones, two fall in the ideas-that-might-work category, and two are proven approaches. You might come up with others of your own, but in any case, check out your plan with state and federal employment regulators before you bet the farm. Federal rules continue to change and so do state requirements, so you'll need to scan the sea before you set sail. Here's the skinny on the six approaches.

- Ignore the rules and just work with little or no salary for all cast and crew. Bad idea. This could earn you big fines and payment of back salaries and maybe even some jail time as a corporate officer or business owner who willfully violated the labor laws.

- Hire all cast and crew as student interns who are paid only a small stipend as they work on your production to learn and earn resume credentials. This might work, especially if your have an inexperienced crew. However, this method should be checked out thoroughly with state and federal employment officials before attempting it.

- Make the entire production a partnership venture, so everyone on the cast and crew would be partners in the production. As owners, they and you could forego salaries. This would be like everyone on the production owning a corner grocery store together, making business decisions together, contributing to the costs equally, and sharing in the profits equally. It could work with the right people, sort of a moviemakers commune. The downside is that this business structure would put your personal assets on the table if there were a lawsuit or some financial liability. ("Daddy, why is that man repossessing my trike?")

- Pay wages and find a way to come up with double the budget for your movie. Also, you would have to do a lot of paperwork for taxes and withholdings. This might spur you to hire a payroll service or payroll staff person.

- Create a limited liability company with the cast, crew, director, producer, and investors all being member (owners) of the company. Members cannot be considered employees, so the wage problem is solved. The

Digital Filmmaking 101 ~ Newton & Gaspard

flexibility of this structure allows you to avoid communal decision-making, and this business structure protects members from personal liability for debts or lawsuits.

- Finally, create a nonprofit organization whose mission would be to offer educational experiences for cast and crew on independent movie productions. All cast and crew could be volunteers on the production. Equipment, supplies, and food could be donated, something that a for-profit business can't accept. This was the approach we chose because it fit with our personal goals of making movies... not making money. And everyone gains experience and resume credentials whether the project is for profit or not for profit. Obviously, this isn't right for everyone.

One downside of the nonprofit approach is that your workers might work harder and better if they see this as an entry-level professional production. If you're asking them to volunteer their time and effort, it could affect how they view the project, and working professionals might be less likely to sign on. This means your crew and cast might be less experienced. But that can be an asset. They won't know that you can't make a feature-length movie for no money.

On *Grown Men*, we found that experienced people and novices still were happy to work on this nonprofit production, and many brought equipment with them for free. For the most part, everyone treated it as a serious production, and only a few people failed to show up. However, we didn't shoot our digital movie on a grueling four-weekend production schedule, so we don't know if this volunteerism and good will would hold up for a month of moviemaking boot camp.

Obviously, the employee issue is going to play a major role in the organizational structure you choose for your movie production. You'll need to select an approach that you can afford and an approach that will let you meet your moviemaking goals. And then you'll want to check it out thoroughly with state and federal employment officials so your movie dream doesn't become a business nightmare.

Rights

The next major factor affecting your business or nonprofit activities is the securing of rights. Not securing all necessary rights for your digital movie is going to put you at a severe disadvantage when you try to distribute it. It might even tie up your production in legal actions. And it's a problem you can avoid.

Rights are a matter that you'll want to pay attention to from day one. A lot of decisions you make will relate to getting rights to present your finished movie, and you'll need to diligently gather these rights as you wend your way through preproduction, production, and postproduction. So fire up the photocopier. There are forms to copy.

Contracts, release forms, and letters of approval are the three ropes you're going to use to hog-tie those pesky rights. The performance rights you're looking for include the screenplay, the performances of your cast, the work products of your crew, the music and sound effects (if they come from a recorded library) in your sound track, any copyrighted material used in the movie (images, such as photos or prints that are more than just background, readings or dialogue from other sources, snatches of music or images on the radio or TV), and the locations you use (excluding public property, but be aware that seemingly public areas such as shopping malls are privately owned). Get the approvals before you commit these items and performances to tape. If you don't and can't get the rights later, you've wasted precious production time.

We started securing rights as soon as the first crew person joined us on our production. Everyone, including the director and producer, signed a release form that gave full ownership of their work to the organization producing the movie. We used this ownership clause to secure rights to the cast's performances, the crew's work, the screenplay, and the music tracks created by our composer. On our first two movies, our composer, who wanted to potentially use the music again, only granted us synchronization rights. Synchronization rights mean you can do anything you want with the music as long as it stays connected to the movie images. If you want to release a hit single, you have to get more rights. Given that we were getting thousands of dollars of original music for next to nothing, it seemed like a fair compromise. We also bought some previously recorded

Digital Filmmaking 101 ~ Newton & Gaspard

music for a few scenes, and for this we also used a contract for synchro-nization rights only.

Release forms also will take care of the rights to use the images of extras, unpaid performers, and locations. If you're shooting in a public place, you technically don't need to get permission to use the images of people who could have been seen by anyone in that public place, as long as you don't highlight them. (Close-ups of people adjusting their under-garments will just buy you trouble.) Some productions post signs that warn people entering the area that they may be included in a movie, but that presumes the moviemakers have gotten permission to shoot in that area in the first place. Guerrilla productions like ours only get permission if there's no permit fee from the city or whomever, so this may draw too much attention to your work. If you decide to feature someone in particular, you better get them to sign a release form or make sure they're not identifiable. Also get signed location releases for every privately owned site you shoot on or shoot at. Do this in advance of your shoot dates to avoid those ugly high-stress negotiations with cast and crew waiting. Samples of individual, group, and location release forms are included in the appendix.

Approval letters are all you need to get use of various copyrighted items. For example, we featured an existing hang-gliding book in one of our productions. To obtain approval, we just wrote to the publisher, explained the movie and the context to them, and they sent a permission letter.

Sound effects from recorded libraries didn't require any forms. When we've used them, we just bought the sound with synchronization rights from a production house and got a receipt. Be sure to tell them you want it for a feature-length movie because some libraries aren't licensed to be used for feature productions. Of course, being in the proper low-budget mindset, you're planning to record all of your sound effects with your DV camcorder.

If in any situation you can't get the rights you need (worldwide, exclusive, without restrictions, in perpetuity), stop. Do not pass go. If you can't persuade that performer, crew person, landowner, or copyright owner, don't even think about using their stuff. Find another solution. Otherwise, you'll regret it when you have to go back and beg that person for the rights so you can sell your movie.

The last point you need to consider about rights is holding on to them once you've gotten them. You or your organization automatically own copyright to your production. Under U.S. law, you don't have to register it or even put a copyright notice on it in order to own your movie's copyright. However, it is advisable to register it with the Library of Congress' Copyright Office to make it clear to everyone who owns the movie and to establish the time when it was created in case any legal disputes arise later. It's also a good idea to put a copyright notice in your movie titles, reading "Copyright (year) (the copyright holder's name)."

Legal Liability

Nobody wants to be sued. As a result, many of your business decisions will be aimed at reducing your potential value as a lawsuit target. For a business on the razor's edge of viability — which we guarantee you'll be if you're trying to make a feature-length movie for eight grand — a lawsuit could mean the untimely demise of your dream. For a nonprofit, it could mean that you have to close up shop as well. And don't be foolhardy enough to think that it couldn't happen to you. Law schools are graduating more lawyers than ever before, so many that their employment possibilities are getting almost as poor as those for moviemakers. But lawyers do have one advantage: A town that can't support one lawyer can support two. They know how to make their own work.

Because of the diminishing job possibilities in companies and law firms, lawyers are now forced to do what screenwriters and other underemployed professionals have always done, which is work on speculation. Just as we have written entire screenplays with the hopes of selling them, lawyers without work will undertake lawsuits just for the possibility of getting a percentage of any settlement. The upshot: Anyone can get a lawyer to sue you today. And lots of people do.

You do have some automatic advantages in this area. For the most part, you'll be in the turnip category, as in "you can't get blood out of a turnip." However, people who automatically smell money around moviemaking may mistake you for a worthwhile candidate, and frivolous lawsuits are as costly to defend as valid ones. The other advantage is that you're small, fast moving, and out of sight quickly — at least one good thing about not being able to maintain a high profile. Because none of these factors will guarantee your safety, it's wise to build in whatever protection you can. There are three steps we took.

Business Structure

If you're going to make this movie for professional sale, you'll end up with some business structure eventually, and by default if you don't actually decide. Basically, you have seven choices: individual proprietorship, partnership, limited partnership, S corporation, C corporation, limited liability company, and nonprofit corporation. Don't go to sleep on us now. There's going to be a test at the end of the chapter.

Now if you embrace inertia and ignore business concerns, you'll probably end up being legally classified as an individual proprietorship, which means that you'll personally own the business and all its assets. A partnership is very similar, except that two or more people personally own the business and divide the assets. Now, even these simple business structures have legal and tax requirements, so ignoring business will put you into some trouble with local, state, and federal authorities. Though these business structures have simplified accounting and tax requirements, they didn't meet our main criteria: protecting homes, cars, and personal assets from being taken to pay business liabilities. So we reluctantly rejected these simpler forms of business.

Limited partnerships have been used to finance many independent film productions. These businesses are made up of two groups of partners. The general partners, usually the filmmakers, run the business and have all the duties and liabilities of a regular partnership. The limited partners just put money into the project for a share of the profits. Because their participation in business decisions is limited, so is their financial risk and liability risk. However, as a general partner, your personal assets won't be protected. Each state has different rules for setting up limited partnerships, and there are federal rules limiting the numbers of partners and how they can be invited to become partners. Limited partnerships are complicated beasties that are set up by lawyers; consequently, they have mostly been replaced by the simpler limited-liability-company structure.

The S corporation is a corporate structure under which the business' assets are included in the shareholders' personal coffers for tax purposes. This simplifies the business income and tax reporting, but complicates your personal taxes. This was a tempting choice for us, but because it intermingles the business assets with your personal assets, a lawsuit or bankruptcy might also be applied to your personal assets ("Sorry about losing the house, Honey."). Too risky for us.

So we bit the bullet and became a real C corporation, just like GM, 3M, and MGM, but without the medical plans and the golden parachutes. This meant that all government agencies viewed our movie-production business as a "person" or entity that was wholly separate from us. As a result, if we wanted to put personal money into the film production, we had to loan it to the corporation or purchase stock shares even though we were the sole shareholders and the corporate officers. It's a little hard to get into this mindset, but you catch on eventually.

As a C corporation, we had to have annual meetings of shareholders (us) and the board of directors (us) and keep minutes of decisions. There was a significant amount of record keeping and tax reporting required (and federal corporate tax instructions are not a pretty sight), but you are afforded almost complete personal protection from lawsuits, bankruptcy, creditors, and the like. However, this doesn't mean you can act irresponsibly. In extreme cases of corporations flagrantly violating the law or endangering employees or communities, the corporate officers have been held liable, even sent to prison. But if you act in good faith and take steps to protect people, the Toyota in your garage should be safe from seizure.

Now, becoming a corporation may seem like a daunting task, but it's actually pretty easy. We had to file some boilerplate articles of incorporation with the state's Secretary of State Office, apply for state and federal tax numbers, and set up stock ownership....

Brief tangential discussion: Stock is tricky and heavily regulated. If you don't sell stock outside of the state in which you're incorporated, if you don't publicly offer to sell the stock, and if offers and sales are only to residents of your state, you are exempt from registering with the federal Securities and Exchange Commission under the "Intrastate Offering Exemption" of Section 3(a)(11) of the Securities Act. On the state level, you'll likely have to file a registration form U-7 that was adopted by the North American Securities Administration Association as a uniform state securities registration form for small corporate stock offerings. But not all states have the same requirements, so check your local laws and rules. Also, the sale of stock on the Internet and other stock-sale innovations are causing the securities laws to change with some regularity in order to keep up, so don't assume this information is still accurate. Use this as a starting point to see for yourself what the latest requirements are. The U.S. Securities and Exchange Commission website is a good starting point. It's listed in the appendix. End of digression and back to our story.

We found a guidebook prepared by a state university that gave us all the steps in lay person's terms for a simplified business incorporation in our state. The federal Small Business Administration website offers similar free help and links to websites that walk you through the process of starting a business as well as providing template documents. Check the appendix for specific sites. Most states also have offices and websites to help small businesses. The Feds and some states offer free training programs on taxes and other business issues. So do universities, business schools, and vocational technical colleges, but not for free. And don't forget the public library; that's where we found the incorporation guidebook. Ask the reference librarians for help. These people love ferreting out information the way you love filmmaking, and they're usually delighted to be asked to use their skills.

If we haven't been too specific about the actual details of incorporating here, it's because it constitutes its own book, and you'll undoubtedly have more, less, or different steps to take where you live.

In the years since we set up a corporation, states have created a new business entity, the limited liability company or LLC. If we were beginning today, we'd start one of these. While they lack some of the fund-raising options available to corporations, they are simpler to create and run, and the paperwork requirements can be easier. Disclaimer time. We've never set up a limited liability company, so all we know is learned from research. Research is something you should do, too, if you plan to follow this route. But from what we've read, a limited liability company is a good fit with independent moviemaking. Here's the scoop:

A limited liability company does just what its name says. It limits the liability for business debts or legal judgments (lawsuits) to the company's resources. The owners' personal resources are safe as long as the owners don't personally guarantee loans for the company or undertake illegal activities while representing the company, such as failing to pay taxes. First business goal met. On to the next.

The owners of a limited liability company, called members, are not considered employees. Rather than receiving wages, members are compensated by receiving their "distributive share" (their share of the profits or losses). If you make your cast and crew into members of the limited liability company, you have a legal way to avoid paying employee wages (which you can't afford with an $8,000 budget). Their work on the project will be done in exchange for a share of any profits. Goal number two met.

But wait, there's more. For tax purposes, a limited liability company is a "disregarded entity," meaning it's considered a sole proprietorship or, if there is more than one member, a partnership. That means no corporate tax filings, unless you submit a Form 8832 to the IRS electing to be taxed as a corporation. (An act of sheer madness! In truth, there can be some advantages, but don't worry about them until you earn enough to need an accountant.) You will have to file a Form 1065 *U.S. Return for Partnership Income* to give the IRS information on how profits or losses are distributed each year. The share of each member should match the percentage of value (cash, capital, or service) that member has put into the company. The company the must give each member a Schedule K-1 listing their share of profits and losses. (You should note that members have to pay income taxes on the company's profits even if those profits are left in the company's accounts and not distributed to the members. Consequently, if your limited liability company earns profits, be sure that members get paid enough of them to pay the taxes.)

You might need to file other forms, too, if you pay income to vendors or if you complicate your limited liability company with employees, non-American members, and such. There's a helpful list of other forms inside the Form 1065 instructions. Taxes themselves are handled through members' individual income tax filing on Form 1040 Schedule E, but income is not likely to be a problem for a while.

Setting up a limited liability company is not difficult or expensive in most states, but it's different in each state. (Apparently, the United States are not as united as we thought they were.) It's not hard to find out the procedures. Just visit the website of the Secretary of State for the state where you'll be doing business. Most have a boilerplate form for Articles of Organization. You fill in the blanks about company name, members (owners), registered agent to receive official papers (it can usually be you in your home state), place of business, whether a manager or members will run the company, and other simple details. Then, in most cases, you pay a fee ranging from $50 to $200, and you're in business. Some states require you to publish a notice that you're going into business. That's all you really have to do, but there's more you want to do.

Obviously, becoming partners with everyone who works on the production is scary since you won't necessarily know all of these people. You may not even find your postproduction crew until the movie is shot, so it will be hard to list them as members when you start up the company. These issues are generally handled by the Operating Agreement of a limited liability company, and it can be a very flexible document. There are samples on the Internet and in books, and we're going to give some ideas on what to include, as well. You can write it yourself, or you can get help from a lawyer. The former is a lot cheaper.

Because the IRS doesn't want limited liabilities to be just corporations in disguise, they limit you to having two of the four features of a corporation: limited liability, centralized management, free transferability of ownership, and perpetual existence. You'll pick your two in the operating agreement that's signed by all members. Because you want limited liability and someone in charge (unless you're comfortable with communal decision-making), then you will need to limit how membership (ownership) is transferred, and you must set a limit on the company's life span, say 50 years. (You'll be lucky to survive that long as a moviemaker!) Members can vote to dissolve the limited liability company earlier if they wish.

Because you're allowed to have members with different rights and participation, we suggest organizing with one or two key members but include in the operating agreement the option for the key members to vote to add associate members who have a smaller share of voting. As long as the key members have over half the votes, they control company activities.

(If you vote to put yourself in charge of daily operations, then the company is manager-managed. It's member-managed if all members vote on decisions.) Since you'll be putting in most of the effort and money, it's easy to justify your high percentage of control. (You may want to buy your equipment personally and lease it to the company for a set cost so that you keep ownership of it if the company dissolves.)

If you also include a clause in the operating agreement that lets the company buy out the shares of associate members after a set period of time, then you can add associate members (cast and crew) in exchange for the number of hours of service they will provide to the company. After they have completed their role in the movie production, the company enters into a contract with them to buy their share of the company. The contract agrees to give them their share of profits if the movie makes any. This gives you a cast and a crew, but no employees you have to pay wages. The cast and crew get to share in any revenue the movie earns, and they are relieved from having to report company income and losses on their income tax returns while waiting for profits to appear.

Since a limited liability company normally dissolves if a member dies, goes bankrupt, retires, divorces, withdraws, or is expelled from the company, you'll want to include a standard clause that allows for members to be bought out (called a buy/sell agreement) and allows the company to continue. There are other clauses that you'll likely want in your operating agreement that will be tailored to your specific circumstances. A small amount of Internet searching and a review of your state's statutes about limited liability companies will turn up a lot of information to help you decide which clauses make sense for your production. There are also companies offering sample agreements that you can customize to your situation.

Here are some of the issues that you should consider including in your operating agreement: the members' percentage of ownership, the members' rights and responsibilities, the members' voting powers. (Votes that match the members' ownership percentages are best.) You'll also want to lay out how profits and losses will be distributed among the members (by percentage of ownership is best), how the company will be managed, how the company will handle buyouts of members who want to or have to leave, how members can sell their interest in the company, and how the company will hold meetings and take votes. (Make sure that a majority of votes decides an issue.)

If a limited liability company sounds too good to be true, it is... in some states. While the organizing fees are quite reasonable, a few states require an annual "franchise tax," "renewal fee," or "annual registration fee," usually about $100. But California, for example, has an $800 "limited liability tax" payable each year. Some others have $300 to $500 annual fees. This takes quite a bite out of a small budget. Be sure to get the full picture on fees before you set up your business tent. In case you're thinking of jumping the state line to organize, you should know that the regular taxes and even some "foreign" (out-of-state) business taxes apply in most states where you're doing business. In addition, you may have to pay some "franchise" fees and hire an in-state registered agent when you organize in a different state. Delaware and Nevada have set themselves up in the business of organizing businesses. They make it fast and easy to set up a business, but by the time you pay the additional fees and taxes to operate in your home state, they may not be any cheaper. Plus, if your company has legal troubles, you'll have to sort them out in a Delaware or Nevada courtroom. For exactly that reason, we decided to set up shop in our home state, and Minnesota only taxes you if you have income, not just for existing.

Even early *Homo sapiens* grew weary of stalking giant cave bears for food and tried a quieter life of growing corn and potatoes. After nine years of hunting for corporate profits and wrestling with the hairy behemoths of corporate taxes and corporate record keeping, we opted to cultivate a nonprofit organization instead — since profits had been elusive and small anyway. Of course, the nonprofit organization would own any movie productions done under its auspices, but a corporation owned the productions we did under its name, so the situation didn't really change much.

There are some definite advantages to being a nonprofit corporation. You have the same protection of personal assets that a C corporation offers, but unlike a C corporation (or any other for-profit business structure) you can accept donations of money, services, equipment, and food, and people can work for you as volunteers — all the stuff you need to make an ultra-low-budget movie. They are no harder to create than a business corporation — as long as you have a nonprofit purpose in mind — and the paperwork can be a lot easier. If you want to try moviemaking as your full-time gig, you'll be happy to know that nonprofit organizations can have staff that are paid for their services. (You can opt out of the corporate rat-race and still seek your fortune. People have done it for years.)

To set up a nonprofit organization, start by reading up on your state's rules for creating a nonprofit organization. Also read the federal rules because you have to meet both sets of requirements in order to qualify for federal nonprofit status and exemption from federal income tax. Following are the general steps for setting up a nonprofit corporation (but remember, like the tourist attractions and the official rock, the rules are different in most states):

1) Your corporation must be organized to carry out a nonprofit purpose. The acceptable purposes under section 501(3)(c) of the federal tax code are: charitable, religious, educational, scientific, literary, testing for public safety, fostering national or international amateur sports competition (but not providing equipment or facilities), or prevention of cruelty to children or animals. (Note that prevention of cruelty to screenwriters isn't a tax-exempt activity.) Get IRS Publication 4220 (*Applying for 501(c)(3) Tax-Exempt Status*) for an easy-to-read outline of how to set up your nonprofit corporation.

2) You must file in your state for a unique corporate name, articles of incorporation (also called "articles of organization"), and corporate bylaws. Some states will provide sample articles and bylaws (check your Secretary of State's website), but you must pass muster with the IRS so check out the boilerplate examples in Publication 557 (*Tax-Exempt Status for Your Organization*) on the IRS website (see appendix). It's best to stick pretty close to the examples so that your request for state corporate status and federal tax exemption aren't denied. It costs money to incorporate — in most cases several hundred dollars — but you usually have to pay to revise your articles of incorporation or bylaws. So do them right the first time and save some bucks. To assist you, there are some nonprofit organizations that helps other nonprofits get set up. (No kidding!) Ask around in the local nonprofit community. There is also advice on the Internet, but make sure it's for the state in which you are

incorporating. A good shortcut is to ask for a copy of the articles of incorporation and bylaws for an existing nonprofit that is similar to the one you plan. You can modify those articles to create yours.

3) File Form SS-4 with the IRS to get an employer identification number (EIN). You'll need this number to set up a bank account for your organization and to do the required filings if you hire any employees. You may need a state identification number as well, such as a sales tax number, so be sure to check with your state.

4) File Form 1023 (*Application for Recognition of Exemption under 501(c)(3) of IRS code*) and Form 8718 (*User Fee for Exempt Organization Determination Letter Request*) with the IRS. The filing fee is based on your likely budget average — a $900 fee if you have a budget average over $10,000 per year for four years or a $300 fee if less. See, you can save $600 by having an ultra-low budget.

5) Annually file a Form 990 (*Return of Organization Exempt from Income Tax*). If you have less than $25,000 of receipts in a year, you don't have to file this form. If your income is more, you have to complete the form, but it's a lot simpler than a for-profit-corporation tax form.

6) Annually file state income-tax, sales-tax, and nonprofit-registration forms. In most cases you don't have to file state income-tax forms if you're exempt from the federal forms, and you only have to file sales-tax forms if you have taxable sales. Be sure to ask your state tax and business officials to make sure you know all the forms you are required to file.

After you have gotten your nonprofit status, make sure you operate within the purpose you set out for the organization. If you don't, Special Agent "Red" Tape may show up at your door in his sunglasses and black suit to discuss how you've erred and what penalty you have to pay. (And don't mention our names. We warned you after all.)

Now if your mind works like ours, the urge to run and hide under the desk is becoming overwhelming about now. Regulations, taxes, legal notices, thumbscrews, and charging mastodons are all listed deep in our primitive brains as things to avoid as fast as our legs can carry us. It's your basic fight-or-flight decision. We could have chucked the entire project when faced with this business stuff, but the rewards from making a movie were great enough that we turned and fought our way through the paperwork and legal language, and we're glad we did. So take heart; success comes to the brave. On the bright side, the remaining steps to protect yourself from legal liability are all easier.

Liability Waivers

The second step we took to protect ourselves from lawsuits was to include liability waivers in all our contracts and release forms with the cast and crew. This was to avoid lawsuits from inside our production group. Of course, we still took steps to minimize risks of injury, but there's always a chance of an accident. These waivers are not iron-clad by any legal definition, but it puts the people you're working with on notice that they are responsible for their own medical and accident insurance and that they have acknowledged that they are accepting any risks of injury. If nothing else, they will all think twice before they ask a lawyer about suing you, and therefore, won't be advised that they could sue you anyway. If they do sue, that's when your turnip status comes into play.

There are a couple of secondary benefits to this waiver. When you get location releases signed by property owners, some ask about insurance (which you don't have). It helped us to be able to say that we had this waiver for every person on the production crew to avoid lawsuits for injury. Of course the waiver won't absolutely prevent legal actions, but lawsuits would probably involve the production company first and the property owner second.

By this point, you're probably beginning to realize that the only real protection from lawsuits that you can have is to make sure nothing happens that anyone can sue you over. To ensure this, take precautions on the set to make sure risks are limited. If you have dangerous-looking scenes, do everything you can with special effects, film tricks, and safety equipment to prevent real injury. In our film *Resident Alien*, an important scene takes place on a roof at night (only a madman would pick such as dangerous setting for a low-budget script), which worried us a lot. The first thing we did was find a one-story building with a roof that had a low pitch, almost flat. We assigned one person to hold the ladder whenever someone went up or down, and Dale, as the producer (and madman scriptwriter) on the set, spent all night reminding people they were on a roof and warning them when they got too close to the edge. Because of technical problems, we had to reshoot this sequence, so we actually did it twice without mishap. We were very, very careful and very lucky.

Shooting for safety on the roof for Resident Alien. *(Pictured, l to r: actor Patrick Coyle and director of photography Scott Lee Dose.)]*

Copyright

Our third step to avoid legal entanglements was scrupulous attention to copyright laws. We're always amazed how many professionals in the media business ignore the laws which protect their own work. In case you have any doubts, YOU CAN'T USE ANYTHING YOU DIDN'T CREATE WITHOUT GETTING PERMISSION! No, you can't borrow that music; no, you can't use video footage running on TV; and no, you can't just lift a few lines from a novel or another screenplay. Granted, there are some gray areas in satire and parody, in public domain material, and in documentary or scholarly usage of material, but you aren't likely to have the lawyerly resources to make sure you have clear rights to use these items. So don't.

For low-buck producers such as ourselves, there are only two feasible options (unless you have free use of a copyright attorney). Create something original or get written permission to use it, which often comes at a cost. Creating something original is easiest. There are lots of creative people looking for outlets for their work. They will love you for asking them to create music, artwork, or poetry for your movie. For example, we had at least six composers ask if they could do our music tracks for free. You can also ask these people to give you permission to use music, art, or writing they've already done.

For minor items, like a newspaper masthead with a column by one of our characters, we just made up a bogus newspaper on the computer. For a club scene that had TVs visible in the background, we ran a video of one of our previous movies. When we wanted our characters pictured on *Entertainment Weekly* magazine, we asked permission, and the publisher granted it after reviewing the final layout. (Of course, this was when the magazine was just starting out and looking for publicity. *Rolling Stone* turned us down flat.) Often pleading poverty and being friendly will get you permission for free if it's not something that's normally sold for performance.

There's one detail that you must not forget. For all the wonderful original writing, music, and pictures, be sure you have a contract or release form signed by every artist stating that you own all rights to that material or at least all rights to use it in your movie. Get these from the composers, painters, musicians, photographers, graphic artists, and everyone else. And then file them away safely. We've never had to pull these out, but we can if there is any question about rights. Don't overlook this essential task.

If something is copyrighted and is identifiable on your set, get permission or replace it with something you have created (and photocopying it is not creating it). It will save you lots of worries in the future.

Even being careful, we got a scary letter on our first film, *Resident Alien*. It was from an attorney for a larger docudrama by the same title. In stern legal language, it warned us that our title infringed on their production. It urged us to select another title.

This was not a pleasant letter. Our production money was gone, titles were done, and our title fit our story perfectly. We also knew that you can't copyright a title unless that title is so famous that you would instantly be stealing sales that rightly belonged to the original production (so you can forget about calling your film *Casablanca*). We definitely couldn't afford an attorney to respond, but we wanted to resolve the issue.

This is where being writers and people who know the value of humor came in handy. We mustered our best legal language and wrote back a letter thanking them for asking whether they would be infringing on our film's title. We went on to say that since our films had different audiences and since we couldn't copyright titles, we felt we could co-exist in the marketplace. We closed by wishing them good luck with their *Resident Alien*.

Fortunately, the attorney and his client appreciated the ironic humor and the validity of our arguments. We got back a cordial letter that parroted our language about co-existing and wished us luck with our *Resident Alien*, which proves that the pen is mightier than the lawsuit.

Our point is, don't mess with copyright. Every distribution contract that's come across our desk has a clause in which you cross your heart and hope to die if you don't own all rights to the material in your movie. This is when you'll be glad you didn't borrow that shot from *Star Wars* and that you remembered to get all those release forms signed.

Tax Obligations

Swallow hard kiddies, and hold onto those armrests. Ready to hear some really terrifying tales? We're going to talk about federal, state, and local taxes and how they affect the business choices you need to make. This is scarier than anything you'll see on the late-night horror show.

Actually, the scary part about taxes is the not knowing. Not knowing if there's a tax out there that you've forgotten to pay. Not knowing if you've filled out the forms properly. Not knowing if the IRS SWAT team is going to kick in the door and seize the paltry gains that you've managed to wring out of your creative efforts. Our advice is to relax and ask questions.

Like most things governmental, there's a lot of fear about taxes that is unnecessary and unwarranted. Dale has worked in government for more than 25 years, and he's not very threatening (unless you ask him to spend money wastefully). And he promises that zombies don't suck the souls of civil servants every morning as they come to work. Government work is just like any other work. Some people are good at their jobs; some are poor. Some are friendly and helpful; some are cranky and officious. The point you need to remember is that the tax man (notice that there's not much clamor for equal gender access to this term?) and tax woman are people you can ask for help.

There are three main types of taxes that may affect you, presuming you don't buy real estate as part of your production: sales/use tax (and this may not apply to out-of-state sales, sales for resale, or when you buy something for your movie that will be taxable when it's sold later); employee taxes (social security, worker's compensation insurance, state and federal income tax withholdings); and state and federal corporate income tax (or franchise taxes for some other business structures).

Taxes have mainly affected our business and our nonprofit corporation in three ways: where we do business, whether we have employees, and what type of accounting we do.

We live in the Minneapolis and St. Paul metropolitan area in Minnesota. We incorporated our moviemaking business in a fringe community because there were no extra sales taxes to pay for a domed baseball stadium (also it was where there was a corner in the basement for an in-home office).

For our business, we operated with no employees except corporate officers, who were the two of us. And the business' corporate officers declined any salary until the company was profitable (which it never was). With no employee salaries, we avoided having to track and pay employee taxes, such as worker's compensation insurance, social security tax, and withholdings for state and federal income tax. For the nonprofit corporation, we've operated solely with volunteers. Keep in mind that taking on that first employee will probably generate enough paperwork to require at least another part-time employee. We've decided if we ever reach the point of hiring employees, one of the first will have to be an accountant-bookkeeper-tax preparer, and if they can sew costumes, that's all the better.

The third taxing effect on our business and nonprofit has been accounting. You will be dealing with large enough sums of money that the state and federal revenue departments will want to know what you're doing with them as a business and as a nonprofit. Even if you've decided to go the individual proprietorship route, you'll still have to keep records for tax purposes. There's no escape. They've got you surrounded. So surrender, and learn how to speak the victor's language. We set up an accounting system designed to keep track of our loans and to tabulate the end-of-the-year information we needed to report on our corporate income tax. This system will be your best friend or your worst enemy or both.

Beyond this basic tax advice, you just need to get the forms and read the instructions. It's all right there in gobbledygook. If you thought personal income tax forms were incomprehensible, wait until you get a look at business tax forms. They don't even try to make them friendly.

(Nonprofit tax forms are much friendlier probably because even IRS employees might need a meal from a nonprofit soup kitchen some day.) But take heart, at least you won't be paying a professional tax preparer to make your mistakes for you. So relax, be honest, and do your best on the forms. That's what everyone else is doing.

It also can be helpful to call the IRS or your state department of revenue for advice when you get stuck. They don't want you to do it incorrectly, so they'll usually help if they can. And be sure to keep a record of the helpful person's name, because surveys have shown that the advice from the IRS tax person is wrong a lot of times.

The problem is that special interests and political deals have made our tax system into a combination labyrinth and morass that no one fully understands. So where the rubber meets the road in the IRS office, there's some poor soul like us just trying to figure out this mess. When you call her or him up, express your fear and your desire to do the right thing, and treat him or her as a person. You'll likely be pleasantly surprised by the results. We were. Time for an example.

We had dutifully applied for a state sales-tax number when we incorporated, but were told to wait until we had a product for sale. So we went into production for three years and reapplied when we had a finished movie to sell. We got the forms, and as we read through them, we realized that the film stock and processing we had been buying out of state was taxable. This was a hefty chunk of sales tax (about $800) since film was one of our major expenses. Worse yet, some of this tax was three years overdue with a 20% per year penalty. Dollars were mounting.

With faint hope that we could avoid some or all of this tax, we called the state sales-tax office and found compassion. The tax guy was actually impressed that we had discovered our oversight (their oversight, too, since they wouldn't send us the information we needed at the beginning) and that we wanted to do it right. He advised us to just pay the tax as if it wasn't overdue. We took his name and thanked him, and avoided more than $500 in tax penalties. This just goes to show you that tax people are human, too, and they respect people who try to do the right thing. They also like it if you don't scream and spit at them.

Now just a word about grants for those of you who are able to pry loose some free money. Remember that even though someone gave you this money to do all or part of your film, you'll still need to operate as a business or nonprofit organization if you want a salable product in the end. If you're a nonprofit, the grant may be large enough to push you into the bracket for filing an income form, and you'll certainly need to show it in your accounting books. If you're for-profit, you'll probably have to report the grant on your personal income taxes and give some of the money away in taxes right off the bat. Because grants are usually given to one or two individuals, not to companies, you are probably going to be an individual proprietorship or a partnership.

Even though the grant money was free, as soon as your business or nonprofit hires people, you get into the employee issue. You'll still need talent and location releases; you'll still need clear rights to music, performances, and images; and you'll still be a target for lawsuits. And if you have the good fortune to make sales of your movie, you'll likely have to pay sales tax and income tax. Sorry. No escape from the business demon or the tax incubus.

We know this business stuff is a big turn-off. But no art comes without suffering, and this is just part of your penance. Hopefully, our experiences can help alleviate some of your pain in going through the process. Also, keep your eye on the goal, a finished and distributed feature movie. Knowing your destination makes a bumpy trip more tolerable.

To summarize, here's a checklist of the business or nonprofit decisions you need to make and tasks you need to do to set up and run your moviemaking business.

Decide:
- Business structure: individual proprietorship, partnership, limited partnership, S corporation, C corporation, limited liability company, nonprofit organization
- Worker status: independent contractors, employees, student interns, members (owners), volunteers
- Location of business
- Cute, serious, funny, or suggestive name for your company

Tasks:

- Read up on starting a business or nonprofit and on basic accounting
- File necessary business or nonprofit start-up papers with a state
- Set up a partnership agreement, a limited partnership agreement, articles of incorporation, or articles of organization if these apply
- Create bylaws (corporation or nonprofit) or operating agreement (limited liability company)
- Sell and issue stock to your shareholders if incorporating as a business
- Get tax and employer identification numbers from the state and federal governments
- Set up accounting books, and begin keeping accounting records
- Prepare contracts, liability waivers, talent release forms, and location release forms, and get them signed
- Get rights to all music, sound effects, images, performances, and work done for your film
- Request the appropriate sales-tax, income-tax, and franchise-tax returns from state and federal governments
- Pay sales, income, and, if necessary, employment taxes (worker's compensation insurance, social security, and withholdings for income tax) on both state and federal level
- File for copyright protection on your script and film
- Lie down in a dark room with a cool washcloth on your forehead

Chapter 5

The Money ~ *"Hello Uncle Burt? You Don't Remember Me, But..."*

When we made *Resident Alien* and *Beyond Bob* (for $28,000 and $26,000, respectively), we thought we'd gone about as low as you could go, budget-wise. So, can you imagine our elation when we realized that we could complete *Grown Men* for in the neighborhood of $10,000? Well, obviously we decided to move right into that neighborhood.

But that $10,000 had to come from somewhere, and so will the cash you need to get your movie off the ground and through postproduction. You've got to buy or rent a camcorder, sound equipment, lights, and tape stock, and you need to get your hands on an editing system. And pay for lots of costs in between.

Yes, you've reached that point. You have the idea; the script is written (or percolating); you've worked out your budget; you've set up your business structure; and now the next big step looms before you. You ask yourself, "How the heck do I come up with the money to do this?"

A darn good question. A tough question. A question with many possible answers. Most moviemakers follow one or more of the following well-worn paths: Investors, Credit Cards, Scrimping, Grants, Favors, and Found Money.

Investors

The biggest problem with investors is that they generally want their money back. It's annoying. Some of them even want their money back plus a profit. Apparently they don't understand movie investments.

While as a moviemaker you're in a position to offer your investors many things — the thrill of being an integral part of an artistic experiment, the joy of watching talent bloom, the sheer excitement of being involved in the moviemaking process and seeing their names in lights — a guaranteed payback is, sadly, not on your list of deliverables.

So when you begin scouring your hometown for investors, you'll want to seek out people who are clearly much more excited about the process of making a digital feature than its actual outcome, profit-wise. If an investor is simply looking for a fast or hefty return, it's best to suggest that they look elsewhere.

However, if they're committed — to you, to your idea, or to a local asylum and have granted you power of attorney — they can become some of your strongest allies.

The other problem with raising money via investors is that, in many cases, it actually costs money to raise money. And on a no-buck digital feature, there is no loose change jingling in your pockets for such shenanigans. Limited partnerships have historically been the financial vehicle of choice for independent moviemakers. However, limited partnerships require voluminous paperwork, and with voluminous paperwork comes lawyers, and with lawyers come fees. You could easily spend $5,000 on legal work to put together a limited partnership for your $8,000 movie.

You see the problem.

If you're determined to take the limited partnership path, find a lawyer who will take care of the voluminous paperwork for free or on a deferred basis. It can be costly and difficult to raise money in other business structures as well, such as taking on stockholders in your corporation (make it less than 25 people and from the state in which you're incorporated), adding members to your limited liability company, taking loans, entering a full partnership, or receiving nonprofit donations. Be sure you understand all the steps before you walk down any fundraising path.

Once you've figured out how you're going to set up your money-raising apparatus, the next step is to go out and actually start knocking on doors to find your investors. (Beware. In some states, there are rules governing how many doors you can knock on, especially for limited partnerships and stock offerings.) Doctors, dentists, business people with a love of movies, women who've outlived their rich husbands, old rich guys with young second wives who are dying to get into movies... these are the traditional supporters of independent moviemakers.

And the beauty of funding an ultra-low-budget movie is that it doesn't take a large number of investors to pull together the cash you need. If your budget is $8,000, all you need are ten friends with $800 each. Or five friends with $1,600 each. Or four friends with $2,000. Or one really good friend with $8,000. The money is out there; you just have to go ask for it.

Once you've found your investors and their money, don't abandon them while you dive into production. Keep them informed of your progress and give them an opportunity to share in the few moments of glamour and excitement that are part and parcel of the process.

They should be invited to the set to watch production, and if extras are needed, they should be asked if they'd like to take part. If you're sending out updates in the form of a newsletter to the cast and crew during post-production, the investors should be added to the snail-mail and e-mail lists. All the investors should certainly be invited to preview screenings, and they should be given a place of honor at the premiere. In short, you should involve them in the process so that they can get something out of it other than a profit (if even that).

Credit Cards

Yes, we've all been tempted. You get one or two or five envelopes a week that exclaim that "You've Already Been Approved!" And who doesn't crave approval?

So you tear it open, and there's a simple form to fill out that will make any number of delightful and convenient credit cards wing their way to your abode. And you look at the generous credit limits — $1,500 here, $2,000 there, trusting souls offering you $5,000 — and you do the math. Before you know it, you've got a plan.

Here's one word of advice: Don't.

Here are two words of advice: Forget it.

Here are four words of advice: It's a bad idea.

Here are eleven words of advice: You're going to lose your shorts and maybe even your house.

Sure, you've heard the stories about moviemakers who put their movies — and their credit ratings — on the line. They rolled the dice, and they won! Yeah, sure. And we've got some prime real estate in Florida that can make you a fortune.

It's not just the risk factor that concerns us. We all know that moviemaking is a crap shoot. We actually like risks. It just isn't a smart plan.

Let's say that you decide to finance a portion of your movie with credit cards, about $5,000 worth. If it's the $5,000 you need to finish the movie, you're in trouble. Why? Because even if you can finish the movie in a month — edit it, do the soundtrack, complete your publicity materials, cutting great deals at every point — it's going to be at least another month before you sign with a distributor (and that's being very, very optimistic). And then there's a minimum of three months before they work it into their distribution schedule (again, wild-eyed optimism). And then there's another four to six months before exhibitors send in the money they owe you (optimistic doesn't begin to describe what *that* is).

That's ten months. You're paying 18% interest (if you're lucky) on $5,000 for ten months — minimum. That's at least $750 in interest, and you still owe $5,000. And what if you can't get the movie finished that quickly? And what if you can't find a distributor? And what if, what if, what if?

Of course, if you want to put yourself in some deeply serious trouble, use the $5,000 to *shoot* the movie. That will tack on another six months or a year to that ever-mounting interest monster you've created.

The stories that have circulated about moviemakers charging entire features on their credit cards are good copy, but they're also simply bad business, grossly exaggerated, flat out not true, or about moviemakers who like to play "chicken" with freight trains.

If you want to boast that you charged your entire feature on your Bloomingdale's card in your press releases, go right ahead. We won't let on. But the next time you get one of those "You are already pre-approved" mailings, do the smart thing. Just say no.

Scrimping

Scrimping is an unpleasant word. Say it out loud once, and you'll see what we mean. *Scrimping*. It has an unpleasant ring, doesn't it? It sounds like a particularly demeaning part of a fraternity hazing. "Yeah, first they shaved our heads, then we had to climb down into the sewers and spend the night scrimping rats."

Scrimping is not fun. It requires sacrifice. It requires discipline. It requires saying no to common urges, such as the urge to eat out, the urge to buy extravagant non-necessities, the urge to get a new pair of sneakers when your current sneakers are only five years old and the holes in the bottom aren't really all that big as long as you stay out of puddles and wear two pairs of socks, which also have holes in them.

Can a person really scrimp together a budget for a digital feature? That depends on the person, their income, and the willingness of their significant other to join in the festive mood of scrimping and living like a pauper. As Ben Franklin said, "Two can live as cheaply as one, but they have no idea how cheaply they can live until they try to scrimp together the money for a digital feature." We're paraphrasing, of course, but you get the idea.

Diligent, concerted, and ongoing scrimping can put an extra wad of cash in your pocket every month, and that wad could add up to a big part of your budget.

Scrimping can take many forms. You can bring your lunch to work instead of eating out. At two to five dollars a day, that gives you an extra $500 to $1,300 a year. You can buy food in bulk at co-ops. You can stop buying those expensive breakfast cereals and treat yourself to oatmeal, the breakfast of scrimpers!

Even when you're scrimping dutifully, money can still slip away incrementally — a few dollars here, a few dollars there, adding up to a big part of your income. You can use this incrementalism to your advantage, however, by having an extra $50 or $100 deducted from your paycheck every two weeks as part of your tax withholding or simply increasing your W-4 tax deduction (creating a sort of forced savings plan).

At the end of the year, your refund will include an extra $1,300 or $2,600, which can buy you all sorts of digital luxuries, like a camera or an editing system.

Of course, many would argue that letting Uncle Sam hold your money for a year doesn't earn you an iota of interest, while even the worst bank savings account will pay you something for the honor of holding your money. True enough. The value of the Uncle Sam savings plan, though, is that once you fill out the form, it's out of your hands. The money is taken out every two weeks, whether you think about it or not. And it's not available for you to use on something else.

Most people don't have the discipline to set aside money every month; if you do, then skip the tax deduction step, and do it yourself. Some companies have employee savings programs that will take a set amount out of your paycheck and put it in a savings account. The result is the same — a bit more money toward making or finishing your movie.

Another scrimping method is to join a car pool to cut down on parking costs. Changing your own oil in the car will also save you some cash. If your climate (and commute) permits, you can simply get rid of the car and ride a bike to work. You'll save on gas, auto repairs, and insurance. As an added bonus, you'll start to get yourself in shape for the grueling rigors of movie production.

They say art is sacrifice. And they also say that scrimping sucks. They're right on both counts.

Grants

Grant money can be a great financial resource for the ultra-low-budget moviemaker, particularly if your project is out of the mainstream or focused on a particularly unique niche of our society. Granters are always looking for non-commercial, personal movies that examine or celebrate cultures, population segments, or lifestyles generally ignored by the commercial media.

While you may not be able to raise your entire budget this way, a grant can help you get started or help you finish, depending on the grant program. Some programs are devoted to supplying seed money, giving you the dollars you need to get your project off the ground but not necessarily enough to complete it. However, one person's seed money can be another person's entire budget. Twenty thousand dollars may be only enough to help a $500,000 feature film set up shop; it's more than enough to get you all the way through production and postproduction, plus enough left over to take a nice cruise.

Regardless of what kind of funding you're asking for, we should point out that there's a trick to getting grant money. Now, this is a secret, so please don't spread it around because then everyone will know about it, and then it won't work anymore. In fact, after you read this section, you may want to tear these pages out and eat them, just to be on the safe side.

Ready for the secret? The trick to getting grant money is this: Follow the grant instructions.

Seems obvious, doesn't it? Yet, every day moviemakers submit grant proposals that blithely, even blatantly, ignore the grant instructions. And not just the fine print. Often the big print as well. In most cases, these grant requests are turned down. Ignored. Or even mocked. Yes, it's true. Grant panels will openly mock incorrectly filled-out grant proposals (behind closed doors) and then unceremoniously discard them. It happens every day in foundation board rooms across the country.

It's a shame, isn't it? Well, no, actually, it's great. Because if *you* fill out the forms correctly and others don't, it will be *their* applications piling up by the dumpster and *yours* that gets moved ahead for further review.

That's the second secret of getting grant money: Grant committees are just itching for a reason not to give you money. It's not because they don't like you or your project. It's because there are so many requests for grant money — and so little money to go around — that they need an easy way to wade through the piles of plastic binders and find those proposals that are completely and totally deserving of their largesse. And the easiest criteria for eliminating contestants from this pool is to toss them out for rules violations.

Let's say they ask for a one-page project summary, and you, in your foolish arrogance, submit a three-page project summary — well, you're outta there! Kiss your grant hopes good-bye! They can now move on to more deserving candidates. Or perhaps their pedantic instructions insist upon three letters of recommendation. And you submit only one. Heads up! Another grant proposal headed for the wastebasket. They shoot... and you don't score!

Submitting your proposal late. Failure to include an innocuous piece of paperwork. Your name at the bottom of the page instead of the top. Who knows what will set off the finicky grant people?

You do, that's who.

You now know how to get the edge over most of the people applying for grants. Read the instructions, and follow them to the letter! Not everyone will. Filling out the paperwork correctly doesn't guarantee you success, of course, but it does put you head and shoulders above the rest of the crowd. At that point, your project and its merits will have to speak for themselves. But at least they'll have an audience.

Favors

Favors are the currency of independent moviemaking. They're the oil that keeps the gears running smoothly. They're the sip of cool water in the middle of an arid desert.

Favors can come from anyone and anywhere. A video producer with a camera package lets you use it on weekends. A relative gives you the key to their empty cabin, a perfect location for your movie. An old friend from junior high who now works at a rental house cuts you a great deal on lighting equipment. Your ex-brother-in-law who has access to some editing equipment comes to your rescue.

While you probably can't produce an entire digital feature on favors alone, regular trips to the favor bank can save you oodles of cash along the way.

Calling in some favors resulted in getting a men's club, dancers, extras, and even a Steadicam during the production of Grown Men. *(Photo courtesy of Granite Productions, Unlimited.)*

Of course, building up an account at the favor bank doesn't happen overnight. You must invest in the favor bank, just like a savings account at a regular bank. You do favors for other people in your moviemaking community by helping out on a shoot, lending some equipment or advice, and offering your talent and your services. All of these favors are an important investment for you and for the rest of the moviemaking community.

By the time you're done with your feature, you'll undoubtedly be overdrawn at the favor bank in a big way. So be sure to get back out there and start investing again, offering your help to those who helped you. Your moviemaking community needs you, and, with any luck, you're going to need them again as well.

Found Money

Found money is great. It's that sudden influx of cash that you didn't expect which suddenly makes it possible for you to get your movie off the ground. Found money was a great asset on all of our feature projects. The trick with found money, however, is to quickly invest it in your movie before you realize that you have some actual need for it — like home repairs, car repairs, or a new pair of sneakers and socks.

Found money comes in many shapes and sizes. Here are some situations that could best be described as found money.

- An ailing, distant aunt dies, leaving you exactly $8,000 (after probate and taxes, bless her heart).
- You win the lottery with a ticket you found on the sidewalk while picking up a nickel because you've been scrimping lately to get a movie project off the ground.
- The hours you spent diligently preparing and mailing in all those Publishers Clearinghouse Sweepstakes entries finally pay off when your mail carrier proposes to you, and you discover that your new fiancé is really an eccentric millionaire with a penchant for independent moviemakers.

Of course, there are moments during the money-raising process that may cause you to feel panic or even desperation. During these moments, you may feel as though you would do anything for money. *Anything.*

There are a few situations that do not qualify in the strictest sense as found money, and we recommend that you don't succumb to these temptations when money gets tight:

- Your distant, ailing aunt asks for a second opinion, and you arrange an appointment for her with Dr. Kevorkian.
- You accidentally place your younger brother's kidney up for auction on eBay.
- You enter a convenience store wearing a ski mask and carrying a prop pistol, and the goofy night clerk inadvertently gives you all the money in the safe.

≈ • ≈

No matter how you slice it, getting the money is one of the hardest parts of the moviemaking process — whether your budget is $8,000 or $80 million.

The mere size of your tiny budget provides you with a slight advantage, but on those dark days when no one is returning your calls and your friends and relatives turn icy when you enter the room, it is little solace. And no longer mere.

Along with distribution hell, the money-raising phase of the moviemaking process is one where you feel the least in control. It follows, then, that this is a time when you are the most vulnerable — to compromise, to inertia and entropy, to complete and total surrender. Resist these feelings with the full force of your psyche because giving in to any of them spells death for your project — and for a bit of your soul.

As Winston Churchill so stoically put it, "Never give up. Never give up. Never give up." If his Prime Minister gig hadn't panned out for him, he had what it takes to be a digital moviemaker.

So hang in there. You never know when you're going to find that lottery ticket, persuade that investor, or receive a knowing wink and a smile from your mail carrier.

Chapter 6

Preproduction ~ *"Being Compulsive Is Not a Bad Thing. I Know. I Double Checked."*

He's making a list and checking it twice. Yes, Virginia, Santa Claus would be a welcome addition to any ultra-low-budget movie's preproduction team. He's cheerful, leaves nothing to chance, gets things done on schedule, and is able to perform miracles.

On our movies, we found that the producer, director, and unit production manager formed a triumvirate that was the guiding force of the production. These are the only three people who see all aspects of production, so it's natural that they do the preproduction planning and follow through. These three members of your production team should be as compulsive as possible.

It's a pity that therapists around the world are trying to control compulsive behavior when independent moviemakers are looking for that very talent in their crews. (Hint: look for people with clean desks and neatly-stacked paper clips, organized by size, color, and age.)

You may want to add the director of photography to this team because so much of the planning is around creating images for your production. You may want to include the screenwriter, who can offer insights into the vision and the intent of the story. In our case, we served as producer and director and were also the screenwriters, so we always had screenwriter input. We included our director of photography in some of our preproduction meetings, but not all because there are hundreds of logistical details that we didn't want the director of photography to think about. She or he will have more than enough to worry about on your production just trying to make sure you've gotten usable and, hopefully, artistic images on tape.

These compulsive three, four, or five people have some basic production decisions to make before the meat of preproduction begins.

Digital or Film

You wouldn't have picked up this book if you weren't giving serious thought to producing a digital movie, but you or your team may still be struggling with the question of whether to shoot digital video or film. Even after we decided to shoot *Grown Men* on digital video, we found ourselves revisiting that decision as new considerations occurred to us. Preproduction is the time when you want to be sure you're committed to your path, so take time to sort out any nagging uncertainties. We'll share the points we discussed.

Video has long had a stigma in the feature-film world that's been a barrier to distribution. If an independent feature was shot on video, it was considered an amateur production and was relegated to cable access or maybe late-night broadcast TV. If an independent feature was shot on film, it was admitted to the next level and considered for distribution. About ten years ago, we were approached by a local novelist who wanted our advice on doing an independent feature-length movie. He had a script, a cast, a crew, most of his props, locations, and a relative who would front him $40,000 to do the project. We were overjoyed for him and told him everything we knew about how to get it shot on film for less than the 40 grand he had available. But he had video equipment available to him, and the video sirens were calling. Although we advised that he would never find a serious distribution offer if his movie were done on video, he ultimately chose video. We heard he completed the project, and that's the last we ever heard of it. No local premiere, no local news coverage, no nothing. Even short films get more attention than that. Our guess is that his efforts fell into the video abyss.

If he approached us today, we'd give him very different advice because the world of movies has changed. You can hardly watch a movie these days that doesn't have some digital segment in it and that wasn't cut on a non-linear edit system. Audiences have paid big money to see all-digital movies such as *The Incredibles*, half-digital movies such as *Sky Captain and the World of Tomorrow*, and mostly-video movies such as that juggernaut of profit *The Blair Witch Project*. And for every one of these movies, there's some happy little distributor sitting on his office floor counting the piles of income. Is it any wonder that the distributors are no longer so picky about what medium you use to shoot your movie? Even if you shoot on digital video, you can easily transfer it to film (though not cheaply) or DVD or streaming web video. The independent movie has become format independent, so choose the format that makes technical and economic sense for you and go forth. If you're checking your car seats for change in order pull together a production budget, we recommend digital video.

The archival longevity of your movie may be an issue, especially if you're planning to become famous by being the last person standing from your era. The reality is that digital video, DVD, and most other digital formats probably won't stand the test of time. Even if you chiseled all those digital ones and zeros into a granite monument so they would never be accidentally erased by a refrigerator magnet, your digital movie would probably be lost. Digital formats depend on two fleeting elements: complex mathematical algorithms to compress and decode the image and equipment that is rapidly changing. Just try to get a 2-inch Quad video-tape from the 1960s played back. You'll find only a handful of Quad machines still operating in this country, and this format was relatively simple by today's technical standards. At the rate of current technological change, most video and digital formats in use today could be difficult to play back 20 years from now. (Anyone remember 5-¼ inch floppy disks?) In contrast, one film archivist commented, "Give me a light and a lens, and I can look at any motion-picture film ever shot."

So you have three choices. Imbed in plastic a copy of your digital movie, a playback deck and monitor, and an early 21st-century power generator… oh, and be sure to include a note in several languages telling how to use them. Or you can pay to have a film transfer done of your digital feature. Or diligently copy it to the newest format every ten years or so. It also doesn't hurt to have it recorded in several formats in the first place as a hedge against obsolescence.

Video Format

After you've decided to shoot a digital movie, you still have to decide what format. ("Will the decisions never end?" you wail. Frankly, no.) For us this particular issue was spurred by the offer of free equipment in DVCPRO and later in Digital Betacam. It might also be sparked by technical considerations such as longer tape length, fewer "drop outs" in the image, high-definition images, and 16:9 wide-screen format. We spent many hours and e-mails talking about the relative merits of tape formats and the production pathways that each would dictate. Which digital format to pick — Digital-8, DV, DVCPRO, DVCAM, Digital Betacam, DVCPRO-50, HDV, HD or some other type?

In the end, all digital formats are good enough to make a feature-length movie (though not all camcorders may be up to the task). Heck, with the right story line, analog Hi8mm footage was good enough to be the backbone of *The Blair Witch Project*. If Hi8mm can do the job, then S-VHS, 3/4-inch U-matic, 8mm, and even VHS could do the job for some stories. Ultimately, it comes down to what you can afford, what's being offered for free, and your vision of the finished project. Just be aware that different formats have different costs and production procedures.

For example, any of the analog formats (VHS, 8mm, 3/4-inch U-matic, S-VHS, Hi8mm, Betacam) will require a media converter or codec (coder-decoder) to translate it to DV format when you digitize it into your non-linear edit system. So you either have to use the codec on a DV camera or deck or buy an analog-to-DV-converter box (such as ADS Tech's Pyro A/V Link at $130, Datavideo's DAC-100 at $200, or Canopus' ADVC-55 or ADVC-110 at $225) as part of your production budget. Once you pick a format, don't second-guess yourself. Just use it the best you can, and make the best movie you can.

Shooting Ratio

As we discussed in the budget chapter, your decision on shooting ratio has a direct impact on your budget and shooting schedule. To stay within an $8,000 budget, rental costs force you to shoot in four weekends. To shoot in four weekends, you have to shoot 12 pages of script a day. If you start doing two takes on every setup — keeping in mind that you'll be shooting 60 to 80 set ups a day — you're not going to get your 12 pages done before the next day starts. So it's pretty much a no-brainer that to make your digital movie for $8,000, you have to decide on a 3:1 shooting ratio. Of course, you'll be able to get some shots in a 2:1 or 1:1 ratio which would allow 4:1 or 5:1 coverage for a few other scenes.

Publicity

Another decision is to publicize or not to publicize. Whether 'tis nobler to suffer the questions of reporters and spectators or to work in relative obscurity and peace. We chose not to do local publicity while we were in production for a couple reasons.

Our budget demanded a non-union production, and we were up front with our cast and crew about this. Several good people who were with the union chose to join us, and we did not want to get them in dutch with the union reps by getting a lot of attention while shooting. (Once you're done, nobody really knows if it was a union shoot or not unless they watch for the union "bug" at the end of the credits.) Most union reps realize that non-union work is where many union actors get their beginning credentials, allowing them to get bigger union work later. So they usually won't interfere if you don't call and ask them if it's okay to use union people on a non-union shoot (they have to say no) and if you don't rub their noses in it with a lot of publicity. (They'll feel obliged to interfere; it's their job.)

We also decided not to seek publicity because it invariably attracts reporters asking questions and taking photos, both of which take the time of a cast or crew person who needs to be working. Reporters and other spectators also can create sound problems and get into shots. Suddenly, you need to have someone controlling the public, too. You may even get the attention of official types who will feel the need to ask you for permits to use a public location you're shooting in. Now, whenever you're shooting out of doors, you can expect visits from the curious. Usually it's just the neighbors or a couple passers-by who'll get bored soon enough and move on. If you publicize it in the local paper, you could see dozens or hundreds of visitors. That's not a good thing for a production that doesn't have time for interruptions. And since we were in editing for more than a year after shooting, we wouldn't have benefited much from that early publicity anyway.

However, you can benefit from a little national publicity. The two major industry trade papers, *Variety* and the *Hollywood Reporter*, both feature weekly "Production Listings," which highlight all the movies currently in production, including their titles, start dates, primary cast members, and major crew positions. Listing your production in the trade papers provides a number of benefits:

- It establishes a start date for your digital movie, which can come in handy when someone challenges the legality of your title. This happened on *Resident Alien*, and it was nice to be able to point to a published start date when someone questioned who had the title first — even though you can't copyright titles.

- It alerts distributors and sales representatives to your existence, and the more aggressive of them will contact you about when they can see your movie.

- It introduces you to other movie professionals, such as composers, editors, and actors — many of whom are looking for work. While the vast majority will be turned off once they learn what your budget is, you may still find one or two who are looking for the experience or are simply turned on by your enthusiasm.

- Finally, it's a kick to see your little digital movie listed alongside the latest productions starring Hollywood's biggest guns.

To get your movie listed, simply contact the papers and ask for a production-guide listing form. We've put the information in the appendix.

Time for a Breakdown

After struggling with budget, business, and preproduction decisions, you may feel ready for a breakdown. That's okay. Preproduction is the only place it's allowed. In fact, it's required.

We're talking about the next preproduction step, the script breakdown. This is where your carefully crafted script, with its interwoven story lines and its fully integrated characters and its gradually-building emotional content, is brutally dissected. When the script breakdown process is done, the script will be lying there in front of you sliced and diced into its most elemental parts, all carefully labeled so you can plan your shooting schedule.

Actually, this process is a peaceful task that's perfect for the detail-oriented personalities on your crew, in our case the director, producer, and unit production manager. This is sitting-at-the-kitchen-table work that requires five distinct steps — four if you cut corners. As usual, we made a few changes to the standard Hollywood technique for breaking down scripts; some steps were simply unnecessary for such a small production. We've listed a very good reference source in the bibliography if you want to learn the Cadillac of script breakdown. We're giving you the VW Beetle version. We will be describing the manual method of breaking down a script because it costs almost nothing to do. If you happen to own spreadsheet software, such as Microsoft Excel, you can build a spreadsheet that will do the sorting much faster. You can save time by copying and pasting scene headings from the electronic copy of your script, too. If the idea of building a spreadsheet gives you the Luddite shivers, use the manual version.

Step 1: Marking Script Segments

To start this process, you'll need a shooting script with scene headings that list scene number, interior or exterior, location, and day or night. You may have been told not to put scene numbers on a script you're trying to sell. True, but now that script is sold to you, and you need those numbers. Scene headings should look like this:

23. EXT. ROCKY CLIFF - DAY

or

125. INT. SHERIFF'S CAR ON ROAD - NIGHT.

If you've never understood why this was the required format for scene headings, you will after you've finished breaking down a script.

"Okay class, pencils up, ruler in hand. You may work in groups." Draw pencil lines across the page at the end of each scene that occurs at the same location and the same time. (Use pencil unless you never make mistakes. Wait, you're the one planning to make a movie for pocket change, aren't you? Definitely use pencil.) Now look at the length of this scene, and mark in the margin next to the scene number how many eighths of a page this scene takes.

We know there's a lot of math anxiety in the world, especially when it comes to fractions. Far be it from us to make this a more anxiety-ridden world. Brief math refresher: A whole page would be eight eighths (8/8). Two pages would be 16/8. A half page is 4/8. A quarter page would be 2/8. And an eighth of a page would be 1/8. Anything less than an eighth of a page is still considered 1/8. Example: A scene running two-and-a-quarter pages is 8/8 + 8/8 + 2/8 = 18/8. Write "18/8" in the margin. (Math wizards, thanks for your patience. Just in case you're feeling smug, remember how many dates this skill got you in high school.)

As you divide your script into scenes, watch for hidden scenes lurking within scene descriptions. Read the following scene description, and look for hidden scenes.

24. EXT. BOX CANYON - DAY

Joe leaps from his horse and leads it to a sheltered spot among the rocks. He then scrambles up the loose rocks to the rim of the canyon. Removing his hat to avoid detection, he peers over the rocks. In the distance, there is a column of dust rising from the surrounding desert. Joe pulls a telescope from his saddle bags and looks again. Magnified, the dust column reveals itself to be Texas Rangers riding single file to hide their numbers. Joe quickly closes the telescope and runs for his horse.

Did you spot them? The first hidden scene is the distant shot of a dust column rising from the desert floor. The second is the closer shot of the Texas Rangers. Because these shots are actually at a different location than the main scene, they need their own scene headings. This is a common oversight in scriptwriting, and you should be watching for it. For the purpose of planning your shooting schedule, hidden scenes may happen on completely different days and locations than the main scene, so you need to break them out separately.

We've found hidden scenes in a variety of places: shots of a television showing an image (the image needs to be shot separately); point-of-view shots of distant scenes; audio voice overs on radios, phones, and intercoms (no image to shoot, but you'll need to record the sound of the performers at some point during your production schedule); and scenes that occur in doorways or looking out windows. This last item may not seem to fit, but consider the situations of using different locations for the interior and exterior of a building in your script. If a scene is viewed from inside the doorway, it is an interior at one location. If it's viewed from outside the doorway, it is an exterior at a different location. Unless you know that you'll be using just one location, list two scenes, an interior and an exterior.

Digital Filmmaking 101 ~ Newton & Gaspard

When we found these hidden scenes without scene numbers, we just added a letter to the main scene number to designate them. In the scene above, the dust column shot would be "24a" and the Texas Ranger shot would be "24b."

After you get into it, this is pretty easy, restful work. Enjoy it while you can. It helps to have more than one person working on it so you can discuss and decide how to shoot any ambiguous hidden scenes. Just plug ahead at this task until all script pages are broken down into scenes and lengths. Even if you're planning to create a production spreadsheet, you should do this step as a guide. Here's an example:

```
                   FADE IN.

        1/8        1.  EXT.  CLIFFS - DAWN

                   The sun is just beginning to cut into dawn's haze.  The only
                   sounds are the WAVES HITTING THE SHORE and the occasional, QUIET
                   CALL OF A SEAGULL.  PERIOD MUSIC is heard faintly from a car
                   radio.  A red Mustang, with a hang glider strapped to its roof,
                   pulls off the road.  MUSIC STOPS as the car's ENGINE SHUTS OFF.

                   BOB gets out of the car.  He is twenty-two, and dressed in old,
                   faded jeans and a baseball jacket. He fumbles with an
        1/8   1A  instruction manual, tosses it aside, and begins to assemble the
                   hang glider. He pulls some tools out of the trunk.

                   On the Mustang's bumper, a bumper sticker that once read, "Honk
                   If You Love Jesus."  It now reads: "Honk If You Love Bob."

        1/8        2.  LATER:  The glider is assembled and straped to Bob's back.
                   Bob pulls out a large paperback book, still in its shrink-wrap.
                   He tears it open.

                   The book's cover reads, "Hang Gliding For Beginners."  Bob pages
                   through the book, rapidly.  He quickly loses interest and tucks
                   the book under his arm, takes a deep breath, then he runs to the
                   edge of the cliff ...

        1/8        3.  BOB'S POV:  We leave the cliff, soaring over the water,
                   gliding, smoothly and elegantly.

        1/8        4.  Bob, in the air.  He dips, he turns, he glides. He pages
                   through the book, getting the hang of it.

                   He looks ahead and registers an expression of sudden concern.
                   He flips to the back of the book to check the index.  The book
                   slips out of his hands.

        1/8        5.  The book falls, tumbling end over end, down and down, faster
                   and faster.  It lands roughly on an outcropping of rocks.  The
                   torn PAGES FLAP OMINOUSLY in the breeze.

        1/8        6.  We return to a wide-shot of the cliff, showing Bob's red
                   mustang patiently waiting his return.

                   FADE OUT.

        1/8        7.  The screen is black.  A title comes up:  "Ten Years Later."
                   The title fades out.  A door is opened and we see that we're in:


                                           - 1 -
```

Step 2: Script Breakdown Pages

Almost all Hollywood productions do this next step, though it's one that we skipped. We were so compulsive and detail conscious as a team and our scenes were simple enough that we felt this step was work we wouldn't use. Turns out we were right. But that was us. If you don't have the kind of production overseers (producer, director, unit production manager) who ask each other three times if they remembered the yellow sweatshirt for scene 16A, then you might want to consider doing this step. It will help you keep track of the myriad details when you get to the set.

This step is simpler, slightly tedious work. You will go through your script again, marking the key elements of each scene. You can underline these elements with colored pencils or highlight them with colored markers. Pick a different color for each of the following categories:

- Cast — speaking roles
- Extras or stunt performers
- Action props — cars, planes, go-carts, horses, etc.
- Props
- Wardrobe
- Special effects, animation, special camera gear
- Atmosphere — raining, foggy, sunrise (These are all difficult to achieve on a limited budget with limited time. Your script should have avoided these items or used them only as scenes that can be shot by the second unit. Day and night by themselves are going to pose enough problems for you.)

You already have scene headings that designate interior or exterior, location, day or night, and length of scene so there's no need to mark these items.

At the same time you are marking these items, you can be filling out the information on the actual script breakdown pages. A breakdown page lists all these pertinent details about each scene. When they are all done, put them in a three-ring binder for your unit production manager. On the set, when the shooting schedule calls for doing scene 16a, the unit production manager will flip to the breakdown page for that scene and be able to see that the yellow sweatshirt is needed. All in all, a useful organizational tool. We didn't really need it ourselves, but there was at least one occasion when it would have saved us some clothing confusion.

Here's what a script breakdown page should look like:

Page # __1__

Scene Breakdown

Production Title __"Beyond Bob"__

Scene #	Script Page #	Length In Pages
1	1	1/8
Location / Set	**Sequence**	**Time Period**
Cliff near river	Bob hang gliding	10 years ago
Day or Night	**Interior or Exterior**	**Season**
Day	Interior	Summer

Scene Synopsis
Bob drives up in his car with hang glider tied on top. He removes hang glider and gets tools from trunk. We see "Honk if you love Bob" bumper sticker.

Cast	Extras / Stunt Performers
Bob — Michael Levin	None

Action Props (Vehicles, Etc.) & Animals	Props
Bob's car (without rust) Hang glider	Tools Bumper sticker Ropes to tie on hang glider

Wardrobe (Cast and Extras)	Special Effects, Animation, Special Camera Gear

Bob's costume:
     Letter Jacket
     T-shirt
     Jeans
     Tennis shoes
	Second-Unit Camera (MOS)

Atmosphere (Rain, Fog, Etc.)	Set Construction
Early morning sun	None

In addition to filling out the script breakdown pages, some people total the number of pages (in 1/8ths) for which major elements are needed: cast, locations, day, night, props, wardrobe, etc. It was less work for us to do this in a later step. The only reason to do it now is if you need to know how long you'll be using some specialty wardrobe. Wardrobe won't show up on the production-scheduling items that are next.

Step 3: Making the Strips and the Production Board
This is nothing like cruising the strip. It's much more fun. Here's where you begin to put every single scene of your movie on little strips of tag board, so they can be sorted into a production schedule. (Spreadsheet users, time to fire up the computer. You'll be designing a spreadsheet with the categories described below.) The first thing you could do is waste $100 to $150 buying a commercially produced production board and strips. Unless you are being paid more than $50 an hour during your free time, don't do it. You can make your own for about $20 in materials (which you may be able to scrounge) and two hours' time.

Yes, it's arts-and-crafts time, class. The materials you need are 15 full-page plastic sheet protectors (top loading); a ruler; a fine-point permanent pen; double-faced adhesive tape; lightweight, white tag-board stock; a paper cutter (optional); a pen knife and straight edge; and enough dimes to make a few photocopies.

A. Cut the tag stock into 11-inch widths. Keep it as long as possible to save time in the next step. You have enough tag stock if you could make about 14 pages that are 8½ inches x 11 inches.

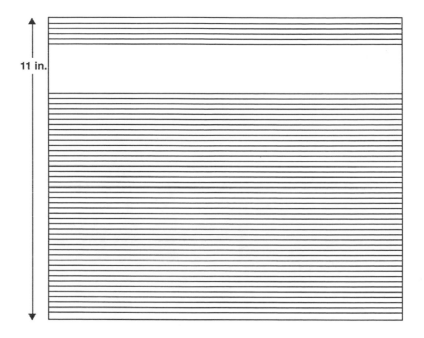

11 in.

B. Next you need to mark lines on the sheets of tag stock as shown in the illustration. Starting from the top, measure down and draw five lines 3/16 inches apart. Next, measure down two inches from the last line, and draw the next line. Then continue drawing lines that are 3/16 inches apart for the rest of the page. This will be about 40 more lines. You can also lay out these lines on a computer and take a printout to the local copy store to get 14 copies on the heaviest cover stock they can duplicate. (Spreadsheet builders, you'll be building this production board on its side. These rows will be your columns.)

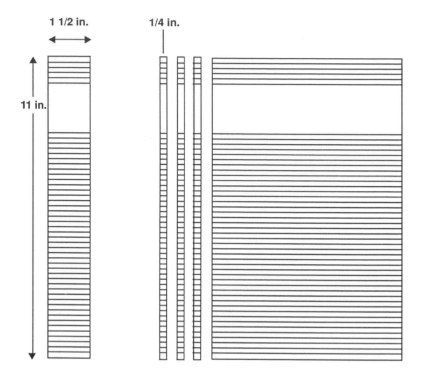

C. As shown in the illustration, cut off one strip from your tag stock that is 1½ inches wide and 11 inches long. This will become the header for your production board pages. Now cut up the rest of your tag stock into strips that are ¼ inch wide and 11 inches long. These will be your scene strips. You can use a pen knife and straight edge to do this, or you can use a paper cutter. Either way, this task is a little mind numbing, so don't daydream and trim off any appendages. You'll end up with a big pile of little strips. (For a spreadsheet, make a header row and ¼-inch rows.)

Breakdown Page #	
Day or Night	
Location or Studio	
Exterior or Interior	
# of Pages	
"Resident Alien"	
Dir. J. Gaspard	
Prod. D. Newton	
Prod. Mgr. K. Erickson	
Scene #	
Cal	1
Leslie	2
Allen	3
Davis	4
Jack	5
Bunson	6
Verner	7
Joyce	8
Doris	9
Deputy	10
Tish	11
Naom	12
Reporters	13
Action Props Cal's Truck	14
Leslie's Car	15
Jack's 4x4	16
Davis' Sedan	17
Locations Motel Ext.	18
Roof Ext.	19
Leslie's Apt.	20
Cal's Apt.	21
Allen's Apt.	22
Newton's Land	23
Sheriff's Office	24
Laundry Rm	25
Vacant Lot	26
Bathroom	27
UFO Detector	A
UFO Debris	B
Alien Spacesuit	C
Geiger Counter	D
Metal Detector	E
45° Effects Box	F
Second Unit Shot	G
Miniature-Animation	H
Monster Head	I

D. It's time to create the header for each page of your production board. Actually, this should be called a "sider" because it goes on the left side of the page. (Spreadsheet users, you have the advantage here. You get to make a "header.") You'll make the header by labeling major elements of your movie on the 1½-inch x 11-inch strip you just made. These elements will then be used to breakdown the scenes in your script. Start out by labeling the top five slots as follows (see illustration):

- Breakdown Page Number
- Day or Night
- Location or Studio
- Exterior or Interior
- Number of Pages

The next slot on the header is a wide one. On the scene strips, this will be used for scene descriptions. However, on the header strip, use this area to list the title of your production and the names of the director, producer, and unit production manager. That way if you lose your production schedule on a bus, the person who finds it will know who is in deep trouble.

The next narrow slot should be labeled as follows:

- Scene Number

Follow this slot with the important scene elements from the next list. These slots should be numbered from top to bottom on the right-hand side of the header strip. To the left of each number, write the name of one of the important scene elements. Don't repeat any numbers because they will be used as shorthand identifiers for each individual item. Fill in these slots with the following:

- All character names
- Extras (this is just one slot)
- All action props (cars, motorcycles, hang gliders, etc.)
- All locations

The next list of items should be identified with letters from top to bottom on the right-hand side of the header strip. Write the name of the item to the left of the letter.

- All specialty props
- All special effects, animation, or special camera gear

If you found yourself uncertain about what to list under some of the categories on the header strip, you may want to go back and do Step 2: Script Breakdown Pages. As you mark the key elements of the script, keep a list of every new item, and use that list to fill out the header strip.

Now you have the completed header strip for your production boards. Make about 15 photocopies, cut them out, and use double-faced tape to attach them to tag stock the same size as the header strip. If you're really into wasting time, hand-write 15 more of these header strips instead.

To finish your low-cost production board, use the double-faced tape to attach a header strip inside each plastic sheet protector along the left-hand side. Save out a couple header strips for holding alongside the scene strips as you fill them out. Now that you've completed your production board, you're ready to move on to making the scene strips that will fill the board. (With the header done, the computer spreadsheet is now ready for its rows to be filled in with each scene's data.)

Breakdown Page #	41
Day or Night	D
Location or Studio	L
Exterior or Interior	I
# of Pages	11/8
"Resident Alien" Dir. J. Gaspard Prod. D. Newton Prod. Mgr. K. Erickson	*Leslie looks at Cal's books*
Scene #	90
Cal	1	1
Leslie	2	2
Allen	3
Davis	4
Jack	5
Bunson	6
Verner	7
Joyce	8
Doris	9
Deputy	10
Tish	11
Naom	12
Reporters	13
Action Props Cal's Truck	14
Leslie's Car	15
Jack's 4x4	16
Davis' Sedan	17
Locations Motel Ext.	18
Roof Ext.	19
Leslie's Apt.	20
Cal's Apt.	21	21
Allen's Apt.	22
Newton's Land	23
Sheriff's Office	24
Laundry Rm	25
Vacant Lot	26
Bathroom	27
UFO Detector	A	A
UFO Debris	B	B
Alien Spacesuit	C
Geiger Counter	D
Metal Detector	E
45° Effects Box	F
Second Unit Shot	G
Miniature-Animation	H
Monster Head	I

E. The tag-stock strips in the pile you made ultimately are going to represent every scene of your movie, so pick up your script and get ready to write. This is another good group activity for the leaders of your production. Just make sure everyone is filling out the scene strips the same way, and make sure you don't skip any pages or miss any scenes that cross multiple pages. (And for you punsters, yes, you do need a scene strip for a strip scene.)

Hold a scene strip next to the header strip, and you'll see that the top five slots on each strip represent the information that's in each scene heading and in the information that you marked on your script. For the Breakdown Page Number on your scene strip, write in the script page where the scene begins. Write in "D" or "N" for Day or Night, "L" or "S" for Location or Studio, and "I" or "E" for Interior or Exterior. (For our productions, the only shots that weren't location were credits and special-effects shots that we did in a studio.) Next, write in the page length that you've written down by each scene heading on your script, such as "3/8." Don't forget to fill out scene strips for those hidden scenes you've found, too.

(Spreadsheet makers, you will be sitting at the computer with your breakdown script at the ready. You can fill in the rows with the information you've written down about each scene in the script. It might be faster to cut and paste scene descriptions or entire scenes from the electronic version of the script into the description column. Don't worry about color coding these rows. The computer will sort without this visual aid.)

As you're filling out these strips, you'll want to color code them with a highlight marker to make the upcoming sorting easier. Pick four different colors to represent day-exterior, day-interior, night-exterior, and night-interior. Common practice is to do day-interior as white (uncolored), night-interior as blue, day-exterior as yellow, and night-exterior as green. Just use the appropriate marker to color the long slot where you'll be writing the scene description.

Next move to the long slot, and write a short phrase that describes the main content of the scene, something like "Cal wakes up" or "Davis' car drives up to motel." Then write the scene number in the next slot down.

Now that you've gotten the basic scene setup coded onto your strip, you need to identify its component parts. Follow down the strip and mark the number of each character who appears in the scene in the appropriate slot on the strip. Use the number rather than just a check mark, so you can tell at a glance that character #3 is in the scene. This is also the reason not to repeat any numbers. When we had a scene where a character was only present as an off-scene voice, we still wrote in the character's number and added a V.O. for Voice Over or O.S. for Off Screen so we were sure to record this dialogue. Many times you'll want the same room ambiance for the off-scene voice, so you'll want to record it at the same time as you shoot the scene or immediately afterwards.

Continue on down the strip, listing the appropriate number or letter for extras, action props, locations, specialty props, special effects, animation, or special camera gear needed for that particular scene. When you get to the bottom of the first scene strip, move on to the next 200 or so strips you have to do. It's not gene splicing, but you have to concentrate and envision the scene and how it's going to be shot.

When you finish going through the entire script, you'll have a pile of tag-stock strips that looks like shredder residue at the CIA. The next step is to make some sense of these color-and-number-coded strips. (Time-saving tip: If you share your dwelling with a pet or child or roommate who likes to chew cardboard, lock the door.)

Step 4: Sorting the Strips

Here's where the hours of tedious coding start to pay off and those enig-matic steps are recognized for their brilliant usefulness. You're going to sort through your strips several times, so clear some table space or shovel the debris of life from the living-room floor.

(Spreadsheet users, here's where you sprint ahead in the race. If you're using Microsoft Excel, select all the data cell rows, but not the header row. Next do a data sort by each column in this order — least to most important to the schedule: special effects, animation, or special camera gear; specialty props; action props; extras; characters; exterior or interior; day or night; and location or studio. Don't sort by scene number, number of pages, or breakdown page number. You can change the order of sorting to fit other priorities, such as an actor's availability being more important than the location. For example, after the main sort, you can select just the rows for a certain location and re-sort for a specific column. The resulting scene schedule will need changes to fit your production days, but you can do that by cutting and pasting full rows. For safety, save an unsorted version of this spreadsheet. After you're done sorting and arranging, use this unsorted version to check that the data for each scene number hasn't been jumbled in the sorting and that every scene is still listed in your production schedule. It's a tedious but critical check.)

Begin by sorting your big pile of strips into smaller piles for each shoot-ing location you will be using. Because you have a separate number for each location, you will be able to just glance at a strip and see if it has a number 20, representing "Leslie's apartment." After doing this sorting, you should have a pile for each location and one additional pile for studio shots. Already that mass of scenes to shoot should be starting to look more manageable.

Next, sort the scene strips for each location into three piles, Interiors (both day and night), Exteriors/Day, and Exteriors/Night. Moving outside to do exterior shots will require several changes in camera and lighting setup as well as time to move the equipment, cast, and crew, so you will want to group these scenes for your location together. For scheduling, you'll need to know how much of your exterior shooting has to be done before the sun goes down and what scenes can't be started until after sun-down, so day and night exteriors are separated. We didn't separate the interior scenes into day and night on *Resident Alien* because we avoided showing windows and modified our lighting to create either circumstance. If you want to or need to show windows with day or night outside, as we did with *Beyond Bob*, you should sort for Interior/Day and Interior/Night, also.

Now that you have each location separated and divided up by lighting and equipment changes, your next step will be to figure out the most efficient shooting schedule. Now is a good time to put the strips into the production-board pages that you've made (the plastic sheet protectors). Later you'll put a strip of double-faced tape inside the top of the plastic sheet protector to hold the strips in place, but for now, you want to be able to shift them around. Just lay the sheet flat so that things don't slide around. Start putting the strips in the production board pages, grouping them by location and Interior, Exterior/Day, Exterior/Night. You can turn over a blank scene strip to use as a divider between sections.

Step 5: Laying Out the Shooting Days

This is the point where your director and unit production manager must be involved if they haven't been so far. You want to organize the shots in your production schedule so that:

1) you don't waste time setting up scenes or moving equipment;
2) you move efficiently from one location to the next;
3) cast members aren't sitting around for long periods waiting to do scenes;
4) you help the cast give the best performances possible;
5) you get the necessary number of pages done each day; and
6) you accommodate any outside scheduling issues.

It's time for some examples.

Scheduling for scene setup: For our film *Resident Alien*, we used a single motel room to represent the three different motel rooms that were about one-half of our shooting schedule. It made sense to set up shop at this motel room and shoot all scenes there before moving on, so we spent two entire weekends shooting at this location. In redressing the room for the three different settings it represented, we started with the setting that required the most changes to the room. We shot every scene that occurred in that setup before we changed the look of the room. Each subsequent redressing of the room removed more props and furniture until we got to the final redressing in which the room was virtually bare.

Scheduling for location: Resident Alien called for a variety of short outdoor scenes at different locations, some of them 50 miles apart. To avoid wasting a lot of production time driving to locations, we would shoot major scenes that were closest to these locations for most of the day. Then towards the end of the production day, we'd hit the road with the cast and crew to pick up these short scenes. That way when we finished, we were already packed up for the day and ready to go to the next day's shooting location.

Scheduling for actors: On *Beyond Bob*, we scheduled our shooting so that we started the day with all the scenes using just one of our principal actors, letting the other actors sleep late. We did scenes that called for six actors toward the middle of the day, and then shifted to scenes involving a different principal actor at the end of the day. This way, actors could leave earlier when their scenes were done, allowing them to get more rest in a weekend of 14-hour shooting days. (The crew was fried, but they didn't have to look good on camera.)

It's nice to shoot scenes in their actual order when possible. Try not to have performers jump from a tense, angry scene directly into a humorous, romantic one.

Also consider the time for makeup changes between scenes. It's hard to go from a bed-head look to knock-dead glamorous in a few minutes' time. Generally, wardrobe changes can be quick, so the only ones we considered much during scheduling were those requiring elaborate costumes or major makeup changes.

Scheduling to stay on schedule: You'll need to consider how many pages of script you have to shoot each day. This is easy to calculate. If you have a 90-page script in standard screenplay format and you know that you'll be shooting on four weekends (eight days) and four Friday evenings (figure ¼ day each), you have to shoot 90 pages in nine days. You need to plan for at least ten pages of shooting per day… and 11 or 12 would be better, so you don't get squeezed at the end if production gets delayed. Just count up the page lengths on the scene strips to see how many pages you're placing in each day's schedule. Be sure to consider how many are night shots and how many are day shots, so you don't schedule yourself to do 14 hours of night exteriors on the heels of a full day of daylight shooting.

Set a fast pace early on so the crew and cast know how quickly they must work. Hollywood productions average two pages per day, so you're going to be working in a very fast lane doing 11 or 12. It's best to make the scenes early in your production schedule some of the easier ones. This lets your cast and crew get used to working as a team at a break-neck pace before they face the more challenging scenes.

Scheduling around other schedules: If you have problems with the availability of an actor, a prop vehicle, a location, or even a time of day such as sunset, be sure to consider this when setting up the shots you'll do each day.

As you're probably understanding, setting up the actual shooting schedule is going to require trial and error. Just take a try at it, and have your director, unit production manager, and producer look it over. Make changes based on problems they see. We set up our shooting schedule in an evening. We also hit some weather problems during production, so we had to move some shots to different days in the production schedule. Using a production board, this was an easy matter of moving a few scene strips to another page. (This is where spreadsheet printouts aren't as convenient.)

Once you've settled on your schedule, put a strip of double-faced tape inside the top of the sheet protector to hold the scene strips in their order. Now you can take these pages and make photocopies for your production crew.

Finished Production Schedule — Production-Board Page

"Resident Alien"
Dir. J. Gaspard
Prod. D. Newton
Prod. Mgr. K. Erickson

10/1/89

		Leslie looks at Cal's books	Leslie and Cal discuss UFO's	Leslie's come on to Cal	Cal and Leslie on Phone	First view Cal's Apt.-Leslie Bursts in	Leslie's bandaged hands dial phone	Cal's PoV-Alien attack	Leslie's POV-Alien Approaches	Cal bursts through door	Alien PoV-Attacking Cal	Cal on Phone - L & A enter	Cal's Apt.-Manuscript	Cal, Leslie, Allen in Cal's Apt.	Allen on Road before UFO	UFO over Alien - Still cut out - Still photo	Allen greets Naomi & Tish	Allen with Naomi & Tish	Allen, Tish, Naomi leave	Alien's arrive	Faces for Allen's dream
Breakdown Page #		41	42	44	54	1	17	53	53	53	53	63	67	76	89	89	90	90	92	89	54
Day or Night		D	D	D	N	D	D	N	N	N	N	D	D	D	N	N	N	N	N	N	N
Location or Studio		L	L	L	L	L	L	L	L	L	L	L	L	L	L	S	L	L	L	L	L
Exterior or Interior		I	I	I	I	I	I	I	I	I	I	I	I	I	E	E	E	E	E	E	I
# of Pages		11/8	9/8	14/8	22/8	13/8	7/8	3/8	3/8	3/8	3/8	12/8	14/8	4/8	1/8	1/8	4/8	2/8	1/8	1/8	1/8
Scene #		90	91	94	11B	2	39	106	106	106	106	121	127	151	128	175	178	180	182	176	110
Cal	1	1	1	1	1	1				1	1	1	1	1							
Leslie	2	2	2	2	2	2	2					2	2	2							
Allen	3							3	3			3	3	3	3	3	3	3	3		
Davis	4																				
Jack	5																				
Bunson	6																				
Verner	7																				
Joyce	8																				
Doris	9																				
Deputy	10																				
Tish	11																11	11	11	11	11
Naomi	12																12	12	12	12	12
Reporters	13																				
Action Props Cal's Truck	14																				
Leslie's car	15																				
Jack's 4x4	16																				
Davis' sedan	17																				
Locations Motel Ext.	18																				
Roof Ext	19																				
Leslie's Apt.	20						20	20	20	20	20										
Cal's Apt.	21	21	21	21	21	21						21	21	21							
Allen's Apt.	22																				
Newton's Land	23														23	23	23	23	23	23	23
Sheriff's office	24																				
Laundry Rm	25																				
Vacant Lot	26																				
Bathroom	27																				
UFO Detector	A	A	A	A	A	A						A	A	A							
UFO Debris	B	B	B	B	B							B	B	B							
Alien Spacesuit	C																C	C	C	C	
Geiger Counter	D																				
Metal Detector	E																				
45° Effects Box	F																				F
Second Unit Shot	G															(G)					
Miniature-Animation	H															(H)					
Monster Head	I							I	I												

Finished Production Schedule — Spreadsheet Page

Breakdown pg #	Day or Night	Location or Studio	Exterior or Interior	# of 1/8 Pages	"RESIDENT ALIEN" Scene Description	Scene #	1 Cal	2 Leslie	3 Alien	4 Davis	5 Jack	6 Bonson	7 Verner	8 Joyce	9 Doris	10 Deputy	11 Tish	12 Naom	13 Reporters	Action Props	14 Cal's truck	15 Leslie's car	16 Jack's 4X4	17 Davis' sedan	Locations	18 Motel Ext.	19 Roof Ext.	20 Leslie's Apt.	21 Cal's Apt.	22 Alien's land	23 Newton's land	24 Sheriff's Office	25 Laundry Rm.	26 Vacant Lot	27 Bathroom	Specialty Props & Gear	A UFO Detector	B UFO Debris	C Alien Spacesuit	D Geiger counter	E Metal detector	F 45-degree effects box	G Second-Unit shot
41	D	L	I	11	Leslie looks at Cal's books	90	1	2																					21								A	B					
42	D	L	I	9	Leslie and Cal discuss UFOs	91	1	2																					21								A	B					
44	D	L	I	14	Leslie's comeon to Cal	94	1	2																					21														
54	N	L	I	22	Cal and Leslie on Phone	11b	1	2																																			
1	D	L	I	13	First view Cal's Apt. - Leslie bursts in	2	1	2																																			
17	D	L	I	7	Leslie's bandaged hands dial phone	39		2																																				
53	N	L	I	3	Cal's POV - Alien attack	106			3																																			
53	N	L	I	3	Leslie's POV - Alien approaches	106			3																																			
53	N	L	I	3	Cal bursts through door	106	1																																				
53	N	L	I	3	Alien POV - attacking Cal	106	1																																				
63	D	L	I	12	Cal on phone - L & A enter	121	1	2	3																																		
67	D	L	I	14	Cal's Apt - manuscript	127	1	2	3																																		
76	D	L	I	4	Cal, Leslie, Alien in Cal's Apt.	151	1	2	3																																		
89	N	L	E	1	Alien on road before UFO	172b			3																																		
89	N	S	E	1	UFO over Alien -Still Cutout still photo-	175			3																																		
90	N	L	E	4	Alien greets Naom & Tish	176			3									11	12																							
90	N	L	E	2	Alien with Naom & Tish	180			3									11	12																							
92	N	L	E	1	Alien, Naom, Tish leave	182			3									11	12																							
89	N	L	E	1	Alien's arrive	176			3									11	12																							

(Enlarged detail)

Breakdown pg #	Day or Night	Location or Studio	Exterior or Interior	# of 1/8 Pages	"RESIDENT ALIEN" Scene Description	Scene #	1 Cal	2 Leslie	3 Alien	4 Davis
41	D	L	I	11	Leslie looks at Cal's books	90	1	2		
42	D	L	I	9	Leslie and Cal discuss UFOs	91	1	2		
44	D	L	I	14	Leslie's comeon to Cal	94	1	2		
54	N	L	I	22	Cal and Leslie on Phone	11b	1	2		
1	D	L	I	13	First view Cal's Apt. - Leslie bursts in	2	1	2		
17	D	L	I	7	Leslie's bandaged hands dial phone	39		2		
53	N	L	I	3	Cal's POV - Alien attack	106			3	

A production schedule obviously can't be done in complete isolation from your other preproduction tasks. To really set a schedule, you'll need to know where your locations are, when you can use vehicles and major props, who the cast members are, and when cast members are available. You can try to get these items figured out before you begin your production schedule, or you can set a tentative schedule and make modifications as these details are settled. We did a bit of both. We had found some locations and knew our cast's schedules, but we didn't arrange for some locations or vehicles until after we'd set a tentative schedule. Sometimes it's easier to get permission to use a prop or a vehicle if you can say specifically when you need it. This leads us to another task that you'll have to undertake sometime during preproduction — a treasure hunt.

Props, Action Props, Locations, and Assistance

The kind of treasure you're after is free, photogenic, and convenient. In the next chapters, we'll describe how to find a cast and crew made up of diamonds in the rough. Right now your task is to find several hundred thousand dollars' worth of personal goods and real estate, just to borrow for a while. This work will have a lot of bearing on the final quality of your movie. We were given full access to a beautiful suburban home as the major setting for our film *Beyond Bob* by a tolerant and gracious homeowner (John's sister). This completely furnished, attractive, multiple-room location easily added $200,000 to the apparent production value of our finished movie. And it didn't cost us a dime. You can get the same kind of screen value from vehicles, props, and wardrobe that you borrow. This is part of the reason distributors thought *Beyond Bob* cost $900,000 to make.

So where do you find these hidden treasures? And how do you get permission to use them? Answers: lots of places, and by asking.

There's a theory that you are no more than six relationships removed from anyone in the world. This means that a client of an uncle of a girlfriend of the mailman of the dentist of your lead actress owns the lime-green Corvette you need to borrow. We found vehicles, houses, wardrobe, camera gear, specialty equipment for props and effects, and furniture just by asking the friends and relatives of our cast and crew.

Start by making a master list of all the locations, vehicles, wardrobe, and props that you need, and then put the word out. You'll be pleased and surprised how willing people are to help you find what you need to make your movie. Feature-length movies are the conjurations of modern-day wizards like you, and people want to catch hold of your cloak in hopes of feeling a bit of the magic. We even received unexpected help from other movie professionals who knew all about the tricks behind the magic. Your vision of your finished movie has the power to bring to you the people and the resources you'll need to finish the project. So spread your vision around, and let people know they can be part of it by loaning you things you need.

The people affected by your magical vision are not just friends and family. Complete strangers who happen to own businesses that are perfect locations for your shooting will succumb to your spell. Just say the magic words, "We're making a movie, and your business would be an ideal setting." Our experience is that business people don't agree to help with a movie because of the potential publicity. They agree because they personally want to be connected with a feature-length movie. In Hollywood, moviemaking magic is so common that it's lost much of its power. Elsewhere in the country, it still fascinates the crowds. Most people are thrilled to be associated with a movie as long as it's not too much trouble.

If you've been a good neighbor in your local production community and helped out other people with their projects, you'll have a much wider group from whom you can ask favors. Many moviemakers own props and have access to locations that will be useful to you. Similarly, you have access to things and places that can help in someone else's movie. A well-connected group of local moviemakers may have combined resources that rival that of a small movie studio. So get on the team.

Other willing participants are local artists, ranging from musicians to clothing designers to painters. Their work can give your movie a piquant local flavor with a unique look. Showcasing their talent won't hurt the artists, and it may actually help them succeed with their own dreams. Look around for interesting additions to your movie, and offer the chance to participate.

When searching for exterior shooting locations, don't overlook public areas, such as parks, wilderness areas, and the local scenic vistas. Bigger movie productions pay lots of money to shoot on locations that are in your neighborhood. These are free and, if you shoot quickly, you can avoid any permits or location releases. Now, if you need to be at one of these sites for an extended period of time with lots of cast, crew, or equipment, you better seek formal permission. It's awkward to have your entire day of planned shooting halted by a park ranger with a demigod-complex. Don't forget that you need a location release for using any property that isn't public land. If you need help finding or getting permission to use a particular local vista, your state or city television-and-film office may be able to help.

While you're out exploring for that pink adobe bungalow for a location and scavenging for that brass seaman's compass for a prop, there are also technical preparation to be started.

Choosing a Look
This is the point where you'll want to start talking to your director of photography about the production and how you're going to achieve the

look you want for your digital movie. As you learn more about locations, the director and director of photography should be discussing the types of shots they want to do, especially if they involve specialized equipment. This is the time to determine the look you want for your movie because there won't be time for this to evolve on the set. Before you roll tape, you'll need to know what kind of images you are trying to achieve and how you will create them. Examining the techniques used in other movies is a good way to get ideas for the look of your production. Movies on DVD are great because you can stop and study how particular images were achieved.

Recognize that you have to create your look with 1/100th the money and 1/6th the time of almost any movie you watch. So consider what time, resources, and money you can commit to creating the look you want. It may be enough to create the visual tone of your movie in a few key scenes and use a simpler and faster-to-shoot style for the remaining shots. Often an audience's memory of a movie is linked to a few monumental scenes. *The Wizard of Oz* has hundreds of gorgeous scenes, but most people's memories gravitate to a few: the tornado; the Munchkins; meeting the scarecrow, tin man, and lion; the audience with Oz; the flying monkeys; melting the witch; and unveiling the wizard. You can't possibly rival the overall production values of a movie like this, but you can create a half-dozen memorable scenes that will stick in your audience's heads.

For example, in our film *Resident Alien*, we knew that we needed to make the crucial collision and climax scenes the visual high points in the production. Even though we were unable to achieve much style in 90% of the scenes we shot, we took extra pains to make sure these key points in the story set the visual tone for the movie. They also had our most elaborate special effects. The result is that most people recall these, our best scenes, when they think of our movie, not the lackluster images our budget forced us to accept for much of the production.

Technical Preparation

In addition to planning the look of your movie, you need to do considerable technical planning. It's no good to get to the location and find that you can't use your lights because you need two-prong adapters for the electrical cords. As you find and get approval to use your locations, do location inspections.

If you wish, you can draw a diagram of each room, its windows, doors, and electrical outlets to help you plan your shots on paper. If the number of locations is small, which will probably be the case for your movie, you can just do a walk-through with the director and the camera and lighting crew. They can see the conditions they will be working in and decide what equipment will be needed to adapt to it.

For example, if half the living room you're shooting in has floor-to-ceiling glass windows, you're going to have a hard time avoiding showing the out-of-doors. This means you'll probably need to shoot day scenes during daylight and night scenes at night. It also means that you'll have to color correct the windows with large gels (expensive!) or balance the lights with daylight gels (less expensive). You'll need more lights and electricity to compete with a bright sun, so you'll have to figure out if you have enough electrical circuits to handle the load. This is the kind of thinking you need to do on the walk-through.

The most important item to locate and examine for every indoor location is the circuit box. Find out if it has circuit breakers or fuses. If it has fuses, note the type and size so you can buy some extras. It's almost guaranteed that you'll blow a breaker or fuse somewhere during your shoot, so you want to be able to find the circuit box and reset it as quickly as possible.

Other things to look at while visiting the location are room modifications that will be needed, where your crew will work, and where meals will be prepared and served. Make sure the owner of the location is comfortable with any changes you wish to make, such as moving the furniture around, temporarily removing a light fixture, laying down dolly track, bringing in furniture and equipment, and demolishing the odd wall here and there. Keep in mind that you are allowed to work at this site only because of the generosity of the owner. Make their wishes and concerns a priority, and be willing to change your plans to make sure they are happy. If they aren't happy, they can pull the plug on you during the middle of shooting. And common decency demands that you treat their property with care and respect. If you can't work within their restrictions, it's better to learn that early and find a different location. As we've said before, we have made it one of our guiding principles that we don't leave behind any owners of locations who wouldn't allow us to come back.

Besides looking for where to shoot your scenes, consider the other

Digital Filmmaking 101 ~ Newton & Gaspard

work areas you'll need. Where will the hair-and-makeup supervisor work? It can't be on the set. Find a laundry room, bathroom, kitchen, or utility room with a sink for them to set up their stool and makeup and to plug in the 47 hair curlers, fluffers, and whippers they need. Make sure it's a room with a door, so they won't interfere with sound recording.

Where will the cast change costumes? A bathroom, spare bedroom, or office space will do. If you have a lot of wardrobe, the dressing room should be near the room or hallway space where wardrobe is stored.

You'll also need to find accommodations for the creature comforts (even if you're not doing a monster movie). Input and output are two major issues. Where will you prepare, deliver, and eat food? What bathroom facilities are available? The kinds of meals you can provide for your cast and crew will be controlled by the kitchen equipment available. If you don't have running water, electricity, a refrigerator, and a microwave oven or stove available, you'll be in camping-food mode: coolers, water jugs, camp stove, grill, sandwiches, and such. If you have electricity, you can bring electric fry pans, crock pots, and coffee pots to create a mobile kitchen.

Limitations in the bathroom area are much more problematic. You need to find something nearby, especially at lunch time. If your location is in a building, this can usually be arranged. If you're going to remote locations, you better give some thought to this issue. If the best you can come up with is a pit stop behind a bush, make sure the people you select for cast and crew can work under those conditions. Otherwise, you'll have very unhappy campers complicating your shooting days.

When you're working indoors, you need to find a place to store actors when they are not being used. You'll be keeping crew people working pretty much non-stop, but the actors are going to have breaks in their work. The last thing you need on a busy set are people who have time to chat. It erodes the work ethic you need, they get in the way, and their talking and horseplay ruin takes. You need to find a reasonably comfortable "green room" for the actors to spend their time away from the set. It doesn't have to be fancy. An unused patio area, a recreation room, or a television room will do. Just a place where they can relax and talk or read while waiting for their next scene. Having a specific room will also help you know where to find them when it's time for their scenes. We suspect that the Hollywood tradition of the star's trailer is not just for pampering the star; it's also to keep them from roaming. (A producer of early Marx Brothers films actually chained them in their trailers to keep them from wandering away, or so the legend goes.)

On the technical front, there are a few more tasks to complete. You need to talk with your sound recordist about the scenes that will be shot at each location so that she or he understands the sound-recording situations that will be encountered. You will realize that even the quietest location becomes much noisier when you actually want to record sounds at that spot. You easily ignore that airplane passing overhead as part of your daily routine, but it becomes a challenge when you start recording sound.

The sound recordist doesn't necessarily need to walk through the locations, though this can be helpful. The main things the recordist needs to know are what equipment will be available and how many people will be speaking in each scene. Sound equipment is pretty lightweight and portable, so the sound is usually the last consideration on the set... to the perpetual annoyance of sound recordists. That's what they get for being flexible.

With all of the technical crew, make sure they understand how to operate borrowed, rented, or purchased equipment. Get a copy of the operating manual for them to read, or get the owner of the equipment to give a quick lesson on operating it. Try to get the crew a little hands-on experience (for free) before they get on the set. Even with this, do a little looking over their shoulders on the set. Ask to hear a little sound playback and have a peek through the camera lens after a shot is framed and focused. Asking the crew people to explain their equipment to you is a subtle way to check their technical proficiency without insulting them. If you think someone is unclear about what they are doing, ask more questions and keep checking their work.

Another important part of preproduction is making lists and lots of them. Most of this obligation falls to the unit production manager, but if the director and producer duplicate this effort, there's less chance that something critical will be overlooked. Each weekend will be the equivalent of a separate production from the logistics viewpoint, so these lists should be done separately for each weekend of shooting. You'll be picking up rental equipment each weekend and checking that every item on your equipment list is included and in working condition. You'll be packing up supply boxes each weekend and making sure the necessary production supplies are inside. Wardrobe will have to be organized and transported each weekend. Props will have to be gathered and delivered to the locations. And each weekend, food will have to be arranged for and served on the set. The only way you'll keep this all organized is with lists for equipment, production supplies, wardrobe, props, and food. Hopefully, your makeup-and-hair supervisor has a list for his or her supplies, too.

The director, producer, and unit production manager should have lists with the names, addresses, and phone numbers of all the members of the cast and crew, just in case someone oversleeps. We also gave these lists to all the principal cast and crew members, so they could call each other for help if necessary. You'll also want to carry a stack of forms: shot log sheets, talent release forms, group release forms, and location releases. It's a pain to run out of these forms when you need them, so make sure you have plenty on hand at all times. We've included samples of these forms in the appendix; however, with your computer, you can customize these forms, make legible lists, and create other useful production documents.

The other documents you'll want are the business version of nagging. For instance, make maps to each location for everyone. We simply photo-copied the appropriate sections of a street map and highlighted the main travel routes. If you're relying on an Internet mapping site (such as MapQuest), double check the directions it provides as errors are common. We also included the address and phone number of the location in case someone got hopelessly lost. If you have cast or crew members who are always losing stuff, pin the maps to their shirts. If you have a schedule that has the cast or crew changing a lot from day to day, you might consider doing a call sheet that lists who is needed for each day of the shoot. Give this out before the start of the production weekend. In our case, the major cast members and all the crew were needed every day, so our production manager just told the supporting characters when to show up. We only had a problem with them not arriving on time about four times in three feature movies.

A useful memo for the cast and crew is one explaining the conditions they will experience on the shoot and a recommended list of personal supplies to keep them comfortable. Because we were working indoors and outdoors in variable weather, our recommended supply list included hat, long pants, shorts, socks, tennis shoes, sunglasses, sunscreen, insect repellent, water jug, and rain jacket. We advised people to avoid bringing along valuables to reduce the chance of losing them. We also let people know that there would be food and drinks provided on the set. In general, try to anticipate problems and annoyances that will make your production company unhappy, distracted, or uncomfortable.

And don't get cocky. Just because everything goes smoothly one weekend, don't assume the next one will. Use your lists. We slacked off for a minute when checking the list of rental equipment, and we ended up using a spare light stand as a makeshift microphone boom pole all weekend. About the only thing you can do to reduce some of your checking and double-checking is to write the contents on the outside of the production supply boxes (spare fuses, black plastic, duct tape, clothes pins, spare batteries, etc.), and then repack and replenish them at the end of each production weekend. On the following weekend, we always checked these boxes before loading them and then made sure they got loaded.

Don't assume anything has been done unless you've seen it with your own eyes, and just to be safe, make sure no one has undone it when you weren't looking. Your major tasks in preproduction are planning, finding, planning, listing, planning, nagging, planning, checking, planning, double-checking, planning, shopping, planning, and waking up in the middle of the night to write down something you left off the list. If at any point you feel like you've gotten it all organized and ready, get nervous. You're probably forgetting something.

We still haven't talked about one of the biggest preproduction jobs, selecting the cast and crew for your movie. So read on.

Chapter 7

Casting the Cast ~ *To Be or Not to Be for Free*

Unless you're working on an Andy Warhol – type movie (an eight-hour static shot of a skyscraper, two hours watching butter melt, or ninety minutes of your computer's screen saver), odds are your movie is going to be populated by characters that need to be brought to life by actors.

So, with both the script and the budget in good shape, it's time to tackle one of the truly enjoyable parts of the process, casting your movie. This is the occasionally magical time when you'll see your story's characters start to come to life before your eyes.

There's a truism that says that casting is 90% of a movie's success. For ultra-low-budget movies, this figure may be on the low side. Odds are that you can't afford huge production values. Instead, you must have well-drawn, involving characters who are beautifully interpreted by skillful actors.

And where will these skillful actors come from? How will you pick the best and the brightest? And how will you get them to work for minimum wage or just meals? Read on.

Finding Actors

If you live in one of the major movie or theater centers in the country (New York, Los Angeles, Chicago, Minneapolis/St. Paul, Seattle, San Francisco, Orlando, and so on), you may find yourself with no shortage of excellent actors. If you live elsewhere — and let's face it, most of the best people do — there are still excellent actors to be found. You may just have to dig a little deeper.

Talent Agencies

Talent agencies may seem like a logical starting point, and in some cases, they are. However, a talent agent's primary mission in life is to earn money from their clients' *paid* work. This may explain why they're not returning your calls.

Plus, because your ultra-low-budget movie will (most likely) be non-union, those agents who work with the unions, such as the Screen Actors Guild (SAG), may be reluctant to work with you. While SAG has attempted to put together options for the low- and no-budget world, the costs still may be outside your budget. Check out their website (*www.sagindie.com*) to see if your project fits their criteria.

With some luck, though, you may find one or two far-sighted talent agents in your area who see the value of getting their actors in a movie — any movie, short of a skin flick — and who don't mind bending the rules a bit to do it. Good actors can learn a tremendous amount about their craft while working on a movie, and smart talent agents recognize that fact and do their best to get their clients in front of the camera.

However, in order to get talent agents on your side, you have to persuade them that your project has merit, is going somewhere, or, at the very least, will be completed.

A good starting point is your script. Don't be shy about sharing your script with talent agents who are willing to look at it. They generally know the best actors in your area, and the more they know about your project, the better their talent recommendations will be.

It won't hurt to give agents some references if they're unfamiliar with you or your work. Good agents protect their clients and want to be sure that they're sending them out on reputable assignments.

The agent may also want a look at your contract or release form. They'll be making sure that their actor isn't signing on for more than intended, and they're looking to see what wages or future share of profits you're offering. After all, they get 10% of it.

These are all reasonable requests and will help to get the talent agent on your side and excited about your project. If no talent agents are available in your area, no problem. There are other sources of actors available to you.

Local Theaters

If you aren't already seeing a lot of plays in your community, put this book down right now and go see a play.

Okay. Are you back? How was it? Did you have good seats?

The point here is that you should be seeing local actors perform. A lot. You should know who's who in your area, and who does what, and how well they do it.

Local theaters — both community theaters and professional theaters — allow you to see a wide range of performers in an equally wide range of plays. They help you to see who has "star quality," who knows how to move well, who seems naturally funny, and who shouldn't quit that day job just yet.

Filmmaker George Romero (*Night of the Living Dead*) found the lead for his vampire classic, *Martin*, while attending a community theater in Pittsburgh. There's no better way to judge talent than to watch it in action. With this information, you'll be in a good position to invite actors to audition for your movie. You'll already be familiar with their work, their style, and at least some of their skills. And in casting, that's half the battle.

Open Auditions (a.k.a. Cattle Calls)

Cattle calls are about as fun as they sound, which is not very. They're insane and noisy and exhausting for everyone involved. But they can be a good way to discover unknown talent.

A cattle call involves bringing in a herd of actors (usually through an announcement in the newspaper), making them mill about for a while in a tight space, and then releasing them into the audition arena (one at a time or in pairs), and having them read short scenes from the script.

Finding the right actors in a cattle call is like finding your spouse-to-be in a singles bar. It does happen, but you may have to dance with a lot of duds to find a winner.

The disadvantage of cattle calls is that there has been no prescreening. Using talent agents or going to theaters to find actors is an excellent winnowing process because you're looking at a pool of talent that has at least some experience in the business. Cattle calls, on the other hand, throw you into a much larger pool, filled with actors who have a widely varying range of skills and experiences.

It's a sink or swim experience, and it's an easy place to drown.

In an audition, you want everyone to get a fair shot. That means adequate time to prepare for the audition and adequate time to perform the audition. When you have fifty people in the lobby, and you only have the room at the community center for two hours, nobody wins.

The solution? Start your open audition through the mail. Ask people to send in or e-mail you pictures and resumes first, well in advance of the audition date. Wade through the material, and get a good sense of who should audition for which parts. Then schedule the auditions so that each actor has adequate time to do their stuff, as well as enough time for you to mix and match actors in different combinations.

This prescreening, while time-consuming, can turn the chaos of a cattle call into a well-organized and fruitful casting session.

Auditioning Actors

When it comes time to audition the actors (whether you're getting them from agencies, local theaters, or an open audition), there are a few things you're going to need to make the day successful.

A Place to Audition

This doesn't have to be anything fancy. It can be the rehearsal space at a local theater, a classroom at the nearby school, or even someone's nicely furnished basement. Some people hold their auditions in conference rooms or suites at local hotels; as long as you get the space for free, more power to you.

There is one requirement, however. You will need two spaces that are adjoining or at least relatively close together: a room for the actors to check in and wait and a room for the actual auditions. These must be two separate spaces; the people waiting to audition should not be watching the auditions. This may seem like nitpicking, but how would you like to have a job interview with the competition sitting around watching? Get the two rooms, and give the actors their best chance to do well.

A Traffic Manager

This can be anyone — your mom, your brother, a friend. Anyone, that is, except you.

You have too much to do to spend time checking people in, giving them scenes to study, pairing up actors, and handling all the other business of the auditions. This is not your job.

There's an advantage to having someone from your production team handle this task. (We used our production manager.) Afterwards, you can get reports on how the actors were to work with when they didn't have on their best audition face. We also got interesting insights into who had good chemistry in the waiting room.

So find someone to handle this chore, or get a couple people to share it. It will keep your auditions running more smoothly, and it will keep you where you need to be, in the other room, watching auditions.

Sides

Sides are simply scenes from the script that have been photocopied and given to the actors to study and read for the audition. The term comes from the Shakespearean age when actors were given only their own lines for a show, plus the cues that precede their lines. This was to prevent the actors from stealing the play and producing it on their own. Since they only had their "side" of any dialogue scene, they were unlikely to be able to swipe the whole play. And that's where the term "sides" came into use. (And, while we're discussing theater history, "sides" were rolled up and given to the actors at the rehearsal, which is where we get the expression "an actor's roll [role].")

There should be at least one good side, or scene, for each of the characters you're trying to cast. Each scene should be two to three pages long. Anything longer won't tell you much more about the actor and will slow down the proceedings. Anything shorter doesn't really give the actor a chance to get up to speed.

Take some care in choosing which scenes you want to use for the auditions. You'll want to pick a pivotal scene for each character — a scene that is dramatic or funny or telling and that really gives the actor something to play. The scene should have a good mix of talking (dialogue and short speeches) as well as opportunities for the actor to simply listen and react to another character.

You should also try to pick scenes that have a small number of characters, preferably two. This will allow you to audition two people at once and get a sense of how they'll play together. Any more than two turns the audition into a crowd scene and usually doesn't give each actor enough to do.

Often people will ask actors to read with someone from the production staff, but we prefer to let actors audition with other actors. It provides a better balance and allows for more spontaneity between the performers.

Finally, be sure to make enough copies of the sides for each person auditioning and some extra copies.

A Schedule-Conflict Sheet

In addition to providing you with a picture and resume, each actor needs to fill out a schedule-conflict sheet at the audition. This document reiterates the planned shooting dates for the movie and has spaces for the actor to fill in his or her name and any work commitments or other conflicts they have with the production schedule.

Conflicts are a good thing to discover up front, particularly if a performer is available for only a few days of your shooting schedule. There's nothing worse than finding the perfect actor to play your lead and then discovering that she'll be touring with *Nunsense!* for half of your shoot.

Video Camera and Operator

Videotape all the auditions. As with the traffic manager's role, you shouldn't act as your own video operator. Your focus should be on the auditions. Rather than using a locked-down wide shot, instruct the camera operator to zoom in on the talent in order to get a better idea of how they'll look in your movie. Review the tape before making any final selections because people come across differently on camera than they do in person. We've been surprised to see seemingly vibrant people lie lifeless on tape while performances we thought were lackluster absolutely sizzled on the TV screen. You'll be amazed to see how the camera really loves some people.

Finally, it's a good idea to hang onto this audition videotape well into production in case you need to cast a replacement for a part.

The Audition

Auditions can be tremendous fun. You'll get to see some wonderful actors; you'll start to see the characters come to life; and you'll begin to move one step closer to making your vision a reality.

However, for actors, auditions can be a real pain. They want to do a good job, and they want an opportunity to really shine, yet time after time producers and directors sabotage the process. This is very frustrating for actors because the audition is their entrance exam. If they don't pass, they don't get to move to the next level.

With that in mind, we offer the following rules to make auditions work for you and for the actors:

The Ten Commandments of Auditions

I.   Thou Shalt Not Be Rude

Put yourself in the actor's Doc Martens. You've got a two-page scene from a movie you know very little about. You're about to go into a room full of complete strangers and prance around, doing your best to breathe life into a scene. Then, in the midst of your best efforts, you see the director or producer yawn, whisper, start to dig into their lunch, or worse yet, doze off.

Wouldn't exactly encourage you, would it?

During the audition, actors are using all of their skills to demonstrate their level of talent. The very least you can do is be polite. And if you can't be polite because it's the right thing to do, be polite because, in the end, it will save you money. "How?" you ask, your ears suddenly perking up. Here's how: If you like what the actor does, you're going to ask them to work for almost nothing. And if you were polite during their audition, he or she just might do it.

So don't do anything during the audition — talk, eat, whisper, sleep or anything else — except glue your eyes and your total attention to the performance. A little politeness goes a long way, and it can net you a great performance for a price you can afford.

Another important politeness tip is to introduce the actors to everyone in the room so that they know for whom they're performing. As one actor told us, "I like to have an idea of who's who in the room, so I know which people to suck up to."

Who can begrudge them that? So make introductions before you start making magic.

II.   Thou Shalt Put Actors at Ease

Auditions can make actors nervous. Why? Because it's their one shot. If they don't impress you in the first two minutes, the odds are against their working on your movie. At least, that's the way they look at it. As a consequence, many actors, even experienced performers, come into an audition a tad nervous. Hyped up. Scared to death.

In order to get the best performance out of them, it's up to you to put them at ease. Talk with them for a couple of minutes before they read. Ask them what they've been working on lately. Ask them about their past experiences. Ask them if they have any questions about the script or the production. Go over their schedule-conflict sheet, and confirm any problem dates.

Then, after they've had a few moments to relax and to just be themselves, ask them to be someone else for a couple minutes and let them read from the script.

III.   Thou Shalt Not Close Thy Mind

Let's say that you wrote a great part in your script for Jim Carrey or Meryl Streep. (Probably not the same part, but who knows? That Meryl's one talented gal). And let's say that for some reason — a mix-up, a time conflict, or lack of bus fare — neither Jim nor Meryl show up at the audition. What do you do? You open your mind, that's what. You'll be doing a disservice to your movie and the acting community if you don't.

The odds are against someone walking in who is a dead ringer for the character you pictured in your mind. The purpose of the audition is to find the actors who are best suited for the parts, not to find people who merely look like what you had in mind or who can imitate a well-known personality.

For example, we once came across this audition notice in the newspaper:

"Actors for student movie needed. Black male, 23 yrs, 6', fit, short hair; white female, 28 yrs, 5'10'', slim, long red hair; black male, 40 yrs, 6', strong, natural hair; white male, 35 yrs, 6', short hair. Unpaid."

Wow. That's not a casting notice, that's a police report. The odds of finding good actors who fit these exacting specifications are extremely slim. Plus, by requesting such exact types, the moviemakers are ignoring hundreds of talented performers whose height or hair length doesn't fit these unnecessary standards.

Keeping an open mind also means considering actors for different parts than the one for which they audition. When you're watching auditions, remember all the roles you need to fill, not just the one that's currently being read.

When director Dan O'Bannon was auditioning people for his zombie classic, *Return of the Living Dead*, he was very impressed with actor James Karen, who was reading for a small part. O'Bannon was so impressed with him, in fact, that he gave Karen a lead part — one that O'Bannon had been planning to play himself!

However, if you decide to ask an actor to read for a different part, give them a few minutes alone to go through the new material. Asking them to read it cold isn't fair or productive.

IV.   Thou Shalt Not Discriminate on the Basis of Race or Gender

There are a lot of things you can't afford at your budget level, and one of them is to let good actors get away. This can happen if you're too narrow in your casting search and you ignore entire populations swimming in the talent pool.

In very few instances, such as when it's a plot point in the story, is race an issue in casting. If you're remaking *In the Heat of the Night*, then race becomes a consideration. Otherwise, you're simply looking for the best actors, and their race should be of no consequence.

You can also overlook great candidates for your cast if you make stereotypical casting choices based solely on gender. The kindly old doctor in your movie doesn't necessarily have to be male; the helpful young nurse doesn't necessarily have to be female. Not all lawyers are men, and not all teachers are women. The person installing the phone can easily be a woman while the owner of the perfume shop could be a cranky, old man.

In fact, now that we think about it, the perfume shop owner might be a lot more interesting if he's a cranky, old man.

On an early feature movie John produced, several auditions were held to cast the part of a tough, no-nonsense cop. The auditions were fruitless — until someone suggested that they try casting the part with a woman. The perfect actress walked into the next audition and walked out with the part. And not one line of dialogue was altered in the script. In fact, it improved several scenes, such as the one where she follows the police captain into the men's room to finish an argument. It added to the scene and to the movie, and it wouldn't have happened if the casting had been narrow-minded.

V.   Thou Shalt Offer Direction

Actors may be many things, but they're not mind readers. (Although many mind readers are darned good actors, but we digress.) All that most actors know about the part they're auditioning for is what they read on the page — unless you tell them more, which is what direction is all about.

If time permits, we usually let the actors perform the scene once without direction. This gives us a chance to see where their instincts take them. Seeing them work without direction tells a lot about their natural skills (and the clarity of our scriptwriting).

Then we offer direction and try it again. At this point, we're not looking at their instincts; we're looking to see how well they can take direction. Of course, this presumes that the directions you've given are good ones. In our case, we never tell an actor how to read a line. If you want someone who can imitate your every word, hire a parrot. Instead, we suggest the intention behind the line or the action, and then let the actor interpret it as best they can.

For example, "Although you don't say it in the dialogue, in this scene you're angry at your wife for forgetting your birthday," or "Right now, your character has not slept for 36 hours, but he's trying to cover it up." These are more helpful directions than telling an actor to say one word louder than another.

In some rare instances, the first read will be perfect without direction. The actor will say every word right, every intention will be clear, and every motion will be poetry. You'll be amazed. You'll be ready to sign the contract and send everybody else home.

Not so fast.

Never hire an actor just because they read all the words right the first time. Instead, take some time and experiment with them. See if they can take direction. Ask them to play the scene in a less obvious way. If it's a romantic scene, have them play it for laughs. If it's an argument, tell them to make it into a seduction.

Remember, you're not looking for someone who can read just this one scene well. You're looking for flexible actors who can take direction. You want to see how they read with other people. Do they listen and respond to other actors in the scene, or are they acting in a vacuum?

If you still love everything the actor does after that (and after reviewing the videotape), then bring out the contract, and break out the champagne — assuming, of course, it was donated in exchange for screen credit.

VI. Thou Shalt Look For Simplicity

There's a technical term for the type of acting you probably don't want in your movie. It's called "Big-Face Acting." (All right, maybe it's not the technical term, but it's what we call it.) It's the kind of acting that plays to the balcony and works great if your audience is a hundred feet away and squinting.

Stay away from Big-Face Acting. On second thought, don't just stay away; run away from it.

The best way to avoid hiring Big-Face Actors is to videotape all the auditions. Then, after the auditions and before you offer anyone a role, review the tape and compare it to the notes you took while watching the actors live.

You may be surprised. Some of the performers who looked great in person, from ten feet away, will seem overblown and unrealistic on tape. That's Big-Face Acting. However, other actors who didn't seem to be doing much of anything at all during the audition may come across as more compelling and interesting on tape. That's movie acting. Those are the ones you hire.

VII. Thou Shalt Give Them a Chance to Do It Their Way

After you've given the actors direction, and they've done it your way, ask them if they want to try it again and do something different. Some actors will jump at this opportunity, with good reason.

At this point in the process, they've done it for you twice: Once just on instinct (the way they think you want it) and once with your direction (the way you think you want it). This third shot lets them combine the two approaches or try something entirely off the wall. They can take the scene right to the edge or even over the edge. They can give it a twist that you had never considered.

These "whatever you like" readings of the scene can be terrific. They give you and the actor a chance to really have fun with the scene and start to see all the possibilities. It's these "off the wall" readings that often give you a sense of whether or not you can bond with the actor and trust them to bring the character to life on screen.

Usually the approaches used during these readings don't make it into the movie, but they can be a great creative springboard for getting deeper into scenes and bringing them to life in unique and memorable ways.

VIII. Thou Shalt Take Blame

It's happened to everyone at one point or another, and it's nothing to be ashamed about.

You'll have twenty actors read the same scene, and none of them will make it work. Your natural instinct will be to blame the actors. "If we had some decent actors in this town, this scene would be working. It's not the script. It's those darn actors."

No. It's probably the script. It needs more work.

However, don't think of this as a negative; this is simply part of the process. It's far better to realize script problems during auditions and rehearsals, rather than during shooting or — worse yet — during editing.

So, make notes during the auditions about which lines are consistently duds and which moments consistently don't work. Since you'll only be using a few scenes for auditions, problems with these scenes should spur you to give your entire script serious, objective scrutiny. If you're too in love with the script to see its warts, get help from people who will call a wart a wart, and listen to their advice.

IX. Thou Shalt Use as Many Actors as You Reasonably Can

This commandment doesn't mean we want you to turn your three-character story into *It's a Mad, Mad, Mad, Mad World.*

It does mean that if somebody really good has auditioned for a role, and they don't get it, you should consider them for other smaller parts in the movie. As we've said earlier, actors live by their credits, and even a tiny walk-on part in a small, regional movie has value.

On every movie we've worked on, we've found great supporting players by offering roles to people who tested for the leads and (for one reason or another) didn't get it. So when you find good actors, give them parts in your movie. It gives them screen time, work in front of a camera, and a couple minutes of footage for their reel. And it gives you performers who really want to be part of your project and who turn tiny roles into small, sparkling gems. Everybody wins.

X. Thou Shalt Not Lie

We don't need to tell you that lying is bad. You're an adult; someone must have mentioned it to you by now.

But often otherwise mature adults, such as movie directors and producers, will tell "little white lies" and even "big ugly lies" during the audition process in order to entice skillful actors to ply their trade in the moviemaker's latest opus.

Be warned: Lying will come back and bite you on the butt. Every time. And your reputation as just another low-life moviemaker will be posted on verbal bulletin boards throughout the acting community for years to come.

Don't lie about money.
We were very clear with the actors we auditioned, and even clearer in the release forms they signed.

We told them if they would get paid or not. We told them when they would get paid. We told them, in no uncertain terms, that the only money they could reasonably expect to see from the project was any "signing fee" or stipend we paid up front. The rest was wishful thinking.

So don't turn wishful thinking into promises you can't keep. It may get you through this project, but people will be less inclined to work with you later when they find out that you were lying earlier.

Don't lie about the nature of the movie.
If the movie involves nudity, the actors need to know this before you cast them and not on the set just before you yell "action!" If the movie will use graphic language or will be explicit in its portrayal of sex or violence, the actors also need to know this before they commit to doing the movie.

Lying to the actors the very first time you meet them is not going to enable them to trust you where you need trust the most, on the set. So be honest about what kind of movie you're making and start building that trust early.

Don't lie about the prospects for the movie.
Like all of us, actors are hopeful people. In fact, they're often more hopeful than the rest of us. Theirs is a business built on hope.

With that in mind, it's a good idea to muzzle your bounding hopes for the project and try to pull it back into the realm of the probable (or at least the possible) when you're talking to the actors.

Don't tell them that the movie will be released by a major studio. The odds are against it. You might get a limited theatrical release, if you're lucky. You might make it to cable. It could go to home video. But a major studio release? Probably not.

Don't tell the actors that the movie will make them famous. The odds are against it. What your movie will give the actors is some experience working in movies and in a role larger than they would be offered if a big Hollywood film came to town. It will look good on their resume. It will look good on their reel. But it won't make them famous, yet. Sorry.

Don't lie about the budget. Don't talk about luxurious motor-home trailers and fabulous costumes and multiple retakes. The actors need to know from the start that this is an ultra-low-budget project. They need to know all the project's limitations, so they can begin planning how to effectively use their talents under these circumstances.

Of course, there are lots of things you can tell the actors. You can tell them that this is going to be an educational experience, that it will help them grow as a performer, and that they will gain valuable acting credentials. You can tell them that you hope this will be the greatest movie in the history of time. That you hope it will revolutionize the movie industry. That you hope it will change the world as we know it. That's your dream, and it's good to share it.

But don't say that the movie will open in New York and L.A. in time for Academy Award consideration, before going national in 2,500 theaters. Talking excitedly about your dream is fine. Lying is not. Be sure you know the difference.

Casting the Cast

Now that the auditioning is over, it's time to officially cast the movie. With any luck, you'll have a problem: Too many good actors, not enough parts. This is a good problem to have. Here are a few pointers:

- Don't cast look-alikes. By this, we don't mean celebrity look-alikes. We mean actors who resemble each other. Unlike a Hollywood movie, with big-name, recognizable actors, your movie will be filled with unknown faces. Don't confuse the audience by casting unknown faces that look similar. If you are forced to cast actors with similar builds, hair color, and features, then be sure to distinguish them with unique costumes and hair styles.

- Offer roles to your first choices first before informing other actors that they didn't get cast. You need to offer the parts to these actors, and have them accept the roles, before you let the other contenders go. Once all the parts are cast — and accepted — you can then start calling the contenders and breaking the news to them.

- Thank the contenders, but don't go into details about why they weren't cast. Don't tell them that they were too tall or too short or too fat or that their nose was the wrong size. Don't critique their acting (unless it's a compliment and unless you really mean it). If you were impressed with their work, tell them that you'll keep them in mind for other movies and that you'll hang onto their picture and resume (and then really do it).

The results of a successful audition, the principal cast of Resident Alien. *Pictured, l to r: Mark Patrick Gleason, Nesba Crenshaw, Patrick Coyle.*

Asking People to "Work for Free"

Years ago, John worked as a writer on a trailer for a proposed low-budget feature. Early on, the producers decided to pay the crew and not to pay the cast. Their reasoning was that the crew would be working for the duration of the four-day shoot while most of the actors would only be working for a day or two.

This saved them money. They thought it was a good idea. It wasn't.

The problem with their approach was that it sent a message to the cast. The message said, "We don't think your time and skills are worth as much as those of the kid holding the light stand." This was a bad message to send.

Did it hurt the movie? Probably. Did it hurt the chances of the producers putting together another project? Definitely. Because the word was out that those guys aren't just cheap; they don't care about the actors.

Well, we're happy to report that the word is out on us as well. We're cheap. We're known for it. Maybe even renowned for it. But we're also known for caring about our actors. For treating them fairly and honestly. And for paying a paltry pittance. Of course, we don't pay the crew any more than that. We pay ourselves even less. We're nothing if not fair. Maintaining equity such as this is a key component in making your project work. It makes it a project fueled by hope, not by mere money.

Initially you'll probably feel guilty about not being able to pay the cast or crew what they are worth. Trust us. You'll get over it, and we're not being cynical when we say that. You may not be handing out paychecks each week, but the fact is that you're offering everyone involved in the project a professional study course that will look great on their resume.

Think about it. There are thousands upon thousands of actors and would-be actors in the world. How many of them ever get to act in a feature? Or, for that matter, play a leading role in a feature? Very few. But you're in a position to offer that to people, and that really is something of value.

So don't sell yourself short. You're giving these actors a great opportunity. As long as you warn them about what they're getting into, you should have a happy set and a productive shoot.

Chapter 8

Corralling the Crew ~ *Assembling the Dream Team*

Production Diary: During the last two weekends, the director of photography has been impersonating Dr. Strangelove behind the camera, the sound recordist and boom operator wore bathrobes and hair nets after being teased about taking naps between shots, the production manager stood on a picnic table operating lights to simulate a UFO landing, and we all worked 14 hours a day. Situation normal.

A little crazed, willing to leap conventional job delineations in a single bound, dedicated to the project — that's the description of a super crew person for your movie. This type of crew member is critical to the success of your production. Finding these people is just as important as finding the right actors for your cast. Without them, brilliant performances by the actors can be lost in a muddle of unusable videotape. Fortunately, there are many people eager to fill this bill.

Some of the steps you'll take to find these wonderful people are similar to the ones for getting a great cast, but it is a different process that is best approached separately.

Finding Crew People

Before you begin your quest, you need to know what the Holy Grail looks like. Who do you need for your crew? The crew positions have already been identified in your budget. Essential ones are:

- Unit Production Manager/Script Supervisor
- Production Assistant
- Director of Photography/Videographer
- Sound Recordist
- Lighting Gaffer/Boom Operator
- Makeup-and-Hair Supervisor

A screenwriter is also essential to your production, and we've discussed how to select one in the script chapter.

Some crew members don't need to be brought onto the project until postproduction. We'll talk about selecting people for the following positions in the postproduction chapter.

- Composer/Music Supervisor/Songwriter
- Session Musicians
- Video, Sound, and Music Editor

Some crew positions are optional and will depend on the nature of your specific project:

- Assistant Unit Production Manager
- Art Director
- Wardrobe Supervisor
- Singers
- Stunt Coordinator
- Special-Effects Coordinator
- Model Builder
- Set-Construction Coordinator
- Animal Wrangler

We haven't mentioned director or producer in these lists because most people who are foolish enough to produce a feature-length movie for a song (or merely a verse) are just crazy enough to direct or produce it themselves. Just in case you've retained a sliver of good sense and want to get someone else to direct and produce your movie, we'll give you some guidelines after we talk about the rest of the production crew.

So where do you find a crew that's strong of back and keen of mind? We found our people largely by word of mouth. We spoke to people who had worked on short films and videos and other low-budget features in our area. Most of them were happy to recommend good people with whom they'd worked. When we called these prospective crew people, they often suggested friends and acquaintances for other positions on the crew. We also watched local productions and contacted people who had done good work on them.

Occasionally, working video and film professionals were afraid of doing a project that broke so many of the rules, so the best recommendations were for people who were just starting in the business. But that isn't always the case.

To find a special make-up artist for a short sequence in *Grown Men*, we called makeup maestro Crist Ballas to see if he had any students he could recommend for the job. Crist asked some probing questions about what we were up to and then said those words that all low-budget filmmakers love to hear: "Sounds like fun. I'd like to do it."

Make-up genius Crist Ballas (left) makes some final adjustments to actress Kate Eifrig for a scene in Grown Men. *(Photo courtesy of Granite Productions, Unlimited.)*

If you don't get lucky like we did (remember, it never hurts to ask), you may find people who are trying to advance to the next level in their professional careers and who will join you to get experience they can't get in their day jobs.

You can also place ads on the bulletin boards at local colleges and film schools and notices on the Internet or in the newsletter of the closest Independent Feature Project chapter. The state or city film office in your area may also have job listings for movie crews. Even equipment rental houses may be able to tell you who's looking for the kind of opportunity you're offering.

Cast your net widely to get names of many possible crew members. Don't be bashful or apologetic because you can't pay real salaries. The type of experience you are offering is rarely available to fledgling movie crew members. You're taking a chance doing this production in order to fulfill your dream. They will happily join you in realizing your dream because their own dreams are attached to yours.

This is a good point to remind you to put on your blinders, the good kind — the ones that don't see color, gender, age, or body type when looking at a candidate, only abilities. There are many good people looking for jobs on movie productions who get these biases thrown in their faces daily. You can use that to your advantage by scooping up those candidates with great skills who have been rejected for irrelevant reasons.

The first positions that you should be trying to fill for your crew are the unit production manager/script supervisor, the director of photography/ videographer, and the sound recordist. These are your key crew members, and they should have some input about who will be their helpers — the production assistant and the lighting gaffer/boom operator.

In several instances on our productions, the key crew people recommended people whom they had worked with before and who turned out to be great additions to the team. So you can save yourself some work by starting with these three key positions. If they don't have any suggestions, then it's a good idea to have them involved in interviewing the other job applicants.

Once you have a list of potential candidates, you're ready to start panning for the gold.

Interviewing the Crew

Your first contact with crew people will probably be a phone call. "Uh, I'm (your name), and I'm making a low-budget digital movie. I got your name from (an acquaintance, someone they worked for, their response to your ad, the editing-room wall at a film school). Are you interested in working as a (mouth-watering crew position) on our production? By the way, there's no pay, the hours are long, and we work on weekends."

If they don't hang up laughing derisively, they will probably ask what type of movie, what format, and what your goals and dreams are for the production. Sell your project to them. As far as you know, they are going to win an Academy Award for their next movie, and it could be yours. You need their interest to find out if they are right for your movie. They'll only consider joining you because your dream is catching, so tell them enough to capture their imagination.

If they are interested, ask them to send you a list of work experience, some references (unless they've already been referred to you), and a schedule of availability. For the sound recordist and director of photography, ask for samples of their work. You need to know that these crew people can deliver results. Be sure to ask what their role was in the sample they send you. For example, if a director of photography candidate only loaned a camcorder to shoot the video sample you're viewing, you have no idea if she or he can even focus a lens.

Once you have sized up the candidates from their resumes, references, work samples, and a little bit of conversation on the phone, you're ready to arrange for interviews. Be sure to look at two or more candidates for each position. That way, the person you ultimately select will give their best work to keep this plum assignment, knowing there are challengers out there just waiting for them to stumble. You'll also get a feel for the range of candidates that is available to you.

Your interviews don't need to be elaborate. They can be done at the kitchen table. You can also do them by phone though you'll usually get a better sense about personalities by talking face to face.

Keep it informal, and start by telling them honestly about your production. It's a waste of time to give the impression that this is a bigger production than it actually is. Crew people will find out the truth as soon as the discussion turns to technical needs, and you point out that you can't afford more than three rolls of gaffer's tape.

Don't forget to mention hard work, long hours, minuscule budget, small crew, unconventional techniques, little or no pay, non-union, and slim chances of the final movie being a financial success. If they're going to be scared off, now's the time to do it.

After laying out the grisly truth of your project and your commitment to it, let them do some talking about their education, experience, their goals, their dreams, their ideas, and why they're right for your crew. You should be listening for the characteristics and attitudes of a good crew member. This list applies to postproduction crew as well as production crew:

Desired Characteristics and Attitudes
- Good humor
- Can-do, problem-solving attitude
- Enthusiasm and respect for your project and ideas to make it even better
- Good work ethic
- Willingness to help with other aspects of the project (loan props, paint sets, find equipment for free, etc.)
- Technical proficiency and basic skills needed for their duties or the ability to learn them fast
- Cooperative, willing to follow directions

- Aware of the challenge, but not afraid to try
- Good vibes (you should have a good feeling about this person and be genuinely excited to work with them)
- Actively trying to improve their skills by volunteering on other projects, working on their own movies, or taking classes
- Owns equipment and uses it (these people are serious about their avocation and could bring equipment they are familiar with to your production)
- Has connections and is willing to call in favors to enhance the project
- Anti-establishment, let's-make-an-end-run, who-says-we-can't-do-it attitude

Granted, it will be rare to find every one of these characteristics in every crew person, but try to find the people who best match this list, and you'll end up with a dynamite crew.

Specialized Skills or Attitudes

In addition to these general characteristics, you'll be looking for some specific skills or attitudes in the positions of unit production manager, director of photography, and stunt coordinator.

Unit Production Manager/Script Supervisor

As we stated in the chapter on preproduction, you want this person to be very organized and conscious of details. If a candidate for this job shows up late for the interview saying they lost the address, look further. This is the one person who has to double-check every step of the project, so make sure she or he is up to the job. You also want a take-charge kind of person, not someone who doesn't move without direction.

This person will be helped by the production assistant. Together they will make sure camera tapes are labeled before being put in the camcorder and are securely stored when taken out. They'll slate scenes. They will keep an accurate log of the shots and will make sure the cast is wearing the proper costumes and hairstyle. They'll check that the right props are on the set, they'll make sure lunch is ready, and they'll keep track of continuity between shots. Obviously, the unit production manager is a busy and important crew member, so make a careful choice for this position. And pick an able production assistant, too.

Director of Photography/Videographer
This person will be your image expert, so the candidate for this job must have a vision of how the movie can or should look and the ability to make it happen. This may not match the producer's and director's vision initially, but if this person can see how to create different looks for the movie, then you have a starting point for some serious visual discussions.

A person who can only create gothic-horror lighting is only useful for that type of movie. You want someone who's familiar with the sorcery that can be performed using lights and lenses and filters, someone who relishes the challenge of making art from nothing, someone with ideas on how to create a big look with no money or time. If you can't find such a person, then you at least want someone who can properly compose, focus, and light a shot.

We found that this position became the leader of the production crew, setting the mood and the work pace for the others. Sure the director is in charge, but if the director of photography is always grousing about the working conditions, you'll have a surly, disgruntled crew.

We've been blessed with good-humored directors of photography, and, with rare exceptions, we've had happy crews even when working long hours in overheated, crowded motel rooms, when circling a skating rink for 20 hours straight, and when shooting on a roof all night in 40-degree temperatures.

The people we've used as directors of photography on our movies have had a "we can do that" attitude for every challenge, and that made our crews invincible in the face of technical challenges. They didn't know it was impossible, and we'd be the last people to tell them.

Just a word on experience. People who want to be your director of photography may have a variety of film and video experience, some of it helpful, some of it not. The trick is to tell the difference.

Working on industrial and training films and videos may not adequately prepare a person to be director of photography on a feature-length movie. If they have only shot corporate videos and done classroom-style training productions, they may not be experienced in how to create a mood with lighting and how to compose a shot for beauty and effect. On the other hand, if they have done productions that use dramatic segments or movie techniques, they may be ready to soar with your project.

Look for examples of their work that show they know how to enhance the tone and the meaning of your script. If you don't see evidence of this skill, don't consider adding them to your team unless you're convinced they will educate themselves a lot before you start production, including doing actual test shots to establish a look for your digital movie.

Stunt Coordinator

Stunts can range from jumping from a ten-story building to a brief fight scene where one character gives another a slight shove. In all cases, safety is the first concern and the highest priority. You may have no need for this position on your project, but if you do, you don't want a devil-may-care risk taker. In fact, the stunt coordinator should be the most cautious and safety-conscious member of your crew.

The right person for this job is someone with a magician's mentality. How can we trick people into believing a stunt is dangerous as heck... without risking anyone's safety? We know of would-be stunt performers who just like the idea of jumping from moving cars for real. Unless you want your production known for its toll in human lives, steer clear of these gonzo types.

Once you've found your top one or two candidates for each crew position, it's a good idea to have a second interview to check your perceptions and to see if they are still interested. (Polite people may not tell you that they think you're crazy, at least not while you're in the same room. Crazy people have been known to snap, you know.)

This interview can be done by phone if you wish. This is a good time to talk about how this person would approach the production tasks ahead if you add them to the crew. Be especially impressed by those who have started preparing for the job. They've done research, they've gotten connections for low-cost equipment rentals, they've learned how to use the equipment, and they've come up with good ideas that will help the production. These are the go-getters you need.

Choosing the Crew

After a couple of conversations with your prime candidates, you should be getting a feel for their personalities and getting some vibes about each person. We've learned to pay a lot of attention to vibes. It's that nagging sixth sense that a person will be a problem, that vague uneasiness about the person that belies their skills and what they say.

Pay attention to these gut reactions. Sure, they could just be that burrito from lunch, but we've found our vibes about people to be pretty reliable. We also get good vibes about people, that euphoric sense that this person will do great things for your movie, and some of those people have become friends who have worked on many of our projects.

Just as when you select your cast, call your first choices for crew members first and get their acceptance before you turn down anyone. If your first choice declines to join you, you can ask your second choice. If you're lucky enough to have two great candidates for a position, consider putting one of them in an assisting position if there's one available. You're likely to create a work team that will have even more good ideas to add to your production.

Now, don't expect that you will have a list of experienced people for every position on your crew. In reality, a small production like yours may not have any experienced people who are interested in working on it. Don't be disappointed.

If you don't have a list of experienced crew people to choose from, you have to be on the lookout for promising people. That describes many of the crew people we've had on our productions. They were people who had worked on movies in lesser jobs and were ready to move up. In fact, some of them had never worked on a movie before.

There are lots of diamonds out there languishing in the rough. You just need to recognize them and give them a chance. You won't be sorry because they will give you their very best work, to your mutual benefit. So consider giving the director of photography position to that production assistant who's graduating from film school or the sound recordist position to that boom operator.

Selecting a Director and Producer

It's likely that you have decided to be the producer or director of your digital film. Retaining control of the project is why most of us decide to make independent movies in the first place. If you happen to be a screenwriter in search of a production company, then you may need to find a producer and director.

Finding a producer won't be that hard. Finding one that's right for your project may take a little more effort. You need someone with experience developing budgets for movies, and someone who can pinch a penny until it bends. Many people in the audiovisual production business know how to do these things. Because most of them have planned video productions, they should be equipped to create a realistic budget for your digital movie. You need someone who will be the guardian of the budget and will calmly and insistently say "no" when the budget doesn't allow for that camera boom. A good producer will then come up with three ways that you can do just as good a shot for no extra money.

Producing is a job that can be learned. In fact, you can do it yourself after having read this book. Dale's experience had been in budgeting and shooting videos for government projects (contrary to popular belief, most government projects are decidedly low-buck). By going to producers' telephone school, he learned enough to serve as producer on feature movies.

What's producers' telephone school? Basically, you call people who know the business, say a video retailer, and try to get a price for a digital-video camcorder for your budget. You'll sound like a moron during the phone call when they ask "Do you want single CCD or three CCD?" and you don't know the difference. Your cheeks will be red as you ask them to tell you the difference and they patronizingly do. You hang up and note how glad you are that you did this by phone.

You go back for your next lesson by calling another retailer and asking for their price on a 3-CCD digital-video camcorder. Those cheeks of yours start heating up again when they ask if you want DV, DVCAM, or DVCPRO. You swallow your pride again and ask them to explain these formats and tell you what models are available. More patronizing education.

You hang up, let your cheeks and pride recover, and then call retailer number three. This time you ask for the price on a Sony 3-CCD DVCAM

DSR-PDX10 camcorder. In three easy lessons, you know what you're talking about.

Actually, most businesses that supply production equipment and services are happy to give you an education about their services. They know a potential customer when they hear one. Some reading and some discussions with knowledgeable people can give a would-be producer enough information to do an adequate job. (There are a number of useful magazines that are sent free to production professionals like you. Check the appendix.)

If you can get someone with experience, you're likely to get better than adequate. Dale's experience producing videos and his own movies meant he could offer many cost-cutting ideas that a less-experienced producer might have missed. If your producer is inexperienced, try to talk over your plans and budget with other producers who have done low-budget projects. You'll get suggestions that will help you control costs on your movie.

If you're not going to direct your project, finding the right director is a much harder task. The director has fingers in every one of the production's pies in order to provide the vision that will guide the project. And that's the challenge. Is it the same vision you have? If your director is seeing how to get laughs from the scene that is your dramatic pinnacle, you've got a double-vision problem, and the two of you won't be seeing eye-to-eye throughout the project. You may even be at each other's throats before you're finished. This is not a good way to work. This is the reason many independent movies have screenwriter/director listed in the credits. It can be very difficult to find someone who respects and shares your vision.

Selecting a director is a type of marriage. You have to have a similar vision if you are going to be able to work as a team to realize that goal. That doesn't mean that there won't be disagreements in this marriage, but it does mean that there's a shared respect for the vision you're trying to achieve. If so, your arguments will only be about the best way to achieve that vision.

Obviously, good vibes are essential in selecting a director. Some lengthy discussions about movies in general and your project in particular will help you figure out if your director candidate is the one. Don't decide until you're sure you've found a person you can trust to take charge of your baby.

Your best choice is also going to be someone who has managed big production projects before, because a feature-length movie has almost endless details that must be remembered while directing. It's usually best if your director has had experience getting actors to do dramatic performances for the camera. Experience directing training videos and industrial films is useful, but different.

If you decide to use a director who lacks this experience (maybe yourself), there are a number of good books on the art of directing which are listed in the bibliography. Read them. It would also be good to practice directing some scenes on video. This will help the director see what the results on the screen look like.

First-time directors can do a good job if they've done their homework. (Orson Welles on *Citizen Kane* is a good, if extreme, example.) Sometimes they even bring a fresh vision to the screen because they haven't been trained to think in conventional ways.

Letting Your Crew Do Its Best

Once you've selected your crew people, encourage them to make suggestions and give ideas on how to improve the production. This can be difficult. You've probably been living with this dream for a long time, and it's hard to let go and share it. It can be even harder to let other people change your dream. Be brave. One of the most important lessons we've learned while making our movies is that dreams grow stronger and more beautiful when other people add to them.

We found that every actor and every crew member brought a little bit of themselves to the dream and added to it. The screenplay that we started with was only the seed, and each person who came to the production made it grow into something better.

The actors brought depth to the characters that hadn't existed on the printed page. The director created compelling scenes that crackled with energy. The camera crew created images that strengthened the messages of the story. The editor created pacing that propelled the story forward. The composer amplified the emotional content of scenes with music.

In the end, our movies were much more than they started out to be on paper because we let others embellish our dream.

Chapter 9

Production ~ *Lights, Camera, Chaos!*

When most people imagine making movies, what they're actually picturing is just one element of that process — production. They envision beautiful actors and actresses in costumes, huge lights, dollies, cranes, cameras, and egomaniacal directors with monocles and megaphones, yelling "action!" and "cut!"

In reality, the production phase is just one element of the overall moviemaking process, though a vital one. Making a digital feature doesn't begin when you yell "action" for the first time on the first day of production or end when you yell "cut" after the last scene is shot. However, if you do your job correctly during the production phase, you can save yourself time, money, and headaches during the subsequent phases.

With that in mind, we've assembled the following production notes to help the director and producer through the production process. This list is by no means exhaustive — the circumstances surrounding your own production are bound to be as unique as the movie you're making — but there are certain common elements and concerns that have a tendency to pop up in all productions.

Training

No, we're not recommending film school. Why spend $25,000 a year to go to a film school (where you'll be lucky to make a couple short movies) when you can create your own feature movie using a third of one year's tuition? And without having to take 12 credits of a foreign language!

By training we mean getting in shape, physically and mentally. Make no mistake, directing is a grueling undertaking. Some people have compared the experience to running a marathon. Of course this is a ludicrous comparison, because a marathon is over in a measly 26 miles while you've got an arduous eight or ten or twenty days of production to survive. Take it from us, your average marathon runner would be begging for mercy after the first half day of shooting, collapsed by the craft-services table, whimpering for Gatorade and aspirin. You must be made of stronger stuff.

The best advice we've ever heard about directing was to "wear comfortable shoes." Directing requires intense concentration and stamina. You'll need to be on your feet most of the day and on your toes at all times.

Taking care of yourself before production (eating well, exercising often) is important; taking even better care of yourself during production is just as vital. This means eating regularly and well (not junk food) during the day and getting as much sleep as you can reasonably get each night.

We also recommend staying away from artificial stimulants like sugar and caffeine because while they will make your highs higher, they will also make your lows lower. And there's nothing worse than finding yourself staring at the ceiling at 3:00 a.m., your brains cells screaming with a "Mountain Dew" buzz, while you curse your inability to sleep and your 5:00 a.m. alarm setting.

It's also a good idea to get off your feet at least once during the day. You can call it meditating; you can call it power napping; you can call it whatever you want; just do it. It will clear your head and increase your energy for the rest of the day.

This break isn't just for the director and the producer, either. In all likelihood, your director of photography will be on her or his feet just as long (particularly since this person is often also acting as camera operator). With setting up the lights, shooting the scenes, tearing down the lights, and preparing for the next set-up, your director of photography rarely gets a chance for a break throughout the shooting day. So find a way to give the director of photography a break whenever you can. This may slow you down for a few moments, but it will pay you back with more energy throughout the day and better results.

Twenty (Thousand) Questions

As a movie director, you will be asked more questions and will make more decisions during preproduction and production than you have throughout your entire life. Director Edward Zwick (*Glory* and *Legends of the Fall*) has said that each day of production involves so many decisions that "I open a

Digital Filmmaking 101 ~ Newton & Gaspard

menu and try to think about what to order for dinner, and I'm ready to burst into tears."

You will quickly find that the questions are constant and they all demand answers: "Do you want him to wear the white shirt or the off-white shirt?" "When you say 'close-up,' how close do you mean?" "Do you want to break for lunch now or in ten minutes?" "Are we going to see that wall or not?" "Is the car needed in this scene?" "What do you want to do next, scene 112 or scene 4?" "Do you want to do a retake?" "Does it matter that he moved?" "Are there any other shots you need or should we send the actor home?" "Are you going to intercut on this shot?" "Are we doing a reverse?" And the question you dread the most, "How did you get this job, anyway?"

You will be expected to have the answers to these and 19,988 other questions on the tip of your tongue at all times during production. In most cases, if you've done your homework (such as knowing the script inside out), the answers will be within easy reach.

However, in some cases, your mind will be blank, and you simply won't have an answer. That's when it's best to fall back on those three infamous words that some people find difficult, if not impossible, to say: "I don't know."

There is no shame in not knowing, particularly if you follow up immediately with, "What do you think?" Keep in mind that the person asking the question is usually someone you hired for their knowledge and skill. They may already have the perfect answer to the question they've raised.

Another good response after "I don't know," is "What are my options?" This gives you choices, which are always easier to deal with. The truth is, as a director, you may not always have the answer, but if someone gives you a choice, you will always have opinions.

Just because you don't have all the answers, it doesn't mean you aren't in charge. The director is the captain of this ship, and this concept must be communicated throughout the crew. This doesn't mean you have to run your set like you're Mussolini on a bad hair day. But it does mean that all suggestions and instructions should flow through the director — and this includes comments from the producer.

The entire cast and crew should look to one person for direction, and if you're the director, that person is you. This is especially important on a fast-paced production like yours. You can't afford the miscommunication and the confusion that result when more than one person is giving instructions.

The Big Lie

You may remember that a couple chapters back we told you lying is a bad thing. Well, we were lying.

There is one occasion on an ultra-low-budget production when lying is not only permitted, it is required. That's when it comes time to "psyche up" the cast and the crew. To do this you must lie. Just this once. Well, actually, twice.

Here's how it works. Before you start your first day of shooting, take the members of the crew aside, sit them down, and give them a pep talk. It goes something like this, "Listen folks, you're the best. I know you can do this. With your help, we're going to make this the greatest movie of all time..."

(So far, it's just hyperbole, which is always acceptable. Here comes the lie.)

"The thing is, though... well, it's the cast. A lot of them are pretty new to moviemaking, and some of them are going to screw up. So, all of you on the crew, who are more experienced, have to work extra hard to make sure that you don't make any mistakes because the cast is bound to. So, when they get it right, we don't want to miss it for technical reasons." Thus ends Lie Number One.

For Lie Number Two, you sit the cast members down, give them the hyperbolic spiel, and then say (here comes the lie), "The thing is, though... well, it's the crew. A lot of them are pretty new to moviemaking, and some of them are going to screw up. So, all of you in the cast, who are more experienced, have to work extra hard to make sure that you don't make any mistakes because the crew is bound to. So, when they get it right, we don't want to miss it for performance reasons."

With two little lies you have psyched-up both the cast and the crew, built up their egos, and persuaded them that the success or failure of the movie rests in their capable hands — which is true. Of course, once you've finished this, you have to go back to telling the truth full time. Or at least until you start dealing with distributors.

Read-Through and Rehearsals

The odds are that your movie will be shot out of sequence; that is, all the scenes that take place in one location will be shot at the same time, regardless of where they appear in the story.

While this is great for your schedule, it puts an extra strain on your actors, who must be able — on nearly a moment's notice — to accurately portray their character at any given point in the story.

In a play, actors have the luxury of following the arc of their character's emotional, psychological, and physical changes from beginning to end, both during rehearsals and in performance. No such luxury exists on a movie set, where actors are routinely required to play widely disparate scenes in quick succession, such as a violent argument followed immediately by a tender love scene.

For example, one segment in *Grown Men* involves a budding romance between a young woman who works in a blood bank and a victim of panic attacks who collapses while he's donating blood. For scheduling and lighting reasons, we had to keep jumping back and forth while we shot, first shooting portions of the early, relaxed scenes between the two characters and then jumping quickly to intense, dramatic, and emotionally exhausting scenes, and then back to the relaxed scenes... often in the space of just a few minutes.

What made these dramatic leaps possible was a thorough read-through and comprehensive rehearsals.

The Read-Through

A complete read-through of the script is an invaluable exercise for the cast and crew, as well as for you. What were once just words on paper come to life during the read-through, and everyone gets a chance to see how the story develops from beginning to end.

Because of the fractured nature of movie production, this is possibly the only time the cast and crew will hear the entire story from start to finish until the night they take their seats at the movie's preview. As such, it's a good idea to gather everyone together for this event. If that's not logistically possible, then the principal cast members and all the department heads should be required to attend (production management, sound, camera, and hair and makeup). Knowledge is power, and the more knowledgeable everyone is about the movie, the more powerful the end result will be.

As with every other facet of your production, the read-through doesn't require any extravagance. Schedule a decent block of time (three to four hours), secure a space big enough to hold everybody (a good-sized living room will often do), provide some food and beverage (bargain pop and homemade cookies), and then start reading from page one.

You may want to tape record or videotape the proceedings, so that you can refer back to moments that caught your attention, either positively or negatively. Otherwise, just sit back, shut your eyes, and listen, imagining the movie while you hear the dialogue and directions.

It's a good idea if someone other than the producer or director reads the directions so that they can concentrate on just listening. And, in order to save time during the reading, you may want to do a version of the script that dramatically cuts down on the stage directions.

At the end of the read-through, you can solicit comments from the group: what worked, what didn't, which parts seemed confusing, and so on. If time permits, you can also go back and have the cast re-read troublesome scenes to help you locate problems and get some ideas for solutions.

The read-through is a very valuable tool because it provides you with yet another opportunity to make changes and adjustments to the script before the meter starts ticking.

Rehearsals

The best feature of our shooting schedule for *Grown Men* (where there were often three to four months between shooting periods) was that it provided plenty of rehearsal time and recovery time. We'd shoot like demons for a couple weekends, then have a couple months to regroup, recover, and rehearse scenes for the next segment.

Unlike the read-through, which was a sit-down affair, the rehearsals allow you to put the scenes and the actors on their feet. Rehearsing is, without question, one of the best parts of the production process because it allows you to do all kinds of experimenting and to take all sorts of risks without spending a dime.

You'll need an empty space for rehearsing, a location where the owners and the neighbors won't mind if you get a bit noisy or work a little late. Chairs for sitting and for use as props are a must, and a bathroom is always a nice perk.

We scheduled rehearsals using the same approach as scheduling the production. If an actor had three scenes to be shot over the course of the upcoming weekend, all three of those scenes would be rehearsed on the same night. This way the actor didn't have to sit around waiting to rehearse.

For each scene, we let the actors do it once without direction to see where their instincts took them, just like we did at the audition. Then we gave them direction and started to refine the blocking (the movements within the scene). As we worked on the blocking, we started thinking about our shots, noting how we were going to cover the scene. Will it need a master shot showing all the characters together? What sort of shots can we do to get the most out of the scene, to make it as visually interesting and effective as possible?

We recommend moving around while you're watching the actors rehearse, observing them from all sides to help find the most cinematic way to execute the scene. If you plant yourself in front of them and watch their actions like a play, you're more likely to shoot the scene like a play, which, although a workmanlike approach, is hardly an effective use of your visual tools. So, just as you've put the actors on their feet during rehearsal, you should stay on your feet as well, circling the action and beginning to make some decisions about how each scene will be shot.

Well-rehearsed actors are a godsend that allows you to accomplish a lot using very little of your precious production time. For example, one of the segments in *Grown Men* had over 20 pages of dialogue that we had to shoot in two locations over three days. (Remember, due to some outstanding equipment deals, we were able to shoot this movie at a more leisurely pace than normal.) In order to minimize re-lighting, many of the scenes were shot out of sequence, meaning that we'd shoot one actor's shot on one day, and then do the reverse shot of the other actor later on the next day.

However, all the scenes played beautifully and came off without a hitch. The actors knew the scenes backward and forward, and they could pick up at any point in any scene at a moment's notice. They knew the lines, and they knew the pace, all because the scene had been thoroughly and rigorously rehearsed.

Of course, you do need to walk that fine line between being adequately rehearsed and over-rehearsed. You don't want the scenes to sound rote or become flat. The key is to rehearse each scene enough so that you and the actors are comfortable, but then stop rehearsing so it doesn't lose its freshness.

Shot Lists

Using your notes from the rehearsal, you can assemble your shot list for each scene. The shot list tells you and your director of photography how you're going to cover each scene. This can be a list of shots ("Two-shot of Daniel and Mary, Mary's point of view of the boxes, single shots of Daniel and Mary as they enter") or crude storyboard drawings that detail each angle.

Keep in mind that every shot is another set-up that will require lighting (or re-lighting), which takes time. The more shots you have, the more time it will take to shoot the scene. And, with the clock always ticking (sometimes louder than others), you may run out of time before you run out of shots. So always do the key shots first, and then plan on grabbing the remaining shots as your schedule permits.

Long Takes

Of course, no one ever said you have to shoot masters and close-ups and then intercut them. You always have the option to compose your scenes as long, continuous takes with the actors moving artfully within the frame.

Cinema history is filled with revered examples of this technique, from Orson Welles' fluid opening shot in *Touch of Evil* (which was parodied in Robert Altman's *The Player*) to Jim Jarmusch's achingly static camera in *Stranger Than Paradise*. Mike Nichols pulled off some remarkable long takes in *Carnal Knowledge*, and directors as diverse as Neil Labute and Michelangelo Antonioni have made them work in movies as diverse as *In the Company of Men* and *The Passenger*, respectively. Even Woody Allen has used this approach, to greater and lesser effect, in many of his movies.

There are, however, drawbacks to this technique. The first is that if it isn't staged properly, it can become visually boring. If that's your point, then fine. Otherwise, the trick to making a long take work is to keep the frame energized by moving the camera, moving the actors, or presenting a very dramatic moment so that you hold the audience's interest without turning the shot into a photographed stage play.

The second drawback is that long takes are risky. A long take requires that the actors and the crew get it right   absolutely, flawlessly right — from the beginning of the take right down to the very last frame. If someone blows it in the last few seconds, you've got to start all over again. If someone blows it on the second take, you start from the beginning yet again. And again. And again.

Long takes are also risky because they give you no options in the editing room. Often a long continuous take will seem great while you're shooting it, but when it's edited into the movie, it will slow the pace or even bring the movie to a dead stop. If you haven't shot any other additional shots (known as coverage) of the scene, you'll be left with no options, which is always a bad place to be.

On the positive side, if you have performers who can do a scene perfectly and a crew who can execute a camera move flawlessly, long takes can save a lot of time and tape during your production schedule. On *Roger Dodger*, director Dylan Kidd was able to burn through 12 pages of dialogue in an afternoon, because his actors were able to play a scene flawlessly, and the crew was up to the challenge of capturing it, all in a single shot. It's just a question of weighing the risks and the advantages.

Abandoning Your Shot List

Of course, the best-laid plans occasionally go awry. You may find when you're on location that the scene you rehearsed and storyboarded so meticulously simply can't be shot the way you intended. You may have lost your original location. There may be technical problems. Or you may simply have run out of time. Whatever the reason, you are now faced with a serious problem in need of a speedy solution.

The best solution that we've found in this situation is to go back to the basics. Ask yourself what your original intention was. What ideas were you trying to convey with the shots you planned? Rather than forcing your shots into a room or a schedule that can't hold them, you need to re-think your plan, using your original intentions but finding a new way to reach your goal.

Often you'll find that the best solution is the simplest. Of course, the simplest solution is sometimes the hardest one to discover. It may not be the one that will make future movie students "ooh" and "ahh," but if it gets the job done and keeps you on schedule, it's the right solution.

For one segment of *Grown Men*, we'd planned on doing an elaborate dolly shot around a bed, showing a sleeping couple as they moved closer and closer to reconciliation. It would show the passage of time, dissolving four times as the dolly moved around the bed, each time showing the couple in different pajamas and bedding, getting closer and closer together.

Nice idea, but when the time came to shoot it, we found that the room was too small to make it work. However, what the room lacked in floor space, it made up in height, sporting a nice, tall ceiling.

Going back to the basic idea behind the scene, we composed four high-angle shots, from four points in the room, where we could see the couple in bed as they moved closer together. Different bedding (and dissolves) showed the passage of time, and we were able to make our visual point, despite not being able to do our original shot. And, in the end, the scene was better for it.

Continuity

The key to continuity at this budget level is to keep a keen eye on the big things and make sure that they match from shot to shot. Try to make the small details match too, but don't sweat it if you miss.

For example, if you have a character exiting one room wearing a blue shirt and entering an adjacent room wearing a red shirt, you have a big continuity problem that you need to correct. That same character exiting one room wearing earrings and entering another without them is less of a problem unless the earrings are the size of hubcaps.

In general, the continuity issue is the domain of your unit production manager, assuming it gets past the actor. (Most actors are remarkably adept at remembering which costume goes with what scene.)

To prevent these potential snafus from happening in the first place, the unit production manager needs to take a Polaroid photo of each of the actors during their final costume fittings or the first time they wear each costume during production.

Each photo should show the actor wearing one of their costumes for the movie. If the actor has six costume changes during the course of the movie, the production manager will have six Polaroid photos of them. On the bottom of each photo should be noted the scene numbers in which the costume appears.

This technique can also be used with special makeup or hairstyles. It then becomes a simple matter to check the photo against what the actor is wearing before each scene to ensure that continuity is being maintained.

It should be noted here that your production is missing one important crew person, the script supervisor. This is the person who makes sure the lines in the script are said correctly and that continuity — at least the major stuff — matches from shot to shot and from scene to scene.

Our unit production manager performed this function during takes. She read along with the script as the actors said the lines, and she noted details, such as which hand the actor used to hold the carving knife.

Script supervisors on big productions keep very detailed notes, but your project will probably be simple enough that the unit production manager and the actors can keep track of continuity issues; however, it's a good idea to have everyone on the cast and crew watching.

Touchups

We mentioned this before, but it bears repeating: Tell your hair-and-makeup person to keep the touchups that they do to the actors to a minimum. Primping and fluffing before each shot wastes time and generally makes no appreciable difference on tape.

That's not to say that the makeup people shouldn't be alert to makeup problems and be prepared to jump in and correct them. You simply must establish up front what you consider to be a problem and what you can live with.

You may not even have a full-time makeup person. Instead, the makeup-and-hair supervisor may stop by in the morning, do the makeup for your key actors, and then disappear for the rest of the day.

If this is your situation, it's a good idea to get this part-time makeup person to create makeup kits for the key actors. Each kit can be as simple as a plastic bag filled with the materials each actor will need to repair his or her own makeup throughout the day. Because different actors may be using radically different shades or types of makeup, creating these individual kits makes it easier to keep all the makeup elements straight and in a place where the actors can find them.

A very quick touchup on the set of Grown Men. *Pictured, l to r: Actress Susan Vee, Unit Production Manager Nicola Muoio, and Executive Producer (and Boom Operator) Dale Newton. (Photo courtesy of Granite Productions, Unlimited.)*

Where to Begin… and Where to End

On your first actual day of production, you may find yourself filled with feelings of trepidation and anxiety. Consequently, we recommend that you lessen your burden a bit and start out your shoot with something simple. And that you start off quickly.

Starting quickly establishes a quick pace for the production, and it establishes the director as a take-charge sort of person. Starting simply gives everyone a chance to get up to speed with a scene or a shot that is not too taxing or difficult.

On some productions, because of the logistics of locations or the availability of actors, you have to start your first day with a dramatically intense or technically complicated scene. In such cases, there's nothing you can do but dive in and do your best. But, as a rule of thumb, don't start with the hardest scene.

If possible, it's also a good idea to save scenes that aren't pivotal for the last few hours of your last day of principal photography. These are scenes that advance the characters without necessarily driving the plot. If you begin to run over schedule on your last day, you can eliminate these final scenes without doing serious damage to your movie. Of course, it's best to have every scene advance both the characters and the plot; however, there are usually a few minor scenes that can be deleted without irrevocably damaging the logic of the movie.

The Geography Lesson

The beginning of the movie is where your audience becomes acclimated to your characters, to the tone of your story, and to the environment in which your story will take place. Part of your job is letting them know who's who, what the relationships are, and where the story is set so that they aren't asking these questions later.

As the storyteller, you want the audience to laugh when you want them to laugh, to be moved when you tell them to be, and to be confused only when it serves your purposes. To that end, it's best to perform a sort of "geography lesson" early in the movie. As the characters are introduced and the situation is established, you also want to teach the audience where everything is located.

In *Beyond Bob*, it was important to establish that the primary location was a lake home situated in the middle of nowhere. This was done with establishing shots at the beginning of the movie and then reinforced visually during early interior scenes by placing characters in front of windows that overlooked the forest surrounding the house. (The "forest" was actually several artificial Christmas trees strategically placed to block out the other homes in the suburban housing tract that was our primary location.)

These early scenes were also used to establish where each room was in relation to the others, geographically laying the groundwork for later sequences. The shots explained where the kitchen was in relation to the living room, where the deck was in relation to the den, and so on.

You need to keep this concept of the "geography lesson" in mind while you're planning your shots, particularly when you're shooting out of sequence. Scenes that take place early in the story — but perhaps late in the shooting schedule — need to present the "lay of the land" more than scenes that take place in those same locations later in the story.

For example, the scenes we just described from *Beyond Bob*, showing the windows and the trees outside, were terribly time-consuming to set up and shoot. The light from the outside had to be color-balanced with the light from the inside; there were only certain times during the day when the light was right; and the trees and the shots had to be positioned with great care to avoid revealing our actual location.

As a consequence, the only time you see out the windows in the movie is at the beginning of the story. Once the location had been established, the windows were either not shown or the shades were drawn. The audience, however, still believed that the story was taking place in a lake home surrounded by trees because this had been established earlier.

Directors vs. Producers

If you've ever sat through the closing credits of a Hollywood feature-length movie, you've probably realized just how many people it takes to make a big-buck movie happen. From the Assistant to the Assistant Director to the Good, Better, and Best Boys, there's a big crowd of folks on the average movie set. That's one of the reasons those movies are so expensive.

Of course, your budget is much smaller, and as a consequence, you will have to deal with fewer people. But don't kid yourself; you will need to deal with them. Part of your job as producer or director is managing the people working on the movie to get the most out of them without killing them.

One of the ideas you'll need to communicate right away is the concept that this is a professional production (the absence of paychecks aside), and everyone is expected to act professionally. That means that you can have fun on the set, but when it comes time to crack the whip and get the work done, everybody does their part.

Consequently, you'll need to decide who is going to be in charge of cracking that whip. Our approach has been a variation of the Good-Cop/Bad-Cop method, adapted for our purposes as Good-Director/Bad-Producer. Basically, this means that the producer is the person who ultimately says no. As in, "No, we can't afford that prop," "No, you can't keep shooting," "No, you can't have a helicopter," and our favorite, "No, you can't have a percentage of the gross." This technique allows the director to maintain her or his rapport with the crew and cast.

Of course, making a movie is a high-pressure situation, and conflicts are undoubtedly going to arise. After long hours of intense work, nerves may become frayed, and tempers may flare. As producer or director, it's your job to keep those conflicts to a minimum.

Digital Filmmaking 101 ~ Newton & Gaspard

One way to do that is to hire charming, funny people who can keep the atmosphere light on the set. We've been graced with some terrifically funny cast and crew members who have helped to keep spirits up and make the long hours move much faster. From joke-telling competitions to dueling impersonations, these folks kept their co-workers smiling and the production moving smoothly.

Despite all the jokes and the fun, you may encounter a situation in which one or two crew or cast members are simply not working out. They may be constant complainers, malcontents, or people who are simply incompetent. Whatever they are, they are trouble, and they can do serious damage to morale and to the movie.

Just as no one likes to be dumped, there are few people who enjoy the act of dumping someone else. But in some situations it must be done, and for the sake of your movie, it must be done quickly and cleanly.

We had a situation with a crew member on one of our movies who was not only verbally disruptive but who also blatantly and repeatedly disregarded our instructions. Although everyone was essentially working in a volunteer situation, there wasn't room for unprofessional and damaging behavior. So the crew member was asked to leave and not return. The person received credit for work done, but it's the last time that person will be working for us.

Tough to do? You bet, particularly when you're in the midst of a complicated shoot and you're losing a key crew member. But that's when you have to do it. To wait and prolong the inevitable only exacerbates the problem.

Sound Advice

Although you're working in a visual medium, don't ignore your sound recordist and boom operator during the planning process for each scene. They need to know as soon as you do what sorts of shots you're planning, so they can find the best and most efficient way to record each scene.

Ultra-wide shots, characters moving within the frame, moving shots, and master shots with characters talking to each other across a wide space can be real headaches for your sound team. So the sooner you let them know what you're planning, the more likely they'll be able to figure out how to record the best sound.

A basic rule of thumb about recording sound is that if you're in a pinch and the sound is bad but the picture's okay, move on. You can fix the sound later. This is generally true.

Bad sound is much easier to fix than a bad picture; however, that doesn't give you carte blanche to record bad sound. You'll want to record the cleanest sound you possibly can while on location. That's the primary concern of your sound recordist on location — getting clean dialogue. Beware of the sound recordist who makes your track sound like a finished, mixed soundtrack. You don't want that. You want dialogue, spotless, pristine dialogue that's so clean you could eat off of it. That way you don't lose any of your sound-mixing options for editing.

A point to keep in mind is that with digital sound, you never want to have the meter on the camera peak at the top of the scale. At that point, the sound turns into an unusable crackle. It is better to run the sound levels a little too low rather than too high. When you get into editing it is possible to raise the levels as much as needed without introducing tape hiss because the recording is digital.

Sound effects are definitely a secondary issue. It's much simpler and often better to add them in post. For example, in *Grown Men*, we have a number of scenes with characters sitting and talking in busy locations (restaurants, offices, bars, a blood bank). For each of these scenes, it was much simpler to shoot them without any ambient sound effects and add them later.

The background extras are quiet during shooting; the sound of a busy restaurant kitchen will be added in postproduction. A scene from Grown Men. *Pictured, l to r: Matthew G. Anderson, Amy Shomshak, and Kate Eifrig. (Photo courtesy of Granite Productions, Unlimited.)*

The same is true of any scenes with specific sounds, such as crowd noises, doors opening and closing, phones ringing, doorbells, crickets, babies crying, and so on. Save yourself the trouble and add the sound effects later. You may want to record the effects as wild sound while you're on location, but it simplifies the editing enormously if you record them separately from the scene itself.

On a related note, make sure that your sound recordist records plenty of "room tone" from each location. Room tone is best defined as the sound you hear in a room when you don't hear anything at all.

Stop reading and listen. What do you hear? The sound of the refrigerator in the next room, the sound of traffic outside, or the "presence" of an empty room.

That's room tone.

Your editor will need plenty of this ambient sound to help cover dialogue edits, so don't leave a location without having everyone stand very still while the sound recordist records two minutes of ambiance. This is also a good time for silent prayer; the quieter the better. (For the ultimate view of what happens while room tone is being recorded, rent the best movie on the subject of low-budget moviemaking, Tom DiCillo's brilliant *Living in Oblivion*.)

You've Been Framed

You may have modest expectations for your movie, hoping it will play at some festivals, get posted for downloading on the Net, maybe get sold to cable television, and perhaps even end up in your local video store in the "Manager's Choice" section. These are noble ambitions, but we recommend that you aim just a little higher, if only during production.

There's always the slim chance that your movie may end up as a 35mm theatrical release. Don't count on it, don't bank on it, and certainly don't borrow against it, but be prepared for it just in case.

That preparation includes framing all your shots so that they'll look decent if your movie gets blown up to 35mm wide-screen format. If you don't, all of your wide shots will cut off your actors at the forehead and ankles, and your close-ups will take on the look of a dermatological examination.

Our advice is to play it "TV safe." The diagram below compares the two most common wide-screen theatrical formats and a standard 16mm or 35mm film frame with the "TV safe" frame of the digital video you'll be shooting. As you can see, if you frame your action a little tighter than the "TV safe" area you'll also ensure that you don't exceed the limits of the wide-screen formats either.

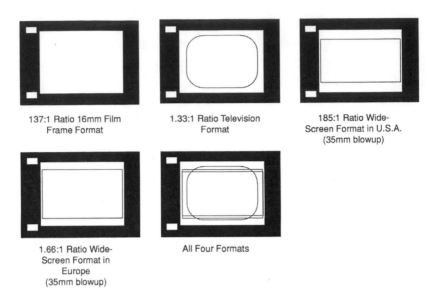

137:1 Ratio 16mm Film
Frame Format

1.33:1 Ratio Television
Format

185:1 Ratio Wide-
Screen Format in U.S.A.
(35mm blowup)

1.66:1 Ratio Wide-
Screen Format in
Europe
(35mm blowup)

All Four Formats

Shooting for a Film Look

When your movie is finished, you may want it to look like a film. To achieve this, the first steps need to be taken during production. To shoot digital video that looks like film, you need to minimize image qualities that are unique to video. There are several ways to do this.

Because video records a smaller range of light than film, it tends to have dark blacks with no detail and bright whites with no detail. To minimize this problem, video is often shot with lots of light and few shadows. In contrast, film images often have dramatic shadows with details visible in them. You can create this look in video by starting with dramatic, shadowy light but then bouncing a little bit of light into the shadows with a white card so some detail is seen. Avoid getting very bright sky in your shots, or bounce sunlight into the scene with your reflector or white cards to better match the light levels of the sky.

Because film's image area is bigger than that of most camcorders' CCD imagers, film often has less depth of field — the range of distance that's in focus — than video. Consequently, video often lacks the out-of-focus background or foreground that medium shots and close-up shots in films commonly use to direct the audience's attention. You can cut down some of the depth of field in your video image by using the neutral-density filters that are common on most prosumer and professional video cameras. Also, shooting fully zoomed in will help throw backgrounds and foregrounds out of focus. Film doesn't look like this in every shot, so mostly try to create a shallow depth of field for your close-up shots.

Often the video "look" has a lot to do with the sharp edges created around objects. If your camcorder has a picture-sharpness setting, you'll want to set it so the edges of objects are slightly soft. When you put a backlight on an actor, don't use a harsh light that accentuates this video edge. Instead, soften the backlight with some of the tough spun in your lighting supplies.

Avoid zooming during a shot. This is very rarely done in a feature film, but it often occurs in videos.

You'll want to shoot your movie as a widescreen production to create the look that audiences associate with "real" movies. If your camcorder doesn't have this capability, you'll need to compose your shots to allow for them to be cropped to widescreen (less top and bottom) in postproduction.

Feeding the Masses

There is one thing you can provide your people that's more important than the opportunity to express themselves artistically, and that's food — hot, healthy food and plenty of it. People will put up with almost anything on a movie set, from long hours to lousy conditions, if the food is good and plentiful. Or even just plentiful.

Regular meal breaks are an important part of your production schedule, as is the easy availability of snacks and drinks. Good food doesn't have to be costly. In fact, nonprofit productions are often able to persuade local restaurants to donate food.

On *Grown Men*, we had a couple local restaurants that regularly donated box lunches to our cause in return for screen credit. So by all means get good, varied food. It shows your cast and crew that you care. (We've provided sample menus in the appendix.)

Extra! Extra!

In order to make your movie look like it takes place in the real world (not necessarily the existing world, but a real world nonetheless), you will discover the occasional need to populate your movie with people other than your primary actors. This population can be drawn from your family, your friends, friends of your friends, friends of your family, and even strangers off the street.

These are your extras.

There are two key things to remember about extras. The first is to be sure to get release forms from *everyone* who shows up to be an extra. Whether they actually end up in the movie or not isn't the issue. You need signed release forms from all the people who might appear in the finished movie, or they don't step in front of your camera.

And second, organize any shooting that involves extras for the maximum value over a minimal amount of time. For a low-budget production, extras create a host of challenges: you need space to keep them when they are not on set; you need crew to control and direct them; you need bathroom facilities for them; and if you keep them too long, you have to feed and water them. We recommend grouping together your scenes with extras. Shoot sequences involving the most extras first, and then dismiss them as soon as you can to limit the number of people milling around. While you can give them some bulk drinks, such as lemonade, and an inexpensive snack, such as homemade cookies, your budget can't feed ten or fifty extra mouths.

On all of our features, we've always scheduled scenes with extras to take place before or after a food break and made sure the extras were thanked and sent on their way before a meal was set out. We've even scheduled two different groups of extras, one before lunch and one after, to keep our meal costs within budget.

Photo Opportunity

One of the first things most distributors will ask about your movie (right after, "Do you have any name actors, any violence, any sex, or any name actors having violent sex?") is whether or not you have production stills.

Production stills are very important to distributors. They are often a vital part of their publicity campaign, and they're hard to create once the movie has wrapped and the actors, costumes, props, and locations have dispersed. Consequently, having decent production stills will make your movie more attractive to potential distributors. Of course, if they hate your movie, it seems unlikely that they'll distribute it just because you have great production stills, but stranger things have happened.

Most Hollywood movies employ a full-time photographer who uses a special camera box to take silent photos as scenes are being shot. Since these photographers are there all day, every day, covering every scene, they burn through a lot of film. As a result, the distributor usually has a treasure trove of photos from which to choose.

You can get some good stills for a minimum outlay of time and money by having a photographer join you (preferably for free) for a particularly photogenic day of production. Or you can set up a later date to shoot staged publicity stills. Be sure to get a creative release from the photographer so you own copyright on the photos.

You can shoot digital photos for virtually nothing if you have a decent digital still camera. If you go this route, be sure to shoot at the highest quality level the camera will allow. It makes for big files, but you may need that level of quality when you hit distribution. Shoot as many images as you can, and store them safely for later use as publicity photos.

A rare good publicity shot captured on the set of Beyond Bob. *(Pictured, l to r: Patrick Coyle, Michael Paul Levin, Peter Moore, Leslie Ball, Julie Briskman, Dan Rowles, and Kathryn O'Malley.)*

Action and Stunts

We can't emphasize enough the need for planning and safety in anything you shoot that could even vaguely be considered an action scene or a stunt. While we don't expect that you'll be creating *The Matrix 7* or *Die Hard 39* on your budget, you're bound to encounter one or two sequences that could potentially be dangerous. Scenes that involve explosions, moving cars, or even a fistfight are all potentially dangerous scenes and must be approached and executed with the utmost care. When in doubt, bring in an expert.

The opening scene of *Beyond Bob* called for Bob to assemble a hang-glider, strap it on, hold his finger out to check the wind, and then step off a high cliff and glide away across the sky. So we shot our actor doing all those things, up to the point of stepping off the cliff. For that we brought in our hang-gliding expert, dressed him in Bob's costume, and shot him as he stepped off a frighteningly-steep cliff and floated away. Our expert has been hang-gliding for years, so his performance, which was breathtaking to us, was just another day of flying to him.

To further ensure the actor's safety, the shots of assembling and strapping on the hang glider were photographed far from anything that even vaguely resembled a cliff. We didn't want to take the chance of a big gust of wind blowing away one of our primary actors.

Fight scenes are another area for concern. Something as seemingly simple as throwing a punch can injure participants who aren't trained in stage combat. Even the simplest fight scene should be choreographed like a tight dance number, with no surprises and little margin for error.

On *Grown Men*, we had a shot of a bar bouncer throwing a customer out of the bar. To ensure everyone's safety, and at the same time to make it look as real as possible, we brought in a stage combat expert to help with the shot.

If someone in your cast isn't trained in stage combat, it's well worth the effort to seek out an expert who will help stage the scene and keep it safe. The end result will be well-staged, believable, and injury-free.

Prelude to a fight: The first rule of this fight club is that no actors get injured. A scene from Grown Men.
(Pictured, l to r: Mark Eckel, David Fields)
(Photo courtesy of Granite Productions, Unlimited.)

Finally, there are many things that happen behind the camera that aren't stunts but are potentially dangerous as well.

In most of our movies, we've had instances where skylights needed to be covered to block out sunlight, and we had one instance when several lawn chairs needed to be placed on the peak of a two-story house. To ensure the safety of the crew in these situations, we came up with a novel solution: We made the producer (Dale) do it.

While he may not have been the most qualified person for the job, there were certain things we knew about him that made him our first and best choice. He had insurance. He wouldn't sue us if he were injured. And if, God forbid, he fell off the roof, shooting could continue unabated.

Seriously, we feel that it's often best to do these dangerous tasks yourself. You're in no position to cover someone else's medical bills, nor can you foot the cost of a lawsuit. This doesn't mean that you should approach these tasks cavalierly; however, you can trust the person doing it, and you can handle the consequences if something goes wrong.

Intimate Scenes

Unless your day job involves shooting photo layouts for Victoria's Secret catalogs, you may find it awkward doing scenes that involve partial and total nudity or intimate moments. These scenes can be as difficult and as tense as staging a stunt or action scene... with the added pressure of having naked people around.

Your first concern in these scenes should be the comfort and privacy of your actors. While they may have learned to overcome shyness about baring their souls, baring their other parts is an entirely different matter and should not be treated lightly. To begin with, they must know up front what is expected; trying to coax someone into disrobing on the set is not only unreasonable, it's unprofessional. It's also not kosher to ask them to disrobe under the pretext that you "won't show anything."

The set should be cleared of any unnecessary personnel, and you should be prepared to be very stringent when you define "unnecessary." In many cases, the remaining crew can simply be the videographer, the director, the sound recordist (if you're recording sound), and the unit production manager.

For some reason, nude scenes attract a crowd like a fire sale, so make sure your unit production manager clears the set and keeps it clear. Be both diligent and vigilant about protecting the actors' privacy during these scenes.

It will probably make the actors more comfortable and will better prepare the crew if you rehearse the scene once or twice with the actors fully clothed. Keep checking with the actors throughout the process to see how comfortable they are with what's happening and what you can do to make it easier for them.

Before we shot a sequence of one character running naked from a lake in *Beyond Bob*, the actor broke the tension by saying to the crew, "We're all adults here. We've all seen 'Willie' before."

That's the sort of attitude that you should pass onto your cast and crew. They are all adults. They've all seen Willie before. So just shoot the scene and move on.

Viewing Dailies

In the old days, you shot the film, sent it off to the lab, and then the next day watched the previous day's work. Hence the term "dailies."

Nowadays, after you shoot a scene, you have the option of playing it back instantly. And repeatedly.

Avoid this option.

Watching each take, or even an occasional take, while on the set will burn up production time like you won't believe and work will stop on the set as everyone comes to watch, too. While it's always a good idea to do some spot-checking during the day (to ensure that you're actually recording images and sound on tape), your time is needed for shooting more footage rather than watching what you've shot.

That's not to say that you shouldn't watch what you've shot. We recommend it, but not while you're on the set. Instead, schedule some time off the set to review your material before you start shooting again.

Some people restrict attendance at these viewing sessions to those on a need-to-know basis (director of photography, camera operator, unit production manager, sound recordist, hair-and-makeup supervisor, producer, director — basically anyone but the actors). Their thinking is that they don't want the actors to freak out when they see themselves on-screen, fearing that it will change the actor's approach and ruin their performance or something. This strikes us as a bit silly. As much as anyone else on the shoot, the actors need a chance to evaluate their work while in the process, when it can do some good, rather than at the premiere, where it's impossible to change things.

On our projects, everyone is invited and encouraged to attend these screenings. Our reasoning is that once people get over the shock of seeing themselves on-screen, they begin to realize that they are involved in making a real movie. This has proved to be the case, especially with the more experienced actors who were somewhat skeptical about our low-buck approach. Our sessions of watching "weeklies" turned into a great support group and morale booster with everyone cheering on each other's work.

After all the effort — the proverbial blood, sweat and tears — they were beginning to see the fruits of their labors up on the screen. Viewing the weeklies after the final shoot, they laughed and cried and said how sad they were to be "done with the movie."

However, for the director and producer, it's only the beginning and far from the end.

Chapter 10
Special Effects ~ *Please Pass the Construction Paper*

The goal of movie special effects is to convince the audience they saw something that really wasn't there. We did one step better than that. We convinced seasoned Hollywood distributors that they were seeing $50,000 of special effects when we had actually spent about $1,000. That's $50 of production value on the screen for each dollar spent. Hollywood producers fantasize about ratios like this when they look at their budgets. Ironically, some of the most visually exciting shots were produced for nothing but the cost to run the camera (and a healthy chunk of our spare time), and some of our most effective special effects went unnoticed, which is the goal of all but the big showy effects, like UFO crashes.

A certain amount of special effects are needed just to make routine movie magic, such as a blender that blasts orange juice into an actor's face, an establishing shot of a building that doesn't exist, or the illusion that day is night and night is day. Some special effects are essential to create a fantasy world called for by a screenplay, such as a UFO encounter or a ghostly manifestation. And most important for all you ultra-low-budgeteers, special effects are used to save on expensive production costs and to let you show images that you can't really afford to shoot. And if these weren't reasons enough, special effects are fun to do, and it's fun to trick the audience.

You may not realize that the majority of special effects are available to you... on your budget. The reason is that most special-effects techniques were developed between 1896 and 1933 using technical resources that are within the reach of today's low-budget moviemakers. Also, a big chunk of today's computer special effects are available to you as part of the video-editing software you'll be using. Add in the image-editing software we recommended, and there is little you can't achieve except 3D animation. And you can buy software for that, too.

This means that, by investing some time and by using older techniques along with new desktop-video software, you can achieve lots of special effects comparable to Hollywood's. We'll tell you about ours to give you some ideas how to do your own.

Miniatures

Miniatures saved us a bundle of money and days of production time. Shots that would have been too difficult or costly to shoot for real were created in Dale's basement for mere dollars. An example of a mundane but completely effective shot is from *Beyond Bob*. The script called for a night shot of a stoplight hanging on cables over a secluded rural intersection. The changing lights on this traffic signal were integral to one of the movie's funniest scenes; however, this type of traffic light arrangement is relatively rare. We only located one in our area, and shooting it posed some significant problems. First, it was hanging 20 feet in the air, making a face-on close-up challenging. It also hung at a relatively dark intersection with no electrical outlets within reach. Consequently, lighting the exterior of this traffic signal would require powerful lights and an electrical generator. Very expensive for ten seconds of footage in the finished movie. So we used a miniature instead.

Dale built a one-fourth scale miniature of the stoplight out of cardboard, mailing tubes, aluminum foil to reflect heat, a three-dollar can of highway-yellow paint, spare lamp parts, and some colored overhead transparencies. The miniature was shot in Dale's basement using utility floodlights with photoflood bulbs for lighting. The end result is a shot so convincing that no one has ever suspected that it wasn't real. Sure, it took a day's work to create, but almost no cash. Renting the equipment to shoot this shot for real could have cost hundreds of dollars. Time we had, money we didn't.

We also used miniatures built with cheap hobby-store materials to create a night shot of a military air base. Cheap plastic jet models were lit by lights shining through hidden holes in the cardboard runway. In the foreground, a miniature chain link fence made from wire mesh completed the illusion for another shot we couldn't afford to light. The key to using these miniatures effectively was keeping their on-screen time brief and making them night shots. Convincing daylight miniatures are much harder to create.

We also used quite a number of miniature signs when real ones didn't exist or conveyed the wrong impression. These signs were usually small so we could take advantage of paste-on letters or computer-generated typefaces on 8 ½ x 11-inch sheets of paper. For example, Skatedium roller rink is a major setting in *Beyond Bob*, but it had an uninspiring soft-drink sign with the rink's name on it. We built our own sign, starting with a piece of white tag board about 8 x 6 inches. We scored it with a knife and damaged the edges to create the look of painted sheets of plywood. Colored adhesive vinyl letters provided the words "Roller Rink," and some salvaged plastic letters from a lobby informational sign were glued on as the "giant" plastic letters spelling "Skatedium." We added a tacky "giant" skate painted on more tag board "plywood" to complete the look. A few nail heads with rust stains dripping from them were drawn in using colored pencils, and a gray crayon was used to give the black plastic letters a weathered look. A sprig of juniper branch intruding into the corner of the shot creates a convincing billboard that helps convey the feel of the setting. Cost was zero thanks to Dale's pack-rat pile of supplies. We used a similar approach to create the sign for a rural sheriff's office. We shaved bark from one-inch tree branches and stained them dark brown to create a convincing frame for this rustic sign.

Miniature signs from Beyond Bob *and* Resident Alien.

Miniatures seem to work best when they are simple. More detail is not necessarily better. If you look at professional matte paintings that are used to create the illusion of larger scenes or fantasy scenes, you'll be amazed how impressionistic they are. For example, the matte painting that was used for one of the closing scenes in Alfred Hitchcock's *The Birds* shows a huge landscape covered with roosting white birds. On the actual matte painting, only a few of the painted birds even look like birds. The rest are nothing more than white streaks of paint. However, the short shot in the finished movie is effective because you expect to see birds. We created a foreground wheat field for one miniature by just making random streaks on a strip of cardboard with yellow, brown, and tan crayons.

You can test your miniatures by shooting test footage and making adjustments to parts that don't look realistic. When shooting miniatures, be sure to use the same camera angle you would use if you were shooting the real thing.

Photographs can help you put people in your miniatures. In *Resident Alien*, we have a wide shot of a character looking up at a hovering UFO. The person is standing still, thanks to a special effects–conscious script. We took a still photograph of our character in the actual setting. Minnefex, a special-effects company which offered its services to the movie, built a miniature of the real setting and suspended a UFO over it. The actor's photo was enlarged to the proper size on a photocopier, hand colored, cut out, and placed in the miniature setting. The result is a shot worth thousands in street value in the movie capital. If you don't have a handy special-effects company to build miniature settings, contact the model-railroad crowd in your area. With a few adjustments, their skills adapt well to movie production. Also, there are many good library books on miniature construction, again, usually aimed at model railroaders.

Mini-Sets

Many times you need a shot in a setting that doesn't require an entire set. You can easily create mini-sets that can convey a sense of a larger location, and the audience then fills in the rest at no extra charge.

In *Resident Alien*, we needed interior shots of a mysterious spaceship showing an unseen person's hand adjusting the ship's controls. There was no need for the entire spacecraft interior, so a control panel was built from painted cardboard. (This is one of Dale's favorite building materials because it's usually free, reasonably durable, and can be shaped easily.) A few lights, plastic parts, colored gels, and a hand wearing a spray-painted rubber glove created the control-panel part of the set. The distant wall of the spacecraft in the background is actually a nearby mini-set constructed of spray-painted egg cartons and cardboard packing material. A little mood lighting created an effective, short scene in the spacecraft. To see how far you can go with sheets of cardboard, check out the extraordinary corrugated-cardboard spaceship sets in the movie *Plan 10 from Outer Space* by Trent Harris. Masterful painting makes them one of the highlights of the movie.

We've also used realistic mini-sets to save the time of doing special effects during full production. For *Resident Alien*, we needed a scene of someone putting bare wires into an electrical outlet, creating sparks. The scene was shot during production without this close-up shot. Later we bought a piece of art board that roughly matched the look of the location's walls and attached it to a scrap of gypsum wall board. We cut a hole and installed a real wall outlet that was wired to an extension cord. Using this mini-set, the character's costume, and Dale's hand, the second-unit did this insert shot several times to get the proper sparks, without danger to the actors or wasting expensive time with the full production company.

Replacement Shots and Continuity Tricks

Mistakes are going to happen when you're shooting up to 80 setups a day. Perhaps there's a close-up you should have done for dramatic emphasis, or you accidentally crossed "the line," and your shot is from the wrong camera angle. At this pace of production, you're long gone from the location by the time you review the footage all together, and you can't afford to take the whole production company back for a reshoot. What do you do? If the shot is of minor importance, you live with what you've got. Those are the breaks in the low-budget biz. But sometimes it's an important shot, so you assign it to the second-unit. For us, that was the director and producer wearing different hats. You take the DV camcorder you bought and shoot replacement shots quickly, efficiently, and cheaply.

For example, we shot a scene of a character falling asleep at a tape recorder while holding a cup of coffee. In the medium shot, the coffee spilling in the character's lap just looked silly, and we had no close shot. So we took the same cup, a similar shirt, and a different person, and reshot the cup spilling in close-up. This improved the suspense of the gradually tipping cup, and when we cut to a shot of the tape recorder's VU meter as we hear the character yell, the scene became funny as intended. The replacement shot works great, and it took us just an hour.

Special Effects

Continuity tricks make the audience believe they are seeing two things together that were never in the same vicinity. An actor on the pitcher's mound can throw a fast ball to a batter at home plate who is performing months later at a different ball field. Careful use of props for continuity can connect the performances.

We pulled off this kind of trick when we couldn't get a sheriff's vehicle and a performer we needed to an out-of-town motel location during the *Resident Alien* shoot. The scene called for the actor to drive up in the vehicle and have a conversation with a passenger while parked in front of the motel. The motel had a front awning supported by white wooden posts. These posts had been seen in earlier shots of the motel, so we just painted a two-by-four white and stood it within the frame where a motel post would be. The sheriff's vehicle pulls up to a post 60 miles from the motel, but you'd never guess it from watching the movie.

It is truly amazing what an audience will believe it saw when it is expecting something. This makes continuity tricks even easier. In the opening title sequence of *Beyond Bob*, a character repeatedly walks past a photo on a dresser. With each pass, we jump closer to the photo. However, only the first two passes were shot with the actor in silhouette passing the actual photo. We then cut to an enlargement of the photo which was shot at another time to allow us to see close-ups of the people in the photo. The actor's body still appears to pass the photo, but it is actually Dale's hand inside the sleeve of a black sweatshirt. Because the first two shots established an expectation, no one has ever seen anything but the actor.

Tricks like these can save flawed shots and can do much to simplify scheduling problems during production.

Poor Person's Process Shots

Let's do a definition first so no one feels left out. Process shots are ones in which a non-existent background is created behind performers or an object, such as a window. This can be done using any of several optical, rear-projection, and digital-effects techniques. An extremely common example is the shot of people riding in the car. Many times the view out the car's rear window is a process shot, and the actors are actually sitting on a sound stage. The image behind them was shot at a different time. In film, these shots are called matte shots. In video, they are called chroma keys and are usually shot in front of a background color that is not part of flesh tones, such as green or blue. Most video-editing software can do a simple version of this. More expensive software can do it better, but it's still a challenge to make it look convincing, and this software is a bit pricey for your ultra-low budget.

However (you're starting to expect this, aren't you?), you can afford a poor person's process shot, and the results are often very good. The riding in the car shot is little hard to do in daylight, so you'll probably shoot it for real and do what we did, scrunch the camera into the rear seat or the passenger's seat and give the camera operator a neck rub when the shot's over. Night time is a different story. For a night shot, you can just drape the windows that are visible in the background with a black cloth. While the actors take their imaginary ride, just have someone occasionally push down on the bumper to create a little road bounce. You can add to this by panning a light that's spotted to its narrowest beam across the car from front to back to simulate passing headlights. Adding sound effects of passing cars in postproduction will complete this illusion.

You can create the illusion of flying during day or night using a similar technique. Just frame your shot so there is a featureless sky with no clouds in the background. You can fly through the air or have an airplane plummet to its doom, and the background view looks okay. We did this with a hang-glider shot. The glider was suspended by a rope from a tree, and the actor was strapped to a board on sawhorses. The pilot's cocoon hid the board. Using a low-angle shot, all we needed to give the illusion of flight was a wind-direction cloth tied on the glider within the frame. We blew the cloth with a leaf blower. This kind of minor, but significant, detail doesn't really register consciously with the audience, but it creates subconscious supporting data that helps make the shot convincing.

That significant detail helped us do another process shot that is common but hard for us independent moviemakers. We wanted a clean cutaway shot of some actors appearing on a television screen. We didn't want picture roll and other TV artifacts that result from shooting a video image on TV. Instead of using a pricey technical approach, our solution was to get the front frame of a TV and put clear plastic across the screen area. The performances of the actors were shot live through this facade. We just lined them up with the camera looking through the frame. A little bit of light was allowed to reflect on the clear plastic to create that significant detail that says "Hey, this is a real TV." The result looked better than the usual matte or chroma-key shot where an image is inserted onto the TV screen. There was no annoying blue halo around the edges of the screen image, and you could see reflections on the "picture tube."

We've also used a very simple version of a "matte" shot to remove a dock we didn't want in a night scene at a lake shore. The sky, land, and water were essentially black except for the pool of light where our shot would take place. Unfortunately, a nearby dock was also catching the light. To eliminate it, we simply hung a piece of black construction paper in front of the lens so it blacked out the offending dock, making it look like more black lake water. Because the paper was very close to the lens, the edges were out of focus, creating a "soft matte" that was invisible in the final shot.

Specialty Costumes

If you're doing a realistic story set in modern times, your costumes will largely come out of the closets of the people connected with your production. Our first movie, *Resident Alien*, was a science-fiction comedy romance, so some unusual costumes were pretty much mandatory for the genre. Knowing this, Dale wrote in scenes requiring a monster costume and space suits.

We used one technique to make all of these costumes, in part because the script called for them to be reminiscent of each other. The monster suit was made from cardboard and foam rubber and then spray painted. Foam rubber is easy to use for these types of soft costumes. Just cut out the shapes you want from sheets of foam that are ½- to 1-inch thick, depending on how thick you want the final costume. You don't have to have seamstress skills to design with foam rubber, though it is helpful. Just hold the sheet of foam rubber up to the person you are fitting, and tuck and pinch it into the shapes you want. Wherever you have to pinch the material together, mark the edges that come together with a marking pen, and then cut out the excess in between with a scissors. In sewing terms, you have created a dart. Usually the ½-inch foam rubber works best for this type of fitting.

To assemble the costume, spread carpenter's contact cement (the nasty-smelling solvent-based type works best) on the edges where the foam rubber will butt together. You don't need to overlap the foam unless that's the look you want. Gluing the edges together will create a seamless look. Let the glue dry to the touch on both edges, and just squeeze these edges of the butt joints together. Voila! Instant seam. If you have the pieces all cut, you can assemble an entire costume in about a half hour.

For larger shapes that need a support structure, such as the monster head, corrugated cardboard is our material of choice. The support structure we used was designed much like the keel and ribs of a wooden boat. The foam rubber is like the outside skin of the ship. Before you spend time making your real support structure, test your design with a small-scale version that you quickly cut out of tag board. (Old potato chip boxes from the recycling bin work nicely.) After your support structure is completed, fit pieces of foam rubber over it, cut the pieces, and glue them together with contact cement over the structure.

The beauty of these lightweight and soft materials is that you can easily modify the final shape to better fit the performer, and you can spray paint or airbrush the entire rig when you're done. One word of caution: sunlight and air tend to deteriorate foam rubber and make it crumbly. We've stored our headgear in plastic bags, and many years later they are still usable.

Producer Dale Newton (right) makes some final adjustments to foam rubber costumes on the set of Resident Alien.

Mechanical and electrical effects can also be added to costumes. For example, we needed a glove with glowing lights in it. We used a painted rubber glove and poked miniature Christmas tree lights through holes in the palm. Wire for the lights traveled from the glove, up the sleeve, and out the back of the costume to the power source. (Be sure this kind of wiring is well insulated to protect the performer; we had to convince our actor that it was safe. Use only DC battery power to minimize the risk of dangerous shock.) In the medium shot we used, the lights weren't visible on the glove until lit, and they glowed nicely on the screen.

Specialty Props

We've used many specialty props to add spice to our movies and to achieve specific effects. One simple specialty prop was a branch that a pigeon had to walk on for a key shot in *Beyond Bob*. We made arrangements to use a racing pigeon as our performer, but we learned that racing pigeons are trained not to land in trees, only at their home roost. So we had trained birds to use, but they didn't like sitting on branches. Our solution was a specialty prop. We used a real tree branch that was attached to a stand. Along the branch we drilled holes out of view and filled them with corn. The pigeon was enticed out onto our branch by the line of corn, and it eventually did a nice little performance for our shot.

Beyond Bob also required a couple ghostly floating effects. In the movie, we used black string to lift up objects that the ghost was moving. Generally, the biggest giveaway for these kinds of "wire" shots is the wires that the audience looks for overhead, so we put our wires out the sides. We stretched two black strings between two wooden handles. We attached the strings behind a tree branch that the ghost was "carrying." Out of camera range on each side of the branch, two people held the wooden handles. With this arrangement, they were able to fly the stick and give it movements, much as you would do with a marionette.

In the story, the invisible ghost uses the same branch to write in the sand. We did it with careful editing and a different technique. We drilled a hole in the end of the branch so it would fit onto a large nail. That nail stuck out of a wooden handle and protruded through a letter "S" which had been cut into the top of a box, much like a stencil. By burying the box under a thin layer of sand, we could move the handle and make the stick appear to write a letter "S" in the sand by itself.

For *Beyond Bob*, we couldn't get permission from a major game manufacturer to use a game board that mystically spells out answers to questions. (Hint: The game's name rhymes with "squeegee gourd.") This forced us to come up with our own connection to the spirit world, and the results were much more fun. Our spirit board looked like an oriental roulette wheel with the alphabet and the words "yes" and "no" printed around the edge of the wheel. A dragon-shaped ticker hit nails around the edge of the wheel as it spun. When the wheel stopped, it pointed to an answer or the next letter in the answer. The entire board sat on a cloth, giving the impression that there was no way of manipulating it from below. Actually, a slit in the cloth allowed us to slide a trigger cable up under the wheel. This cable lifted a Velcro pad up to hit another Velcro pad on the underside of the wheel. We just moved the pad on the wheel to match the letter we wanted to stop on. All this was invisible to the camera, and it allowed us to show a continuous shot of the actors spinning the wheel and it stopping on the desired letter. Very convincing, very simple, very cheap.

The Spirit Board created for Beyond Bob.

In *Resident Alien*, we needed to show a rigid chunk of UFO debris become pliable when an electrical charge was applied to it. The debris itself was easy; two prop pieces were used. A rigid one was made from auto-body putty, and a pliable one was made from foam rubber. We painted and decorated them to be identical. The rest of the trick is in planning the sequence in which electricity is applied to the debris. We designed the natural points where edits would occur — such as going to a close-up of poking the electrified debris — as the points where we would switch the props. As long as all the edit points seemed to be ones naturally motivated by the other actions in the scene, the audience didn't realize that we were using them to switch the props. In fact, audiences are so used to this kind of editing, many of them don't even realize an edit has been made. Just ask a non-moviemaker to tell you how many shots are in a fast-paced soft-drink commercial, and they will usually guess about ten. What they actually watched may have been 50 edits. You can use this obliviousness to editing to help your specialty props create some surprising effects.

A more mundane type of specialty prop was a jail-cell door. For *Grown Men*, we needed a five-second shot of a cell door sliding shut on an actor.

It would have been a schedule killer to try to shoot this at a real jail, even if we could get permission. Instead, we reused a jail door we'd built for *Resident Alien*. Its bars were made from electrical conduit inserted into holes drilled in two-by-two-inch boards. A few screws to hold them in place, a wooden box for the lock, and a coat of black spray paint create a convincing cell door. A PVC pipe was screwed on the top to allow the door to slide on a smaller pipe. At one of the main locations, this rig was set up in the basement parking garage against a stark concrete wall. The door was just slid into place in front of the actor to throw him in the slammer. Interestingly, while visiting the set of a television western for which he was writing, John spotted a jail-cell door constructed the same way. The lesson is that specialty props don't have to be elaborate to be effective.

Simple jail-cell door in use in a scene from Grown Men. *(Photo courtesy of Granite Productions, Unlimited.)]*

We've also used vinyl adhesive sheets to good effect. In *Beyond Bob*, a car needed to be aged ten years. We considered starting with a rusty car and paying for it to be repaired to a ten-years-earlier look, but that was too expensive. Instead, we painted brown rust on pieces of clear adhesive plastic and applied them to the car's fenders, wheel wells, hood, and trunk. This easily knocked a couple grand off the resale value — temporarily. (The car later rusted in the spots we had predicted.) Paste-on letters and decals cut from colored adhesive sheets also helped us transform a family car into a convincing police vehicle.

Animation and In-Camera Effects

Optical-film-printer effects and digital computer effects are the standard techniques for creating many special-effect shots in the movie industry. However, many times an effect that is achieved completely in the camera is more believable than all but the most expensive lab tricks. Digital computer effects can lose almost indiscernible bits of reality, a bit of haze here, a shadow or reflection there. While it's hard to put your finger on the specific loss, something in the audience's subconscious sees what's lacking and spills the beans to the conscious mind. Because in-camera effects and animations really occur before the lens, they retain more of these intangible trappings of reality. In the early days of film, most special effects were done in the camera, and it has worked well for us, too. Watch the original *King Kong*, which has animation by Willis O'Brien and special effects that primarily were done in the camera. While the animation is a bit choppy by today's standards, hundreds of other special-effects shots still look great. Many times, animation, split screens, rear projections on miniature sets, and glass mattes (scene elements painted on a pane of glass in front of the camera) were all used within the same scene, creating stunningly realistic special effects. The use of more than one technique can distract and confuse the audience's subconscious minds, preventing them from figuring out any of the tricks.

Some in-camera effects are time consuming and elaborate, others are laughably simple. Here's a simple one that we did.

We wanted to show space travelers being transported by a beam of light from their ship to the ground. To accomplish this effect, we relied on a technique that was pioneered in a 19th-century magic trick called *Pepper's Ghost*, which was used to conjure up an apparition. It's a simple effect that uses a thin pane of glass placed in front of the viewer (or camera) at a 45-degree angle. The diagram below will show how it is set up. You've probably seen this effect if you've ever opened one of those casement windows with a hinge on the side. On a bright day, you'll see an image reflected in the glass from the left or right of the window.

We created a light beam that delivered our space travelers by installing the 45-degree-angle glass in a cardboard box painted black inside. The front and the back of the box were open so the camera could look though the 45-degree-angled glass. One side of the box was also open but covered with a piece of black construction paper. The shape of the light beam had been cut out of the paper, and the hole was covered with some Rosco tough spun (tissue paper would have worked too). We put a light with a dimmer behind the paper cutout. Then we covered the cutout with a piece of cardboard hinged with tape to the bottom of the box. We started the shot seeing only the empty location. By slowly lowering the hinged piece of cardboard, the light beam was revealed from top to bottom, so it appeared to drop down from the sky. The light beam's image reflected in the 45-degree glass was brighter than the night location, so the beam couldn't be seen through. At this point, we stopped the camera and brought in the actors to stand behind the beam. The camera was started again, and we dimmed the beam's light source, revealing the actors. We shortened the shot in editing, but other than that, the effect was done completely in camera.

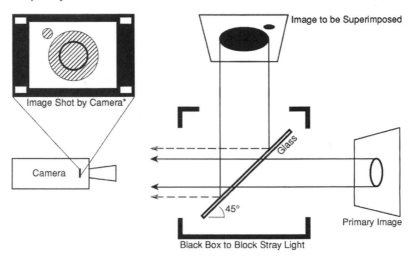

*(Note: Superimposed image is reversed and less bright.)

We used simple single-frame animation to help achieve some shots that were beyond our technical expertise to do for real. Because it's always a struggle to make animations look realistic, using computer tools is not particularly a disadvantage here. Let us give you an example of an animated effect we did when we worked on film and tell you how we'd do it today. We wanted a night shot of a military jet landing behind a military air-base sign. The sign didn't really exist, so we made a simple miniature and placed it in front of a night sky that consisted of aluminum foil that was spray-painted black and then attached to a glass window. (We know you can buy expensive black aluminum foil, but you didn't really expect us to

Digital Filmmaking 101 ~ Newton & Gaspard

do that, did you?) A light source and some Rosco tough spun to diffuse the light were placed behind the glass. Small holes poked in the aluminum foil created a starry night sky. Because we were working on film at that time, we shot a first pass of the sign against a star field background one frame at a time. We animated a black cutout of the jet across the background to create an unexposed hole in the star field so no stars would show through the jet. Then we wound the film back and did a double exposure to animate a flat painting of a jet across the darkened sky and behind the blacked-out sign in the foreground. Of course, we had to use the camera's frame counter and keep an accurate log of what happened in each frame. The result was a jet flying in front of a star field and behind a sign in the foreground.

One of the big problems with animation is that it looks too sharp. Real motion images are slightly blurred in individual frames. The big special-effects companies use special motorized equipment to slightly move models during single-frame exposures to create this blur. For our jet, we just painted it with blurry streaks coming off the trailing edge of the image, so each frame already had this blur. The final shot isn't perfect, but because it's short, because it's a night shot, and because there is a jet-landing sound effect matched to it, no one has noticed it wasn't a real jet landing behind a real sign.

Thanks to computer tools, we would no longer do this shot hunched over an animation setup for hours. Today, we would be hunched over our computer screen for hours as we used our video-editing software and image-editing software to do the same trick.

We would start with still-frame images of the sign, the starry sky, and the jet (scanned photos or digital photos). If we could take a still photo of a real jet, then we'd blur it using software tools. Otherwise we would use the original painted artwork. Using the photo-retouching software, we'd use the stars as a full background layer. Then we would cut the sign and jet from their backgrounds and make each of them separate layers of the image, with the sign being the front layer. We'd do any adjustment of brightness, contrast, or color, to make sure all the base elements worked together before we moved on.

Using the motion tools available with most editing software, we'd set up a move for the jet layer only, so that it passed above the star layer and beneath the sign layer. To help make the shot seem more real, a slight jiggle could be added to all three layers to give the impression of a slight tripod shake. Such little flaws often make effects look more real. Then just sit back while the computer renders out the frames for the final shot to the length you've set. Add a jet sound effect to complete the final shot, and thanks to the wonders of computer technology, you wouldn't have an animator's backache... though you might be going a little bit blind in one eye.

These tools can serve other practical uses, too. Working as fast as you will be, you may get a boom mike or an unwelcome reflection in a shot. This used to be a major problem, but today you can fix these shots with digital software. If the boom appears in a stationary shot, just capture a still frame from the video before the boom dipped into view. Most video-editing software will let you overlay this still image on the original shot. Then use a "garbage matte" filter or image-editing software to crop the still image so it covers the boom mike. If the shot is moving, you can export the frames where the mike appears and use the image-editing software to paint out the mike. Import the still frames as a new video sequence to replace the bad one. The same methods work for offending reflections.

If you want help doing cartoon-style flat animation, you can use a technique called rotoscoping. Shoot video of real things moving, capture it in your editing system, and export it as a sequence of still images. (Again, check the manual to make sure you can do this on your system.) Then, using the layers of your photo-retouching program, you can draw your animation on top of the live-action images to get realistic motion. Then delete the live-action layer, and import your sequence of still images as a video clip. For the title sequence of a video, Dale used this method to animate a stylized image of a deer running. Some of you have already realized that this method allows you to combine animation with live-action performances. Think of the possibilities.

You'd take a different approach if you needed a three-dimensional animation, such as a flesh-eating Martian spider sneaking up on an unsuspecting author as he toils at his computer. (Yikes! Take that, arachnid!) For this kind of scene, you would use an animation puppet that can be posed, just as you would with conventional 3D stop-motion animation. Instead of using a film camera to capture the frames, you could use either a digital still camera or use the photo function that's included with many DV camcorders. If there is a remote-control trigger, use that to avoid shaking the camera. Some camcorders actually record a few seconds of any still you shoot, so you'd need to capture still frames from this video using your editing software, and then put them together in editing. A word of warning: Live-action video on a DV camcorder is often recorded differently (interlaced-scan video) than digital stills on a camcorder (progressive-scan video), so live-action footage and animated stills of the same shot may not match when put side by side. For images from a digital still camera, you'd use the same approach, except that you could just import the image files rather than capturing them. Of course, there are many kinds of 3D animation software available, too. But in addition to the money and time it would cost to buy and master this software, it takes a ton of skill and computer processing power to create realistic-looking objects and put them in a believable digital world. It's a lot less trouble to create creatures and objects in the real world and animate them.

Conventional cell animation or cut-out animation can also be done. Use a digital still camera or a camcorder with a photo function instead of the usual film camera on the animation stand. Then combine the stills in editing.

Titles

Titles can make or break the first impression an audience or a buyer has of your movie. It's important to do them professionally, and thanks to computer editing, they are a snap these days. However, there are a few points to keep in mind.

Look at some television titles and then look at the titles on a feature-length movie. You'll notice a difference. Wide-screen movie titles tend to be smaller text and often don't fill the entire screen unless they are scrolling. They would just be overwhelmingly large if they filled the big screen. TV titles tend to fill the entire screen so you can read them off your 20-inch screen across the living room. You want your audience to mentally put your production in the movie category, not the sitcom category, so make your titles look like theatrical ones. Also, not using the entire frame will help you protect your titles for the possibility of a theatrical release in wide-screen format.

It's always nice to select a typeface that conveys the spirit of your movie. If you can't find one that does this, go for a simple block style that won't clash with your movie's content.

Digital techniques available on most editing software allow you to do stunning opening titles. While it may take more effort to produce them on the editing software you can afford, long hours can deliver just about anything you can think of for an opening title. The low-budget German movie *Run Lola Run* has a very clever opening title. An overhead shot follows a soccer ball as it's kicked straight up over a crowd. As the shot moves upward, it reveals that the people in the crowd are grouped so that they spell out the title. Very cool.

The movie *Four Weddings and a Funeral* uses another title technique that is stylish and easily done. The titles were inspired by the movie's subject matter. Title cards were done as wedding invitations and were shot as part of a table-top arrangement of wedding paraphernalia. This approach could be easily adapted to many movies. For example, titles for a children's story could be scrawled in colored chalk on the sidewalk along with kids' drawings. Titles for a college-days drama could be written as notes in the margins of textbooks. A movie about the tribulations of waitressing could have titles written on restaurant order slips that are clipped to an order carousel and rotated into view. You get the idea. These types of titles can be simple to do and can really add spark to your title sequence.

Camera Rigs and Effects Gear

It's very likely that your script will call for some type of special gear to create an effect or special camera rigs to create a shot. Some of what was once specialty gear is now considered routine equipment. Camera dollies and wind machines are some examples. Sadly, this equipment is usually too expensive for ultra-low-budget producers to rent, and it's too cumbersome to fit our hit-and-run shooting schedules. Of course, we've come up with some inexpensive alternatives.

We built our own low-cost, easy-to-move dolly after seeing one advertised in a filmmaking magazine. The basic concept was to use light PVC pipe as the dolly track and to attach special wheels to a sheet of plywood to make the dolly. The commercial version costs $500. We built our own for $80. It can only roll in a straight line, and for sound shots, you need to put talcum powder on the PVC pipe to stop squeaks, but it adds a lot of production value by creating some very acceptable dolly shots. The heart of the dolly is the wheel sets that hug the PVC tracks. We made our plywood sheet smaller and hinged so it would fit in our car trunks, but you can add these wheel sets to just about any platform. We cut hardwood on a table saw to create the angled base for standard cart wheels with their own brackets. We made four sets with two wheels each and just bolted them to the plywood base. See the diagram below for creating your own wheel sets.

For the actual dolly track, you can use ten-foot lengths of PVC pipe. We improved ours by cutting the PVC pipe into three-foot lengths and using connectors that fit inside the pipe to allow the pieces to butt together. This allowed us to carry 24 feet of track in a car. We added some threaded metal rods with wing nuts as spacers to hold the tracks at the same width as the dolly's wheels. The completed dolly and track can be assembled in less than 15 minutes, it can be easily picked up and carried around the location, and it all fits in a car trunk.

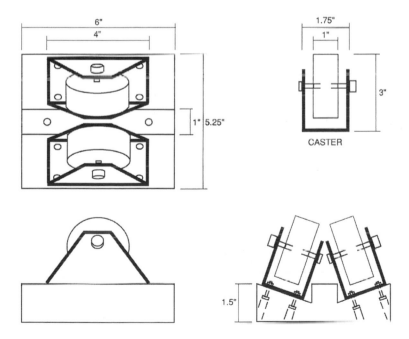

A low-buck but effective camera dolly.

On *Resident Alien*, we needed a wind machine to simulate the concussion from an explosion. Our solution was a leaf blower, which is a ridiculous use of technology for removing leaves, but which makes a great portable wind machine for a limited area. We simply aimed it at the actors' faces, turned it on, and we had an explosion concussion that would blow the rug off a Hair-Club member.

We've also seen other slick home-built equipment, such as a skateboard with a tripod head mounted on it for those "I feel so low" dolly shots and simple camera stabilizing gear for hand-held shots. Just look through the equipment advertisements in an *American Cinematographer* magazine to see some of the latest low-cost camera systems. If you're a bit handy and willing to trade chrome and aluminum for wood and PVC pipe, you often can build your own versions of these wonders for tens of dollars. True, they won't be quite as streamlined or attractive, but who are you to be so picky?

In addition to this general-use equipment, you may need something very specific for a scene in your movie. The first step to designing this type of equipment is freeing yourself from any thoughts of how professional it has to look. The only thing that matters is what the result is on the screen. For *Beyond Bob*, we needed a blender that sprayed orange juice on one of our actors. The actual blender wouldn't throw it effectively, so we built an orange-juice squirter. It was made entirely of scrap parts in a half hour. A nozzle of pinched-off copper pipe was stuck in the end of plastic tubing that led to a piston made from two plastic pipes, one inside the other. The inner pipe had adhesive tape over its hole so when the pipes were pushed together, they squeezed the contents of the other pipe out the tubing. We taped the nozzle behind the blender, filled the piston with juice, and squeezed the piston together to douse the actor. It was primitive and ugly, but highly effective. You can achieve all kinds of effects with simple apparatus like this. Just remember, it only has to work for the shot, and it doesn't matter how cobbled together it is.

We've also created some equipment that helped us speed up production and trim costs. In the opening sequence of *Beyond Bob*, we needed to show a car repeatedly passing highway signs that are in the same position in the frame. To compose the shots identically, we attached under the camera a thin board that extended in front of the camera lens out of view. To this board we bolted a small square of clear plastic that sat in front of the lens. For the first shot of the sequence, we marked the plastic to show the position of the sign and the roadway. We removed the plastic square and did the first shot. Then we composed each subsequent shot using the plastic square, removing it before shooting. The shots matched beautifully. The moral: Don't be embarrassed by any equipment that works.

Chemistry and Science Effects

You can create a variety of interesting effects using simple kitchen and bathroom chemistry. Dale once poured vinegar mixed with food coloring over baking soda to create a sink drain that frothed up with colorful bubbles — a no-cost effect that worked well on camera.

A chip of dry ice or seltzer tablets and water inside a small container, like a 35mm film canister, can create mini-explosions. The ever-popular dry ice is also great for making boiling brews and mist effects.

A word of caution: Be sure you know the effect of chemicals you plan to mix together. If you whip up a batch of ammonia mixed with chlorine bleach, you will become the star of your own snuff movie. Remember that the carbon dioxide given off by dry ice is not breathable, so use it with proper ventilation. Be careful. There are a number of good books on effects for theater and movies that will give you tested, safe ideas. If you're thinking about creating that *Star Wars* explosion, read on to the next section.

Don't-Try-This-At-Home Effects

During our first film, we were very fortunate to be approached by a relatively young special-effects company called Minnefex. The two owners offered to do our spaceship and explosion effects for cost. Most of the time they were creating effects for television commercials, fun things like break-away bags of charcoal briquettes, and they wanted to do some challenging dramatic-movie shots. We struck a deal, and they delivered some great special-effects shots with spaceships, explosions, and miniature sets.

Minnefex co-owner Dave Weiberg puts some finishing touches on a spaceship model for Resident Alien.

The point is that the people who do special effects professionally rarely get to do the really interesting jobs that first attracted them to the business. Most of them have a closet full of *Famous Monsters of Filmland* magazines some-where. (Our special-effects guys now have John's collection as a thank you for their hard work.) This means that many of them will do whatever possible to help you with your digital movie just to get a chance to do the neat stuff. So if you need to do some of the dangerous tricks like explosions, ask some of the professionals. They may be willing to do it for fun. That's a lot better than hoping you won't lose a hand while you learn the art of miniature pyrotechnics.

As you can see from our examples, there are many types of movie magic that are available to you on a low-budget production, especially if you have a script that is designed to make good use of simple, well-placed effects. If, as you've read through our examples, you came up with better ways to do the effects we described, you're on the right track. Once again, creativity and ingenuity will greatly enhance your production values where money can't.

Chapter 11

Postproduction ~ *The Light at the End of the Tunnel: Completion or Oncoming Train?*

Whew! It's finally in the can (actually, on tape, but you know what we mean). You've made it through production in one piece, and the hard part's over, right?

Sorry. You're probably beginning to suspect they're all hard parts. How astute of you.

Postproduction now lies before you, and it can be just as grueling and exhausting as production, but in a different way. If production was like boot camp, postproduction is like months of cross-country marching that slowly (and sometimes painfully) moves you toward completion or makes you go AWOL.

Of course, there is some fun along the way. Editing is filled with equal parts of pleasure and pain. The process allows you to finesse and perfect your movie while at the same time it magnifies all of its inadequacies.

Your rough cut will let you see your movie as you've never seen it before, all together and in one continuous piece. The addition of sound effects and music then takes the movie to the next level. But we're getting ahead of ourselves. Suffice it to say that the end is in sight, but it's only visible with high-powered binoculars.

The postproduction process consists of a number of occasionally overlapping phases: editing the rough cut and the fine cut; sound-effects editing; dialogue looping; music scoring; sound mixing; and then creating the final master tape.

Editing

Finding Your Editor

In outlining how to find and work with an editor, we're making the big assumption that you're not planning to edit the movie yourself. At this budget level, it's a very common practice for the director to wear a couple of hats, sometimes a whole hat rack. Director-writer, director-composer, director-actor — you can find plenty of examples of these combinations working and even working quite successfully. The same can be true of director-editor.

And, with the advent of so many different (and affordable) digital-editing options available to you, you may think that there's no reason to turn your movie over to anyone else for this final phase. And you may be right.

With that said, we'd like to champion the idea of bringing on an editor. Not just *any* editor, of course. You need to find someone who can work with you in partnership to shape the movie and get the most out of the footage you've worked so hard to shoot. As with everyone else who has been involved in the project, an editor will bring something extra to the table. He or she can take what was shot and get the most out of it, often finding things in the material that may have slipped past the director.

That's because the editor brings a fresh set of eyes to the movie, another perspective that is entirely divorced from the travails of the production process. Good editors don't care how tough a shot was to get; they only care about making each cut and each scene work the best way possible, regardless of what went into shooting the footage. A good editor becomes a partner with the director, helping find the great movie trapped within the raw footage.

So how do you find this partner? The same way you've found everyone else: by grapevine, word of mouth, and networking. Put the word out in your production community and get a sense of who's good, who's great, and — most important — who's interested. Editing a feature movie is a major undertaking, roughly equivalent to a second full-time job, so you need to find someone who is as committed to the project as you are... if such a thing is possible.

An editor who owns an editing system is a plus, but that alone isn't sufficient reason to sign them on because nowadays just about everybody owns an editing system.

What you're really looking for is someone with a philosophy similar to your own. When it comes right down to it, editing is as much about philosophy as it is about technique. Talk with candidates about what movies they like. Find out who their favorite editors are and why. Start to get a sense as to whether or not you "click" with this person. You're going to be spending a lot of long hours with them, so rapport is required.

Looking at their past work is helpful but also problematic because the best editing is often seamless. If it's done right, you won't recognize how an editor may have saved a scene. Conversely, a beautiful and dramatic montage on their demo reel might be cut exactly as the director story-boarded, with little real input from the editor.

Looking at a number of their past projects will begin to give you a sense of their work; however, the best editor for your project may not have much appropriate material to show you. Instead you may be looking at work samples that include documentaries, industrials, news stories, and student films. In some cases, potential editors may have no dramatic examples on their reels. So how do you know if they'll be right for your movie? Again, it comes down to philosophy and rapport.

Like everyone else who's signed on so far, the editor may be looking at this project as a way to take a step up the ladder and learn more about their craft. If they're committed to the movie and you feel a philosophical connection, you may have found your partner.

One advantage of computer-based editing is that you can let the editor cut a scene or two as an example of their work. If you don't care for the results, both you and the editor have only wasted a handful of hours. And, if you like their work, then you're already on your way.

Editing Equipment

If you find an editor you like and can work with and they already own a digital-editing system, then your choice of system is already made and you can move on. Good for you.

Don't feel you need to invest in a new system if your editor's system (or your system) is not strictly "state-of-the-art." There's always a price tag attached to state-of-the-art gear, and this could be your only chance to substantially reduce your movie budget. As long as the system can produce a quality DV output, has basic features for editing multiple tracks of video and audio, and includes controls to correct common video and audio problems, you're in good shape.

If you or your editor are tempted to buy a high-end editing system, remember your budget. You can drop a lot of money on systems that do much more than you'll ever need.

If your movie truly demands the purchase of a higher-end (and higher-cost) editing system, read everything you can on all the current (and not so current) systems to determine which features you really need and which ones would just be fun to play with. Consider these points.

- What's the learning curve on each system? A more basic system with which your editor is already proficient may be the most practical move.

- What is your ultimate plan for the finished movie, and how will this system help or hinder your plan?

- Can you fit it in your budget? If not, are you prepared to up the ante? Remember, the odds of your movie earning a profit, or even recouping your investment, are slim. Don't burden yourself with unnecessary debt.

- Can you put the editing system on a paying basis? Can you use it to edit wedding videos, corporate videos, or other people's movies to pay for the system? Research these opportunities before you buy anything.

The key, as with every other step in the low-budget digital-production process, is to understand the difference between what you *need* and what you *want*. As the Rolling Stones pointed out a long time ago, you can't always get what you want. But if you do your homework, sometimes you get what you need.

Working with Your Editor

Often the hardest part of working with an editor is simply letting him or her do the job. The urge to micro-manage the process may be great, but we recommend that you resist it. Leaning over your editor's shoulder critiquing every cut will drive both of you batty and one of you off the project.

Instead, sit with your editor and review all the footage for a given scene, talking about what elements you like and what you don't like. Once you've reviewed the footage, let the editor go off and put the scene together using your comments as a starting point and adding his or her own creative "zing" to the process. Then review the work, offer suggestions for changes, and let the editor take another crack at it. Keep doing this until both of you are happy with a scene, and then move on to the next one.

We've found that this approach works well for both parties. It allows the director to come in and look at each scene fresh, without any baggage about how difficult it was to edit. And it provides the editor with some creative license to work without someone watching and second-guessing each move.

Take it from us, you won't get the most benefit from the relationship if you simply look upon your editor as an order taker. Just as you have with the other creative people who have joined your project, you have to let editors stretch their creative muscles. It will be good for your editor, and it will make your movie better.

Editing for a Film Look

During production, you may have taken steps to shoot film-like images on digital video. When you start editing your footage, there are a couple more ways to enhance the film look.

Most films still use cuts and dissolves as the standard transition between shots. The other transitions available with video-editing software will make your movie look more like video, so avoid them except in very special cases.

Audiences are accustomed to seeing films in widescreen format. If you've shot your footage in a 4:3-ratio format (standard TV frame), you'll want to add a 16:9-ratio widescreen mask with your editing software to give the audience the look it is expecting.

Finally, you can process your standard video footage with some of the filters and effects that come with most professional editing software. With the right combination of filters, you can get a film look that is as good or better than the ones produced by many film-look softwares. We'll give you some starter setting, but don't be afraid to experiment if they don't give you the desired result with your footage. Keep handy a DVD movie with the look you want. Use it for reference as you try out different adjustments. Also be ready for some long render times to process your adjusted footage. (This can be a good time to get reacquainted with people you haven't seen since you started shooting your movie.)

The following settings produce a passable film look. Start by de-interlacing your footage. This step alone does a lot to create the feel of film. Next adjust the blacks in your footage using the gamma setting. This will be only a slight adjustment, say from 1.0 to 1.2. You might have to go the opposite direction depending on how the video was lit and shot. Top off a basic film look by using a tiny bit of Gaussian blur with a radius of 0.2. It helps knock off the harsh video edges.

You can go further to recreate the look of older color or black-and-white footage. Use the desaturate filter to create a look of aged color footage. You might also want to adjust the color balance to reduce the blue and green levels. To create black-and-white, apply a tint of black. To make sepia-tone footage, apply a tint of brown. Adjust the percentage and color of the tint to your taste. If your footage needs to look like it came from a hand-cranked camera or an old home-movie camera, you can add a slight strobe effect.

The Rough Cut or First Cut

Nowadays, with non-linear-editing systems, the differences between the rough cut and the final cut are not nearly as distinct as they used to be. Since most systems allow you to do many of the visual effects (dissolves, fades, and much more) and often have room for multiple soundtracks, the rough cut can look pretty fine indeed. On an $8,000 budget, you will produce your final cut on your edit system.

In the early stages of the rough cut, you often make a real switch in your thinking. You stop trying to make the movie you set out to make, and you begin to define the movie that you've made. All the pieces are there; it's up to you and your editor to assemble them in the most effective way.

For some, it's a major overhaul, where the movie is quite literally remade in the editing room. (See Ralph Rosenblum's excellent account of the editing-room re-creations of *Annie Hall*, *A Thousand Clowns*, and *The Night They Raided Minsky's* in his book, *When the Shooting Stops, the Cutting Begins*.)

For other movies, it's a question of juggling, moving things around, and deciding to add or subtract some elements. (See Charles Grodin's very droll description of the editing of *11 Harrowhouse* in his fine book, *It Would Be So Nice If You Weren't Here*.)

Whether the surgery is major or minor, it's important that you keep an open mind and be willing to make the painful cuts in order to make a better movie. That said, it's just as important to make sure that you don't throw out good material that simply hasn't been perfected yet.

A good example is the seance scene from *Beyond Bob*. From the beginning, this was always one of our favorite scenes. It had atmosphere, it had humor, and it also had a couple of powerful character moments. However, in the rough cut, the scene stunk.

The problem started with the sound and just got worse. On the night the scene was shot, there was a problem with dialogue recording that made half of it unusable. The rough assembly of the scene was painful to sit through as sound jumped from bad to indecipherable, making the scene nearly unwatchable.

Even if it had perfect sound, it appeared that the scene was clearly a turkey headed for Thanksgiving. John was ready to toss it out and cut our losses. But Dale and our editor argued for it and eventually won out. The scene stayed, and repairs were made.

As it turned out, the only real problem was the sound, but it was such an overwhelming problem that it masked an otherwise good scene. In the end, with a number of the lines in the scene re-recorded by the actors and some terrifically creepy music added by our composer, the scene played great and is a high point of the movie.

The lesson here is to use your rough cut as an opportunity to take a cold, hard look at what's working and what's not working, and make decisions accordingly. At the same time, make sure you understand why the scene isn't working before you decide what to do about it.

This process of refining the movie — shortening and cutting scenes, moving sequences around, shaping each scene so it has the utmost impact — may take many weeks or months. For some movies, it takes years. But after all the pruning and preening, you will eventually arrive at a major destination, the Fine Cut.

The Fine Cut

There's no question that, left to their own devices, some directors and editors would never reach the fine-cut stage. They would instead spend the rest of their lives tweaking and futzing with the movie, making imperceptible changes here and there, completely unwilling to throw in the towel and call it done. And non-linear editing only adds to this problem, by making it possible to create multiple versions of every scene and forestalling the final decisions for eternity.

One of the best ways to determine if you've actually reached the fine cut is to screen the movie for a small group. The ideal audience is one that doesn't know anything about the story; however, by this point the only way you'll find anyone who's unaware of all the minute details of your movie is to pull strangers in off the street. This is the approach we took with *Beyond Bob*.

With the help of our local Independent Feature Project chapter, we got the use of a local theater with a video projector and advertised a special "sneak preview" of a locally produced movie. To get an unbiased reaction from our showing, we held an earlier, invitation-only screening for cast, crew, family, and friends. This private screening ensured that these people wouldn't show up for the public screening and skew the audience reaction. Although a few of them stuck around for a second look at their work, their reactions didn't seem to affect the crowd.

After the screening, our test audience was asked to fill out comment cards, but this was of marginal value. Most of what we needed to know had been learned simply by watching and listening to the audience while they experienced the movie for the first time. And we learned a lot.

The screening was great because it gave us a better sense of which scenes moved too slowly (too many of them) and which ones moved too quickly (almost none). It also told us which jokes were drowned out by laughter from previous jokes (an enviable problem), which plot points were obscured by laughter, and which scenes got laughs we didn't intend. The screening helped us identify big problems, such as scenes that had to be shortened or eliminated, and little problems, such as sound that needed further repair or music that wasn't quite right yet.

Our showing was more elaborate than most. You can also get good results just by sitting several people in front of the computer.

Sound-Effects Editing

Throughout the picture editing process, you (or your editor) will probably also be adding the different sound-effect tracks you'll need to give your soundtrack a full, "lived-in" sound. A sparse, hollow soundtrack is a dead giveaway that yours is an ultra-low-budget movie, but with a little work and ingenuity, you can spice up the track and give the entire project a bigger-budget sound for very little money.

The system we used for editing *Grown Men* had up to 99 soundtracks available, which we never came close to using. However, as with the movies we cut on film, we did establish a pattern for the tracks, which made it easier to work on the system.

The first four tracks were used for dialogue. When the movie was just about finished, we also went in and removed all the sound effects from the dialogue tracks and moved them to the separate sound effects tracks. These tracks also included sound effects that we added in postproduction and room ambiance.

We also duplicated any sound effects that were intermixed with the dialogue and put them on a separate track. This track was turned off unless needed to produce a music-and-effects-only soundtrack.

The next tracks were the music tracks, which we divided into source tracks (music that the characters could hear in the movie, such as a song played on a radio) and underscore (music that only the audience hears). Keeping them on separate tracks made it easier to cross-fade from source music to underscore.

This consistent approach made it easier to turn sound or music on and off as needed while working on the soundtrack. If we wanted to hear just the effects and music, we simply switched off the first four tracks. If we wanted to test how a sound effect played against the dialogue, we could easily switch off the music tracks. If we were putting in dialogue recorded in postproduction, we could toggle back and forth between the original and the new dialogue tracks to test the sync.

Finally, this system made it easy for us to create a foreign music and effects (M&E) version of our soundtrack should an overseas distributor want to buy the movie and add their own foreign language dialogue.

Dialogue Looping

While you're recording your sound effects and doing your foley work (creating effects to match actions in the movie, such as walking sound effects), you may also need to "loop" or rerecord lines of dialogue that were not recorded cleanly on location.

On *Grown Men* we had one entire scene — seven minutes long — that needed to be looped, because the actress lost her voice on the day of shooting. Needless to say, this was not an ideal situation. However, we heeded our own advice: When the picture is good and you can't get good sound, shoot it anyway and fix it later.

We did this by creating our own looping system for re-recording dialogue that resembled, in a small way, the ADR (automatic dialogue recording) systems used in Hollywood.

Because she lost her voice the day of shooting, actress Susan Vee had to loop all of her lines for this scene after the fact. A scene from Grown Men. *Pictured: Susan Vee, director John Gaspard. (Photo courtesy of Granite Productions, Unlimited.)*

In the Hollywood version, the actors go onto a recording stage where they watch the scene they're dubbing and hear the original sound on headsets. The system is set up so that they can watch and say the same line again and again until they're able to re-record it perfectly in sync with the picture. (To see this system in action, look at the climax of the film *Postcards from the Edge*, where actress Meryl Streep re-records a scene for director Gene Hackman.)

You can create your own version of this process using your editing system.

First, create a repeating loop of the lines that need to be replaced. In the case of the *Grown Men* looping session, there were fifty separate lines that needed to be re-recorded. It took very little time to create a tape of all fifty lines; each of the lines was repeated five times in a row, to give the actor five opportunities to get it right. Create this looping audio and video (we did a slate between each section with the text of the line to be spoken), and then export it to a VHS tape or DVD for playback.

Then find the cheapest recording studio or in-home studio that can record a computer audio file (.wav, .aiff, .mp3, or Quicktime .mov file), a DAT tape, or even a reel-to-reel tape. You can also record it directly into your DV camcorder, which has CD-quality sound.

The studio should have a separate soundproof recording booth with a viewing window. Set up a video monitor (playing back the VHS or the DVD) so that the actors in the booth can see the television screen through the viewing window. (You don't want the monitor or the playback deck in the sound booth because both make noise.)

The sound from the playback deck needs to be routed into the actors' headphones so they can use it as a reference, to help them sync up their voices with the original track. Just keep rewinding and replaying the video-tape or the DVD until the actors get it right.

If there's no cheap recording studio in your area or no studio at all, then you'll just have to make your own for dialogue looping. Don't worry, this isn't time for carpentry. It's time for creative reinterpretation of your living space or any other space you have available.

A space without room tone will let you record clean dialogue that can be adjusted to fit any scene once the scene's room tone is added. (Remember, we said to record room tone at each location? This is where you'll be glad you did it.)

You'll want to find a room that doesn't get much outside noise from traffic, aircraft, neighbors, construction, nearby garage bands, and such.

Check the room by recording some sound in it so you can hear those hums and rattles that you're mentally filtering out. Below-grade rooms (such as basements) and rooms with no windows (such as bathrooms and closets) are good candidates. Make sure they don't have performing plumbing or noisy appliances you can't turn off. If your home has a 1950s air-raid shelter buried in the back yard, you've got a good start on a makeshift studio and on first-strike survivability.

Next you'll have to deaden any hard surfaces that reflect sound. Fluffy rugs on the floor and heavy fabrics (towels, blankets, drapes from Tara or the von Trapp household) hung on the walls will do the trick. You can usually skip the ceiling. You don't have to do an entire room. Just use the fabric to divide a corner off the main room. (And your parents thought that building blanket forts in the living room wasn't a useful skill!) If there's a large walk-in closet filled with clothes, you have a ready-made sound booth.

Just as you would at a sound studio, set up a TV and playback deck — VHS or DVD — to show the dialogue loops. Run the sound to headphones for the actor. Use your shotgun microphone, or rent a decent desk microphone, and put it on a stand so the actor can say the lines while standing up. Make sure that the actor doesn't get too close to the microphone, which will make the lines sound unnatural. The cable from this microphone should go to your DV camcorder to record the new sound. You may need some adapter cables to get this all working.

Obviously the TV, playback deck, and camcorder should be outside your sound booth. The TV is trickier because it makes a good deal of electronic noise but has to be close enough for the actor to see lip movement and visual cues for the start of the lines.

If you have a room divided by a French door, you can just put the TV outside of the glass. Otherwise, you can get a cardboard box larger than the TV (so it doesn't overheat and burn you and the actor to cinders), and cut out a hole so just the screen shows through. Put the open back of the box outside of the sound room for ventilation, and then put thick blankets and pillows around the part of the box inside the sound booth to muffle the TV sounds. It may not look pretty, but your makeshift sound booth is ready to do the job.

One final note on looping: When you cut your replacement dialogue in with the existing location dialogue, you'll probably need to dirty up these new lines. Generally, the dialogue you record in a recording studio will sound a lot cleaner, so your looped lines might not mesh well with your original dialogue. By using the filters and equalization controls on your non-linear editor or by adding some sound effects to the entire scene (such as street noise), you should be able to balance these two different tracks. The end result will be a consistent-sounding track, and the audience will be none the wiser.

Music

Few things are as important to the success of your movie as music. Music can enhance the emotional content of a scene, build suspense, link a scene to previous scenes, reinforce comic or tragic moments, help set the time and the place, and much more. The right music score can improve a mediocre movie and can often save a weak scene. Conversely, a bad or inappropriate music score can really drag down an otherwise good movie, so plan on putting a lot of effort into this part of the process.

Music is going to cost some money. How much depends on the amount of music your movie requires and how it is created and recorded. However, at this point in postproduction, your checking account has probably dipped into the low triple or double digits — or even lower. Because the creation of the music score usually comes near the end of production, it is the most vulnerable to budget cuts. This is unwise; "borrowing" against your music budget for other production elements will weaken your final product, perhaps measurably. So strive to keep money set aside for music, and then make sure that's where it ends up.

Using Existing Music

The odds are really against you having the money to put recognizable music into your movie. That's because, with the exception of the classical music of Mozart, Bach, Beethoven, Brahms, and that ilk, most recognizable music is not in the public domain. Even "Happy Birthday to You" is owned by someone, and it will cost money for you to use it even if it's only hummed or sung a cappella.

Leslie Ball sings a song written especially for the movie in a scene from Beyond Bob.

If you do find music that's in the public domain, you can't just take it from your favorite record or CD; you must pay the people who recorded the music and the people who distributed the recording. This often costs lots of money. And at this point in the production, you'll be lucky to have enough money to jingle in your pockets, let alone to get a jingle on your soundtrack. Your only option for using public-domain music is to have it recorded by your own musicians.

Some music publishers and record companies will allow you to use existing music on a "festival-only" basis, which means what it says: You can license the music for a small fee, but you can only show the movie at festivals. If you end up striking a distribution deal, you'll have to pay full rate for the music, which may end up being a deal breaker, depending on the final cost of the music.

However, don't let these facts persuade you that using existing music is entirely out of the question.

Recordings of the original music of bands and musical groups in your area are excellent sources of music. If you aren't connected with your local music scene and the musicians in it, find a local critic, club owner, or music fanatic who can introduce you to the right people and the right sound for your movie. It's a win-win situation for everyone. The artists get some excellent exposure for themselves and the music they've already recorded, and your movie's soundtrack moves up a couple notches. It doesn't cost the musicians or you anything, and you both might share some profits down the line.

Finding a Composer

As with the other professionals and soon-to-be professionals you'll gather to help make your movie, finding your version of James Newton Howard or John Williams may take equal amounts of perseverance and luck.

In our case, we got lucky. We stumbled upon the Hope Diamond in the rough. When our composer joined us for our first movie, he had never scored a film, but he did possess an encyclopedic knowledge of music and a burning desire to compose for features — a winning combination. He has since moved out of our budget range, which is Hollywood's gain but our loss.

As with the other people on your team, you need to look for a composer who is passionate about her or his role and committed to your movie. By this late point in your production, it's possible that you've been contacted by composers eager to ply their trade on your project. During our productions, we received inquiries from both coasts and many places in between from composers who were willing to work on feature projects, even one as low-budget as ours.

If you haven't received any inquiries by the time you've begun editing, then it's time to start beating the bushes. Some of the best sources are industrial composers in your area or the nearest large city. These are composers who create jingles and write music for commercials and industrial films and videos. They are working professionals who understand the process, have a lot of the connections that will help get the music produced, and who are already doing what you need, albeit on a smaller scale.

It's possible that one of these industrial composers will leap at the chance to do a dramatic music score for a movie that doesn't star bug spray or bathroom tissue. Of course, the only way to find out is to track them down and ask them. Once they learn what your budget is, some will lose interest. Be persistent. Make a list of the best composers in your area, and go down it until you find a composer who connects with you and your movie.

Every time you're turned down, be sure to ask if they know of someone who might be interested, a new composer, a promising assistant, or an unknown waiting to blossom (like the one we found). As with every other facet of this production, the more experienced people you can get, the better the end result will be. However, enthusiasm and talent can make up for inexperience, a lesson we've learned many times.

Besides tracking down industrial composers and networking through the grapevine of your film community, you can look to local schools and universities. Schools with a music arts program can be an excellent resource not only for finding your composer, but also musicians to perform the music and maybe even recording engineers. And don't forget: both students *and* teachers are potential candidates.

What to Give Your Composer

Composing for movies is a very precise art. In order for your composer to create a finished score that fits your movie like a glove, you'll need to provide an accurate copy of your movie. By "accurate," we mean that the picture should be locked, with no further changes.

Once your composer has started scoring the movie, let him or her know if you make any changes. Even trimming a few frames from a scene can throw off a music cue, so it's essential to provide a new tape of any sequence that you've changed once the composer has started.

You can give the composer a VHS or DVD copy of the whole movie or just the segments of it as you finish them.In either case, be sure to add a timecode burn to each scene for timing purposes. The composer doesn't necessarily need the sound effects, but all of the dialogue is essential. The composer needs to know exactly when characters are and aren't talking in order to get the right timing for the music.

If the composer is using a computerized scoring system, you may only need to provide compressed Quicktime versions of each scene, along with sound files (.wav, .aif, .mp3, to name a few) of the soundtrack. The composer will load these into their system and be able to create the score in sync with the image.

Working with Your Composer

Just as you've done with the writer, the actors, the editor, and all the other creative people who've brought their skills to your film, it's essential that you give your composer some latitude in creating the score. It's best not to dictate musical instructions or give the composer a temporary score filled with existing music and ask them to duplicate what they hear. This isn't a good use of their time or their talent.

The first step you'll go through with your composer is the spotting session. This is where you sit down and watch the movie, pointing out where you feel the music should go. Why is this called a spotting session? We don't know. It might be because you're trying to "spot" the best place to put the music, but that's a guess. However, it's an important and fun part of the process.

Before the spotting session, watch the movie on your own a couple of times. By this point you've seen it a million times, but now you're looking at it strictly from the standpoint of its musical needs. Take notes as you think about when, where, and why you want music. What do you want the music to do? What should it accomplish?

A good preparation for this part of postproduction is watching other films. Figure out why and where they have music, and see the effect it can have on scenes. Listen to movies, and watch scenes with the sound off to figure out what role the music is playing.

Rent some DVDs that allow you to turn off the dialogue and sound effects on a movie and just listen to the music while you watch the picture. This can be an education in itself. Then you'll be ready to sit down with your composer and go through your movie scene by scene and sequence by sequence.

Steve Martin has been quoted as saying "Talking about music is like dancing about architecture." It's true; talking about music can be tough, particularly if you don't have the vocabulary to do it. You may be tempted to give your composer very precise directions ("I want to start with a minor chord here, and then move into a ninth over this part"), but unless you have a master's degree in music, you're really talking the wrong language.

A better approach is to talk about the emotions you're looking for in each scene ("I want some tension here," "The mood needs to be lighter in this scene," or "We need a jolt right now"). It's the composer's job to translate those emotions into music, and they'll know the best way to create what the scene needs.

That doesn't mean you can't play examples for them. We always played music for our composers that had the mood, spirit, or orchestration that we were thinking of for certain parts of our projects. They never duplicated what we played for them, but instead used it as a form of research for the score they were producing.

For the main theme for *Beyond Bob*, John had an idea of what he wanted, but didn't have the vocabulary to define it. But when the opening credits for the movie *Garbo Talks* came on TV, he knew that was it. He called our composer, told him what channel to turn to, and a few moments later the composer returned to the phone and shouted triumphantly: "I get it. You want a *waltz*!" He slammed down the phone and the next day played us the perfect theme for our movie.

You can also create a temporary music track with existing music. A temporary score is a fine tool for your editor to cut against, and it will give your composer a strong sense of the mood you're after.

The drawback is that you'll get used to the temporary score, and you may want the composer to duplicate it instead of reinterpreting it. That's the situation composer Alex North found himself in after Stanley Kubrick fell in love with the temporary score full of classical music he'd put on *2001: A Space Odyssey*. North's finished score was set aside and never used because Kubrick was unwilling to let go of his temporary score. Of course, since you can't afford to pay for the existing music on a temporary score, this won't be a big problem for you.

The Final Output

When you're all done editing, it's time to master your movie to the various formats you'll need.

Most festivals and distributors will happily accept a DVD as the preview copy of your movie. DVD production has become a simple process, with built-in programs like iDVD (if you've kept your movie under 90 minutes) or other off-the-shelf programs.

The key is to make your DVD clean and easy to navigate — no overly complicated menus, no bizarre Easter Eggs (hidden menu functions). You want distributors and festival programmers to concentrate on your movie, not your marketing moxie. (For more in-depth details on how to create that DVD, we recommend that you turn to Chris Gore and Paul Salamoff's great book, *The Complete DVD Book: Designing, Producing and Marketing Your Independent Film on DVD*.)

You will also need to make the full-size DV tapes of your movie for theater screenings and future mass-duplication. To do this, you will be renting (or borrowing) a professional model DV deck, which takes the longer full-size tapes. While you have a rented DV deck, you can also use it to make some VHS screeners of the movie. If your DV camera offers "pass-through" capabilities, you can run the movie out of your computer editing program, through your video camera, and out to your VHS deck instead. As an alternative, you could spend a couple hundred dollars on a small digital-to-analog converter box, which will allow you to make VHS copies from your computer anytime you like.

Of course, with any luck your editor will have all or some of these options at his/her disposal, in which case mastering the final tapes and DVDs will be a snap.

Keeping in Touch

The postproduction process we've just outlined can take from three months to three years, depending on your degree of patience and the depth of your pockets.

While you may be quite busy working on the movie during this time, many of the people who worked on earlier phases of the project may begin to think that you and the movie have dropped off the face of the earth. Nowadays, with TV docudramas turning up on television only weeks after the actual event, most people don't realize how long it can take to complete a feature, particularly a feature that's darn near out of cash.

In order to keep your ever-growing list of supporters updated on the progress of your film, we recommend creating a regular or irregular e-newsletter that you e-mail to all the participants. It doesn't need to be elaborate. It's enough to give a one-page recap of the film's current status, the upcoming steps in the process, and maybe news about what's going on in the lives of the cast and crew.

This can even take the form of a website devoted to the project. It can feature periodic updates on your progress, photos, and even an occasional clip. For *Grown Men*, we created a photo site so that cast and crew members could view and download the shots from the most recent shoots.

These are all simple ways to keep in touch and they allow the people who've contributed their time and talents to follow the moviemaking process to its inevitable (and almost interminable) conclusion.

Chapter 12

Distribution ~ *Meet the New Boss. Same as the Old Boss.*

Ah, how times have changed.

In the old days, there used to be only one kind of distribution. You'd sign over the rights to your movie to some (occasionally slimy) individual or company, who would in turn market and sell your movie to various venues (theatrical, home video, cable, and broadcast) around the world. Maybe you got some money. In most cases, you didn't.

It was a good, solid system. They made money. You didn't. Everyone knew what to expect.

Then came the Internet... and everything changed. Or did it?

Well, there certainly are a lot more marketing opportunities for independent movies now because of the Internet. If you can get fans (and potential fans) to your website, you can show them clips from your movies, entice them with photos, and maybe even sell a few home-grown DVDs to the more daring buyers out there.

We've done it for years with our movies at our website, and although we've met a lot of nice people, we haven't gotten rich from the endeavor. Which is fine by us, because we recognized the limited money-making potential of independent moviemaking a long time ago. If you want to get rich, there are a lot easier ways to do it than by making movies.

That being said, the primary purpose of making your movie was the desire to tell your story to an actual audience, and that's where distribution comes in.

First, it's time for a little painful reality.

The reality is that most independent movies never find distribution — and when we say distribution, we're talking about a system that gets your movie to an audience and gives you a cut of the profits. Some statistics suggest that only about 10% of the feature-length movies made each year ever find any sort of outlet.

That means 90% of all the ultra-low-budget, low-budget, medium-budget, and even the occasional high-budget movies never see the light of day. With the additional output coming from the new wave of digital moviemakers, these numbers may be even higher.

Of course, there are those rare few who break through, reach an audience, receive acclaim, and pave the way for the moviemaker's next project. But for every one of those success stories, there are another nine (or more) stories with less-happy endings.

The road to independent-movie success is strewn with movies that got this far and then petered out. What went wrong with these movies? Did their makers simply lose momentum? Were the finished movies unmarketable? Did the distributors refuse to take a risk and let these movies die before they ever really had a chance to live?

Yes. Yes. And yes. Plus a thousand other reasons.

Distribution is its own special level of hell, different from the raising-money level of hell, the production level of hell, and the rough-cut level of hell. The primary cause of this torment is that when you start looking for a distributor, your movie changes from being a personal expression of your own imagination into a mere product, which will be marketed and sold alongside Crest and Spam.

But unlike those well-known brand names, your product is the one and only, a prototype without an audience. Of course, this problem is not unique to independent movies. This is true of all movies, and that's why distributors love movies with pre-sold elements, such as big-name actors, a well-known director, a screenplay based on a famous book, or nearly any title that's followed by Roman numerals. Unfortunately, your movie will likely have none of these elements, which will make it more difficult as you make your way through the distribution obstacle course.

The one thing your movie can have that will make it attractive to distributors is a great story. An involving story. A surprising story. In talking to distributors about what they look for in movies, we heard again and again that the more excited they are about your story, the less concerned they are about big names and big production values. In short, you don't need to blow up buildings, but you do need a story that explodes onto the screen with characters an audience can care about.

So if you're reading this chapter before you've dived into production, double your efforts on your script, and make sure it's the very best it can be. There's usually a long time between when you write your script and when you start knocking on doors to find a distributor, but your early efforts on the script will pay off when it comes time to sell your finished movie.

The Distribution Stream

For years and years, most dramatic feature movies followed a similar path through the various levels of the distribution system. The Internet and web-based distribution have threatened to change all that, but as of this writing, only the truly die-hard are downloading movies, and NetFlix — while offering a wide selection — is still catering to traditional, name-brand movies from the traditional distribution stream.

For now the typical, well-worn path for a movie is a theatrical release in mainstream or art-house theaters. This is followed by an appearance on one or more of the pay-per-view systems and airline in-flight movies.

Once these venues have been exhausted, the movie moves onto the pay TV channels (that is, premium cable channels, such as HBO and Showtime). At about that same time, the movie will show up on video-store shelves. Next, it's on to the basic cable networks, network television, and then finally syndicated TV.

Steven Soderbergh and his pals at 2929 Productions have attempted to break up that stream, with the same-day release of their movie *Bubble* into theaters, pay TV, and home video all at once. Only time will tell if they can break the traditional pattern.

Of course, a movie can jump into this distribution stream at any point. For example, many low-budget independent movies never get a theatrical release or even make it to pay-per-view. Instead, they start their distribution life on cable channels or go directly to video stores.

When Should You Approach Distributors?

There are two answers to this question: As soon as your movie is perfect or when it's completely done. Whichever comes first.

Showing your movie before it's entirely finished is not a wise move because distribution people, like many carbon-based life-forms, are notoriously literal-minded. They see what is, not what might be. As a result, it can seriously hurt your movie's chances to screen it for them in rough cut or unmixed form.

Showing a rough cut with a partially-mixed soundtrack to an audience to gauge their reaction is one thing. Showing the same, unfinished movie to distributors is entirely another. No matter how many caveats you issue before the screening, once the lights go down or they press "play" on the DVD menu, your movie will be judged as a finished product and not for its potential. And once distributors have looked at a movie and passed on it, very few will reconsider the same movie later. The demands on their time are just too great.

How to Find Distributors/How to Be Found

Before you can start tracking down distributors, you need to decide what sort of distributor you want; that is, at what point in the distribution stream are you going to dive in?

To do that, you have to step back and take a cold, analytical look at your movie — not the movie you set out to make, not the movie you hoped to make, but the movie that you've actually produced.

It's no small task to divorce yourself from your movie and look at it completely objectively. You have to look at the movie in realistic terms to determine where it is likely to fit into the distribution stream. Otherwise, you will waste a good deal of money and time barking up the wrong distributors.

Of course, everyone wants their movie to receive a big, splashy theatrical release with 1,200 prints opening in multiplexes throughout the country simultaneously. While this is a nice wish, it's not a particularly realistic goal. Even if your movie is released theatrically — a darned big "if" — it's more likely to be rolled out with a small number of prints, territory by territory. So you need to establish some realistic, attainable goals.

After looking at your movie realistically, you may conclude that it's not theatrical material. Instead, it may be better suited for cable television or home video, and you may wish to concentrate on those venues.

Or you may realize that your movie has little commercial potential and is better suited to the festival circuit. Or, as we mentioned earlier, you may decide that your movie is best suited to living on the web, available to anyone who wants to take the time to download it.

There's nothing wrong with recognizing your movie's limitations. It's a whole lot cheaper (and less demoralizing) to realize this before you spend tons of time and money looking for the wrong kind of distributor.

There's no great trick to finding distributors. Most of them actively want to be found because they need a constant flow of new product to keep their doors open. Almost all distributors will look at your movie because they're afraid they might miss The Next Big Thing if they don't. Imagine yourself as one of the distributors who passed on *The Blair Witch Project* at the Sundance Film Festival, and you can see why the distribution business is run on paranoia and fear.

As we mentioned previously, you can list your movie in the trade papers, *Variety* and the *Hollywood Reporter*, at any point during production or postproduction. These listings run every week and are a primary source for distributors looking for new movies. As soon as your listing appears, some of them will call and write.

Besides the trade papers, there are five tried-and-true methods for getting your work in front of distributors: film markets, festivals, the direct approach, website promotion, and getting someone else to do it.

Film Markets

A film market is like a supermarket for movies. Buyers come, squeeze the melons, read the ingredients, and try to find the freshest, ripest produce in the store.

Sometimes a market is attached to a film festival, like Cannes; sometimes it's a free-standing event, like the American Film Market.

For an ultra-low-budget feature, there currently is no better venue than the IFP (Independent Feature Project) Market, the industry component of the Independent Film Week, put on each fall by the New York chapter of the IFP. It's over-crowded, over-booked, and exhausting. But a handful of movies have been "discovered" at the IFP Market, so it's worth investigating.

As of this writing, the market is divided into three categories: emerging narratives, documentaries, and international co-productions. Housed in the Angelika Film Center in New York City, the market runs for seven days, screening movies from 9:00 a.m. to 5:00 p.m. in all of the Center's six theaters.

Throughout the day, the lobbies are packed with moviemakers trying to corner buyers. The buyers, meanwhile, are racing from theater to theater, trying to find The Next Big Thing. It's a zoo, but most of the buyers are actual buyers, and the reality is that some movies do get discovered, bought, and distributed based on their showing at the IFP Market.

Several words of advice before you go to the IFP Market (or any movie market, for that matter):

- Be sure you need to go. It can be an expensive proposition, particularly if you don't live in the city where the market is held. With our usual low-budget approach and free lodging, we still managed to spend around $3,000 at the IFP Market on entry fees, plane tickets, and promotional items, money we're not convinced was well spent. For that reason, we didn't include a visit to this market in our sample budget. Check out other options before making this trek.

- Track down attendees from previous years and get tips from them about how to attack the market. For the IFP Market, check with your local IFP office for names of people from your area who have attended. Recent attendees can give you an idea of what promotional tricks seemed to work, who was buying, and what to do (and not to do) to get your movie noticed.

- Target the buyers you think would be right for your movie and work on getting them to your screening. Don't spread yourself and your resources too thin by trying to get all the buyers to attend. Peruse past market catalogs to get an idea of who buys what.

Digital Filmmaking 101 ~ Newton & Gaspard

If you do decide to attend a market, consider the following advice:

- When you're at the market, attend as many other screenings as you can. Talk to the other moviemakers, compare notes, trade horror stories about production, and invite them to your screening. To get the best reaction possible for your movie, you'll want to pack the house with as many sympathetic bodies as you can, and for the most part, other moviemakers are a very supportive group.

- Keep a firm handle on your expectations. Walking away from a market with several offers would be nice, but you may end up with nothing but memories. As you look through materials from previous years, compare the number of movies that have any name recognition to those that don't ring any bells at all. You'll see that the majority of movies are in the latter category.

- Don't sign anything without talking to a reputable entertainment attorney first. (We'll tell you where to find such an attorney later.) We were offered one contract that had potential obligations that would have cost us ten times the payment we'd get.

- Finally, try to have some fun. A movie market can be a very intense environment, buzzing with hundreds of people who all have a lot on the line. So relax. See some movies. Meet some people. And try to enjoy yourself a bit. A good time may be all you get from a movie market.

Festivals

One benefit of the IFP Market is that it is attended by representatives from many of the big film festivals, including Sundance, and it's a good way to spark their interest in your movie and start some buzz about it.

If you're only looking for awards, then it makes sense to blitz all the festivals that are a good fit for your movie. If you're looking for a buyer, then you're better off selecting those events at which your movie is likely to be seen by the right people. Check with a festival's promoters and moviemakers who entered in previous years to see how much buying takes place at each festival.

As always, the hottest festival ticket is the Sundance Film Festival. Everyone wants to attend, and everyone wants to have their movie entered, accepted, screened, and then sold to the highest bidder. It's happened to other ultra-low-budget movies, and there's no reason why it can't happen to yours.

But don't think Sundance is the do-all and end-all of film festivals. There are plenty of movies that never got into Sundance that went on to long and semi-successful lives thanks to other film festivals. With the right movie, you could spend a year or two traveling the world (sometimes on the festival's dime, sometimes on your own), screening your movie to happy crowds in far-flung locales.

Often, if you're successful at one big festival, you'll be invited — without the need of an entry fee — to an ever-cascading series of festivals. Until that happens, be careful how you spend what few grocery dollars you have left on festival entry fees. (You'll have long ago run out of budget money.)

The fees run anywhere between $25 to $50 for each festival, and when you add in postage, the cost of promotional materials, screeners, and just sheer hours spent, submitting your movie to festivals can quickly drain your bank account and personal energy.

Many festivals today require submissions to come through an on-line clearing house, *www.withoutabox.com*. This site is designed to save you — and the festivals — time and effort by streamlining the submission process. As a result, you'll only have to fill out one master entry form, and for an extra fee, you can post electronic files of your promotional materials for easy downloading by festivals.

This site will save you a ton of time — once you get your materials uploaded — but be careful of its ease of use. It's so simple to enter multiple festivals that before you know it, you could drop several hundred dollars in entry fees to festivals that aren't really a good fit for your movie.

So go slow, research each festival, and then choose wisely.

The Direct Approach
The third approach to finding a distributor is the most direct. Find the

distributors you feel are right for your movie, contact them directly, and send them a DVD of your movie for review.

Not so surprisingly, this approach — like all the methods we've outlined — has an upside and a downside.

The upside is that it's generally faster and cheaper than pouring money into prints, cassettes, DVDs, publicity and entry fees for markets and festivals. The downside is that there's nothing like screening your movie for distributors in a theater with an actual audience reacting to your story. Watching the same movie in a five-by-six cubicle on a twelve-inch screen under fluorescent lights is hardly an ideal viewing situation. Particularly when you realize that many distributors watch screeners with one eye on the clock, one ear tuned to their cell phone, and one finger hovering above the "fast forward" button.

It's also important to remember that distributors are people (really, we've heard this to be true), and that they all share the very common human trait of not wanting to be the first person to dive into the pool. They want someone else to test the water for them.

With that in mind, it's best if you can provide them with reassuring information that makes it okay for them to like — and want to distribute — your movie. The best tools are great reviews and awards from a variety of festivals. It may take you a year or so to create this paper trail, but it's time well spent if it says to a distributor, "Come on in. The water's fine."

Researching distributors is the key to successfully using the direct approach. Don't waste your time and their time by sending your movie to distributors who are not suited for your project.

- Look through back issues of *Variety* and the *Hollywood Reporter* to learn who is distributing what. Each publication puts out special issues several times a year, right before the Cannes Market, the MIFED market (an international audiovisual market in Milan, Italy — Mostra Internazionale dei Film e Documentari for you purists and Sophia Loren fans), and the American Film Market, with ads from all the key distributors touting their movies.

- If you're looking for a particular venue (such as a theatrical release), make sure the distributors you approach are in that business.

- Learn what types of movies they release, and then approach those distributors whose movies are the same genre as yours. If you're approaching a cable channel directly, make sure you've watched that channel and understand the kinds of movies they buy. The same is true of home-video buyers.

- If you're targeting basic cable channels (such as Lifetime, USA Network, and the Sci-Fi channel) and broadcast channels, keep in mind that they present movies in two-hour blocks. This means your movie needs to be between 90 and 92 minutes long (the other 28 to 30 minutes are devoted to commercials). Sending them a 120-minute movie tells them that you don't understand their business.

- Many basic cable channels have standards-and-practices departments (a fancy word for censors) just like the broadcast channels. Consider this if your movie's content requires any serious cleaning up before it can be aired. A four-letter word here and there can be cut out, but wall-to-wall swearing, explicit nudity or sex, or over-the-top violence are not what they're buying.

After you've picked the distributors who are most likely to be interested in your movie, send each of them a short inquiry letter or e-mail. Briefly describe your movie, and include copies of any reviews you've received from premieres, screenings, or festivals. Don't send a screener DVD until they ask for it. It's a waste of your limited money to give screeners to people who haven't asked to watch them.

After you've sent out the preview screeners, be a little patient. In most cases, you'll be approaching small companies with small acquisition staffs. One person may be in charge of doing all the screening, all the negotiations, filling out the paperwork, and helping out with other projects. But you should check in on a monthly basis, or whenever they say to call back next. A polite, brief nudge every so often keeps your movie from becoming part of the bottom sediments on the desk.

Website Promotion

A solid website can put some power behind your movie and get the attention of distributors at the same time.

A well-designed and well-executed website that promotes your movie doesn't need to be expensive to be effective. It just needs a clear point of view, interesting graphics, and enough information to whet the viewers' appetites and make them want to see more.

The site can take a lot of different forms, from an ongoing diary chronicling the making of your movie, to a polished promotional vehicle that clearly introduces your movie to the web audience. Photos, sound files, a trailer... all these elements are a great way to introduce the world (and distributors) to your movie.

As with your movie, it's best to wait until your site is finished before you send out invites for visitors. A distributor is unlikely to visit an incomplete website more than once.

You can also save yourself the hassle of creating your own site by placing a trailer or short from your movie on one of the many independent-movie sites. While these sites can't do all your promotional work for you, they can help get your movie to a wider audience, and they may, in years to come, join festivals as the first stopping place for the new movies. We've included a list of some of these independent-movie websites in the appendix.

Getting Someone Else to Do It

Up to this point, making your movie has been pretty much a do-it-yourself affair. However, finding a distributor is a time-consuming process, requiring you to become a promoter, a salesperson, and a negotiator. You may simply not want to do this. Maybe you want to focus on your next project or recover from this one. In that case, you need to find someone else to help you sell your movie.

The people who help moviemakers sell their movies go by many names: sales representative or rep, sales agent, producer's representative, and others. Often these are people who've spent some years in the distribution business and now are out on their own. Some are people who have spent time selling their own projects.

Most work out of their homes using only a phone, fax, e-mail, their good judgment, and their industry connections to make their living. The best ones are very aggressive and knowledgeable about the business. However, don't ever confuse aggressiveness with knowledge.

As with all professions, some reps are better than others. To find the ones who do the best job of selling, talk to the buyers. Place a couple calls to key theatrical distributors, buyers at cable networks, or large home-video distributors and find out whom they know and — more importantly — whom they trust.

Sales reps generally work on commission. Some have set rates that they use regardless of the project. Others slide their commission scale, depending on how much or how little work they think they'll need to do to sell your movie.

If they like your movie (or even if they hate it but think they can sell it), they'll want the right to sell the movie in all the territories they cover, and they will want to be able to sell these rights for periods of up to 20 years. As with all contracts that you sign during the distribution process, you should have an experienced entertainment attorney look over any sales-rep agreement before you sign it.

The Budget Question

One question you may be asked by many potential distributors is "What was your budget?" Even after the success of ultra-low-budget movies such as *The Blair Witch Project*, *Clerks*, and *El Mariachi*, there are still some distributors who feel that a movie can't be worth their time if it cost less than a decent European vacation.

Of course, the viewing public doesn't really care about a movie's budget. They may be curious about a movie that's being advertised as a dirt-cheap production, but if the story doesn't grab them, then the budget won't either.

So when a distributor asks the question, you can do one of four things. You can lie outright. You can tell an alternate truth. You can skirt the issue. Or you can tell the complete truth.

Lying

This is a bad idea. It always trips you up somewhere down the line, and it puts you on that slippery slope to becoming yet another Hollywood lowlife. If you insist on lying ("Our budget? A million three, plus deferrals."), keep in mind that most distributors are pretty smart. They've looked at hundreds of movies and perhaps have produced a few of their own. They know what it costs to make a movie. So, if you lie, you better stay within the bounds of reality.

An Alternate Truth

You can tell an alternate version of the truth by figuring out what your movie would have cost if you had actually paid everyone. Then, when you're asked the budget questions, you can say, "A quarter of a million, including deferrals," and you'll be telling the truth. Mostly.

Skirting the Issue

We're big fans of skirting the issue by turning the question around and asking, "What do you think the budget was?" With *Beyond Bob*, only one distributor came close (guessing "around $50,000, with lots of deferrals"). As we've bragged before, one knowledgeable person even went as high as $900,000, which was obviously way off and which also made our day. This approach can also be educational because it will give you an objective assessment of your production values.

The Truth

Telling the unguarded truth about your budget will have more impact if you skirt the issue first and let the distributor guess. The person who guessed $50,000 felt good about himself when we told him the actual cash budget had been under $30,000; he was also impressed by what we were able to achieve for that budget. The person who guessed $900,000 was enormously impressed with us when we revealed our true costs. In both cases, we got the maximum benefit out of telling the truth.

The big fear about the truth is that it will come back to haunt you, particularly in the form of a low offer from the interested distributor. Don't be afraid; simply stand your ground. The production budget of a movie has no bearing on its market value; witness *The Blair Witch Project* and *Waterworld* as the two sides of that coin.

At this point in the process, your movie is worth whatever the market will bear.

The Deal & Other Details

Once a distributor makes an offer, you need to do two things: Check them out some more, and if they pass the inspection, hire professional legal talent.

We can't overstate this enough: Don't accept any offers or sign any contracts without the aid of an experienced entertainment attorney. Distributors buy movies all the time, week in and week out. They write the contracts. On the other hand, this will probably be the first time for you. Who do you suppose has the advantage in this situation? Don't take any chances. Get yourself some expert advice.

Your local Independent Feature Project will have the names of lawyers who are both experienced in entertainment law and sympathetic to your cause. Some work for free or on a sliding scale. Others may accept a deferral or perhaps a credit in the movie in exchange for their services.

But before you get to that stage, you need to investigate the distributor a little further. You need to find out how they've dealt with other moviemakers in the past. Ask for the names of people they're currently doing business with who can vouch for their business practices. Call everyone on the list and question them in detail about the deal they got, the results they've achieved, and their overall impression of the company.

Then disregard everything you've heard and dig deeper.

Find out what other movies they've released and track down those moviemakers — the ones who didn't make the reference list. Ask them the same questions.

We followed this approach with one distributor and didn't even need to get off the reference list. We sent a letter to one of the moviemakers, and she phoned us a few days later. She was out of town at a retreat miles away from a phone. But when she got our letter, she drove into town and called us immediately to warn us away from the distributor. Needless to say, we didn't sign with that company, and a few months later they disappeared off the face of the earth.

Just as every movie and every distributor are different, so too is every deal. What's a standard contract item in one medium is something you may need to fight for in another. Here are some of the things that are the same and different in each venue:

- It costs money to distribute a movie. In the case of a theatrical release, it can cost a lot of money. With low-budget independent movies, it's not uncommon for a distributor to spend two or three times the movie's production budget on prints and advertising (P&A). It cost hundreds of thousands of dollars to get the ultra low-budget *The Blair Witch Project* in shape for its theatrical release. The sound mix alone for *Clerks* was twice the movie's production budget. A home-video release also requires considerable capital for advertising, duplication, and packaging.

    That's why distributors resist paying a cash advance for a movie and frequently offer the producer a smaller percentage of the movie's profits, such as a 60/40 split or less. Of course, profits don't happen until they make back their costs, which could take a long, long time.

    For distributors who are sharing percentages of profits with you (such as theatrical and home video), find out in advance what expenses are going against the revenues. If all the distribution costs are being subtracted (including distribution-staff salaries) you'll probably never see profits. A better deal is one that gives you a percentage of the revenues. In either case, ask for quarterly reporting and payments. They may try to negotiate an annual reporting structure, which basically allows them to keep your money longer. Don't let them do that.

- Large distributors, such as those run by the studios, have lots of ways of burying losses and cross-collateralizing their movies. A small distributor can't afford to simply break even on a movie; each movie must make back its costs plus some more. It only takes two or three bombs to put a small distributor out of business.

In order to protect their investment, both large and small theatrical distributors are probably going to want to hang on to all the other rights as well, including home video, cable, and anything else they can think of. Their argument will be that the theatrical release of the movie is the locomotive that pulls the rest of the train, publicizing the movie for cable and home-video release. They may want to be able to make cable and home-video sales to offset any losses from a theatrical release.

So if you're planning to splinter your rights (sell theatrical rights to one distributor while retaining other rights to sell elsewhere), you may be in for a big fight with your theatrical distributor. If you insist on doing this, you'll be in a better position if you go into the negotiations with these ancillary rights (like home video and cable) already sold. Even then, the absence of these rights may break your deal with a theatrical distributor.

Depending on the movie and the distributor, you may have an easier time holding onto the rights for things like a soundtrack album, book publishing, or merchandising, although you'll probably fight tooth and nail over all that stuff as well.

- For lump-sum deals, such as a contract with a cable network, the distributor or buyer may try to spread out payments as much as possible. For example, you may ask for the first payment to be due upon delivery of the movie. They may counter by making the first payment due on the first air date. If they lock up your movie with a contract and have no required air date, you could sit around for the duration of the contract and never see payment. Stand your ground and make them pay for the right to tie up your movie. They can be pretty tough about this, but it's just another technique for holding onto your money a little longer.

- If a basic cable network wants your movie, they're probably going to want it exclusively, and they're going to want it for a long time. A five-year exclusive contract is not uncommon. Their reasoning is that they have to be able to offer product that viewers can't find anywhere else in order to stay in business. Otherwise, they'll be swallowed up in the mass of cable channels and eventually disappear. So find which network is right for your movie, and don't expect to accumulate sales across the cable dial.

- As more and more cable channels are added, the prices paid for movies go down, not up. Sure there are more buyers of movies, but as each network is added, the ratings (market share) go down for everyone because there are more of them dividing up the same audience. As the ratings go down, the budgets shrink proportionally — the pieces of the pie keep getting cut smaller and smaller. The positive aspect of this growth of cable channels is that more channels need more product, particularly exclusive product. Although they won't necessarily be paying as much for the movies they buy, it should increase your chances of making a cable sale.

What You'll Need to Provide

Again, the specific requirements of what each distributor needs will change, depending on the company and their venue. But some things are true across the board.

- Many distributors are going to want errors-and-omissions (E&O) insurance to ensure you have ownership or use rights to all elements of your movie (as we discussed in the chapter on business). Who pays for this insurance is a negotiable point. With their access to blanket policies, distributors are in a better position to put up the money, but since that adds to their overhead, they're often resistant to doing it. However, in many cases the deal can't proceed until it's resolved, so if they really want your movie, they'll cover this cost.

- Foreign distributors (theatrical, home video, cable, and broadcast television) may need for you to provide a music-and-effects (M&E) track for your movie. This is a special mix of your soundtrack which includes all the sound effects and music, but none of the dialogue. (That's why we told you to put all the dialogue on separate tracks and to create one sound-effects track that replicates any sound effects that were intermingled with the dialogue.) Using this M&E track, the foreign distributor can create foreign-language versions of your movie for each country in their territory.

In addition to the M&E track, the foreign distributor will also need a continuity script. This is a word-for-word transcript of your finished movie, which will be the basis for the foreign-language translation.

- Publicity stills and promotional material. This will vary from venue to venue. As we mentioned in the chapter on production, theatrical distributors desperately need quality production stills to promote your movie in newspapers and magazines. And they have to be smart stills — photos that really capture the tone and mood of the movie, not snapshots of actors and crew mugging for the camera (unless that really captures the tone and mood of your movie). Not having these professional stills will make your movie less attractive to buyers because they'll need to do more work to promote it.

Home-video buyers also need stills for DVD-box art, but these photos generally need to be more stylized, with slick, well-lit images and a lot of attention paid to hair and makeup. Spend some time in a video store and look at a lot of different boxes to get an idea of the types of photos used to sell movies in this venue. If your time and budget allow, schedule a photo shoot for right after you've finished with principal photography (before the actors, costumes, and locations disappear) to shoot some high-quality images. This will make your movie more attractive to the home-video market, where the artwork on the box is often more important than the movie inside.

Cable television has less need for photos because they usually promote movies using on-air promotions (which are short trailers of footage from the movie) and the synopsis that is printed in the cable guide.

- Incidentally, don't expect to have much say about the promotional campaign your distributor puts together for your movie. Most will listen to your thoughts, but it's not a contractual right that they're likely to give to you. It would mean that if you didn't like their campaign, you could hold up the release of the movie. In the distributors' defense, most moviemakers are not equipped to put together an effective trailer or a powerful poster. That's what distributors are good at doing, so don't be surprised when you're left out of this loop.

- Some distributors (and movie markets and festivals) may ask you for a press kit on your movie. This is written information about your movie — the story, the cast, the crew, the production history, and reviews — that will be given to the press (the entertainment news media) for promotional purposes. Publicity photos are also included. You may also use elements of the press kit to entice distributors to look at your movie and to promote any local premiere that you do for your movie. In short, it's a selling tool and should be approached as such.

  If you've created a website for your movie, many of the materials may already be in place for your press kit. If you're creating a press kit, you'll have many of the materials for your website. It's just a matter of moving them from one medium to another.

Every press kit has a few basic elements:

~ Cast List: This is a list of your principal cast members, along with the names of the characters they play in the movie. In a movie such as yours, which will be populated with unknowns, this is how movie critics will know who plays which character. This is also where the critics will go to find out how to spell the actors' names, so proofread it twice, and then get someone else to proof it, and then proof it one more time yourself.

~ Production-Team List: Same as above, this time featuring everyone behind the camera: producer, director, writer, director of photography, editor, composer, and so on.

~ Story Synopsis: This is a one- or two-page synopsis of the key elements of your story. Some moviemakers prefer to tell the whole story in the synopsis; others use it to set up the story and leave the reader hanging, so as not to give away the movie's ending. This second approach is a better selling tool. It entices the reader to want to watch the movie, and if the reader is a potential distributor, that's a good thing.

~ Production Notes: This is something of a catch-all where you can highlight the biographies of your key players and present interesting anecdotes about your movie. Although every part of your press kit should be professionally written, the production-notes segment needs to shine. The better it is, the more likely newspaper writers are to simply retype it and print it as is, which is exactly what you want them to do. (Newspaper entertainment writers are notoriously willing to let someone else do their work, except for those few who review books about movie production. Those writers are the best in the business.)

~ Production Stills: All your best shots, with captions (actor name, character name, movie name, copyright info), should be included. Since you will likely have an electronic press kit, these will be on CD. Just make sure that they are of high quality, properly captioned, and readable on both Macs and PCs.

~ Video Diary: These are becoming more and more common. This is basically a short documentary about the making of your movie, including behind-the-scenes shots and interviews with primary cast and crew members. You may not include it in all press kits, but it should be part of your website. This video diary could also be used as a special feature on a DVD release of your movie.

Keep in mind that all this promotional material — which will help with your local premiere and may pique the interest of a distributor — may be tossed out, rewritten, or edited by your distributor if your movie gets picked up for distribution. If you've done a really stellar job on it, they may follow the example of the newspaper writer and simply slap their logo on it.

Self-Distribution & Self-Flagellation: How to Tell Them Apart

Despite your best efforts, you may not find a home for your movie with any of the big or small fish swimming in the distribution stream. You may have been turned down flat at all venues, or you may have received some proposed deals that offered more harm than good. Whatever the reason, you may now feel like the proud owner of a fairly expensive paperweight.

Don't despair. You're not dead yet.

Self-distribution is a viable alternative for you and your movie. On the positive side, it allows you to control how and where your movie is shown, and it eliminates that pesky middleman who seems to come out ahead on most deals. On the negative side, you have to commit to distribution in the same way you committed to production, recognizing that this is nearly a full-time job, requiring as much faith and stamina as the production process did.

One of the reasons that traditional distributors insist on errors-and-omissions insurance is that they don't want to get sued. If you cut out the middleman and release your movie yourself, you will be solely responsible if your movie defames, libels, infringes, violates, spindles, bends, folds, mutilates, and on and on. In short, since you can't afford the insurance, you need to make doubly sure that you haven't trampled anyone else's rights while making your movie.

The most likely markets for self-distribution are theatrical, home video, and the Internet. Before you dive into any of them, consider the following:

Theatrical

- Theatrical distribution is the most risky of the three because it generally requires more capital, such as renting a theater, renting video-projection equipment (fortunately, more and more theaters are adding video projectors... just to save you money), spending lots more to make a 35mm blow-up print , and buying advertising. None of this comes cheaply, so try to think of ways to cut costs. For example, rather than four-walling (renting the entire theater and keeping all the hoped-for profits), strike a deal with a local theater owner. Split the house and let him keep all the concessions, which is where the theater makes all of its money anyway. However, you'll have to persuade the theater owner that you can draw in an audience before he or she will be willing to make that deal. If your movie falls in the cult category, you can offer to make it a midnight movie on weekends, so it doesn't cut into the theater's prime time.

- Use articles and reviews in the local media as your advertising. Don't stop with the major newspaper; do some legwork, and make sure you get mentioned in the alternative press, in neighborhood papers, on local radio, cable, and broadcast television shows — anywhere! A press release written in news style will often be picked up by neighborhood newspapers, which are well read by their audience. This sort of publicity is cheap and will pay off with paid admissions at the door.

- Don't blow the bank on elaborate posters with expensive photography and graphics unless the theater is located in a high traffic area where the poster will serve as advertising. Otherwise, go with a simple, elegant (meaning cheap) poster that lets people know they've made it to the right theater.

Home Video

Home video is cheaper to break into than theatrical, although not necessarily easier. You can rent space in a movie theater; you can't necessarily buy your way into a video store unless you want to own the entire store. More and more, video stores are only looking for the "A" titles (big-name movies with big-name stars) and the "B" titles (exploitation and action pictures with semi-big-name stars). This often leaves the "C" titles (small, independent movies with no-name stars) out in the cold.

There are some things you can do, however, to get your movie into video stores on a local, regional, and even national basis:

- Generate interest in your movie, so that store owners will see a value in buying your movie. Stage a local premiere and get as much publicity as you can. Then approach local chains and dealers about buying copies of your tape, using the publicity and reviews as supporting arguments that prove there is a demand for your movie.

- If cast and crew members are from out of town, send video copies of the movie (and any reviews you've already gotten) to their local papers to generate publicity. Then use that publicity to persuade video-store owners in that area to stock your movie. By the same token, if you shot in any towns outside of your own, be sure to generate some publicity in those towns as well, and then start hitting on those local video-store owners.

- Work with your area's film commission to persuade all the video chains in the your state to create displays in their stores of movies that were made in your state — the big-buck Hollywood movies that have passed through the state and the locally-produced movies such as yours.

- Create a great, eye-catching box. To find out what sorts of designs work, walk through a couple video stores, and see what catches your eye. If you're not a graphic designer, don't pretend to be one. You've done a lot for your movie so far, but don't feel that you have to do absolutely everything. Find yourself a graphic designer to create the right look for your video box. Get a friend of a friend or a promising student at a local art school, or call ad agencies in your area and see if they can recommend someone looking for the experience. You need to make your box look great, and you may need a professional to do that. Also, try to get them to do it for resume experience with you covering the production costs.

- You'll also need great photos. If you didn't shoot them before, then shoot them now. On two of our movies, we ended up shooting photography for the video box long after the movies had wrapped. It can be a hassle to get the actors back together. If they have moved on, you'll have to use your imagination. In the case of *Resident Alien*, one of our key actors had moved to Los Angeles, so we used a stand-in wearing the large alien "bug head" we had created for the movie, which was actually a more eye-catching approach!

Staged publicity photos from Resident Alien *and* Beyond Bob.

- Keep your price point low. If you're charging $30 for your DVD, and a store owner knows she can get two "A" titles or four "B" titles for the same price, what do you think she's going to buy? To keep your price low, use the same methods you used during production. Never pay full price for anything, cut deals at every turn, and use your networking skills to get the most bang for your buck. Fortunately, there are DVD replicators who will produce 300 totally professional DVDs in cases with artwork for about $1,600 ($5.33 each) or 1,000 for $1,800 ($1.80 each). Take note that you want *replicated* DVDs — not *duplicated* DVDs

— just like the big distributors make. You have to order a minimum of 300, but they are compatible with almost all DVD players and computers; duplicated DVDs are not.

- Contact all the libraries in your state. Many buy videos and will be interested in locally produced movies, particularly if those movies have garnered some local publicity.

- Be persistent. Be very persistent. This is a hard way to make sales, one to a dozen at a time. You'd probably make more money flipping burgers for the hours you'll invest, but then you'd miss all the glamour of show business.

Internet

More and more moviemakers are turning to on-line stores to sell their features.

Currently, most of these on-line video stores — like Film Threat DVD (*filmthreatdvd.com*) and *BuyIndies.com* — only offer DVD and VHS sales. But as technology improves (and it always does), it's likely that buyers will turn to sites like these to download movies to their computers and iPods as well.

As broadband and streaming video become increasingly available, more sites will present movies, and more people will be hitting these sites to watch (and buy) these movies.

Even if you can't sell your movie, making it available on the Internet may be a good way to promote your crew, your cast, and yourself. It could be a good stepping stone for the careers of everyone in your movies.

It's a great time to be an independent moviemaker. With your digital movie just sitting in your computer, you will be well positioned to ride this digital wave.

There are a couple things to watch out for, however:

- As with any other form of distribution, you need to be vigilant about protecting your rights. The technology for getting your movie to the masses may be in place before the mechanisms for recouping your investment have been built. It may be okay if *no one* makes money off your movie, but it's hardly fair if *someone* (like a distributor or website provider) does and you don't have a piece of it. As with any other distributor, make sure you don't sign anything or commit to anything without the proper legal advice.

- Be very careful that you understand the terms of your agreement with a website provider. Many may want exclusive rights to sell or show your movie, and they may want those rights for a good long time. If you're using the web exposure to move your movie up the food chain, you may be trapped in that web when a bigger distributor shows interest in your movie and you can't sell it to them because you've signed away the exclusive rights.

≈ • ≈

We're not giving away any secrets when we say that distribution is perhaps the toughest part of this entire process. This is primarily because, for the first time, most of the control is out of your hands. However, you are not without some advantages. The biggest is that, from the financial point of view, you don't have to do a lot of business to be successful.

A producer with a movie that has a $500,000 or million-dollar budget has to earn back a lot of money just to break even. You don't have that problem. You don't have to make a killing to pay back your investors, your child's college fund, or your retirement savings.

By the same token, your movie can be attractive to buyers simply because it doesn't cost a lot; you don't need to demand big advances and large percentages in order to be profitable.

The final advantage you have is one of patience. Depending on how you raised your money and who you raised it from, you probably won't have high-rolling investors breathing down your neck. They won't be insisting that you unload your movie as quickly as possible to get them a return on their money.

You can afford to be selective and patient as you look for the right distributor and the right distribution deal. This is good because you may need to be patient. Perhaps *very* patient.

Afterword

Congratulations. You've made it all the way to the end... unless you skipped ahead to see how things turned out. We've been honored to be your guides on this travelogue of ultra-low-budget movie production. If you've stayed with us this far, you've probably caught the bug to take this trip yourself.

This book can be your ticket for starting that journey, if you wish. We guarantee that making your own movie will be like nothing you've ever done before. It's leaping off the 30-foot diving board. It's walking on stage in front of the world. It's joining a club of adventurers who have scaled a peak that other mortals just look up at with whispered wishes.

As in any good adventure, you'll have to use all your skills and wits. At times, it will be gut wrenching. It will demand teeth-gritting courage. It will require determination undergirded by iron willpower. It will take everything you've got to see it through to the end. Most importantly, it's an adventure that will let you realize a dream and feel the confidence that comes from mastering an arduous trek.

Some of the best experiences we've had as a result of writing this book are meeting other moviemakers. We've especially enjoyed it when they've told us how our book has fanned the flames of their personal moviemaking dreams. We've had so much fun fulfilling our own dreams that we can hardly wait to hear how theirs work out.

It's nice to know that there are others traveling the same path.

We wish you the best of luck on your adventure. We know you'll have stories to tell when you return, and we look forward to hearing them.

Keep following your dream. It's worth it.

John Gaspard
Dale Newton
www.graniteproductions.org

Enlarged Appendix

(Not a useless appendage with inflammation along your digestive tract. Instead, a useful appendant of information to digest along with this tract.)

<u>RESIDENT ALIEN</u>

An Original Screenplay

by

Dale Newton

14.   EXT. ROOFTOP - NIGHT

Cal is on the flat roof of the apartment building. A
clamp-on work light casts a pool of illumination around
him. Stars fill the night sky behind him. The apparatus
seen earlier is now sitting on an overturned milk crate,
and Cal is perched on a folding chair next to it. He has
the control panel open and he's using a volt meter to test
the wiring.

                    LESLIE
                    (o.s.)
         You can't hide from me! I hear you up there
         every night.

Cal looks over to the side of the roof where a permanent
ladder is attached and then turns back to his work. From
the ladder, there is the sound of irregular shoe steps on
metal, accompanied by huffing and puffing.

                    LESLIE
                    (slurring)
         Hey! Stop shaking the ladder.

Cal finishes his tests and closes the panel. He flips a
switch and it glows to life with various colored lights
reflecting off his face.

15.   INT. SPACECRAFT - SPACE

Another control panel with odd, fluid shapes and buttons
suddenly begins to flash wildly. An unearthly wail of a
siren is heard with intermittent bursts of sound. The
entire room begins to shudder.

16.   EXT. ROOFTOP - NIGHT

Leslie slowly appears at the top of the ladder, weaving
slightly. She's obviously spent the afternoon getting cozy
with her whiskey bottle.

                    LESLIE
         My plug's still tubbed.

CALL SHEET   Date _____

Production Title _____

Location and Address	Scene Numbers

Cast Member & Role	Makeup Call Time	Set Call Time	Remarks
Extras	Makeup Call Time	Set Call Time	Remarks

Notices of Changes or Future Schedule

GROUP RELEASE   Date _____

In exchange for screen credit under the names listed below, each of the undersigned grants [PRODUCTION CO.] the right, but not the obligation, to use her or his
name, voice, likeness or any simulation thereof, or any film or photographs taken by
[PRODUCTION CO.] of each of the undersigned individually or with others in
connection with this production, tentatively titled

_____

These usage rights are given forever and throughout the world, and include, but
are not limited to, the production, distribution, advertising and exploitation of this
motion picture by any means whatsoever by the [PRODUCTION CO.].

Name (Print)   Signature   Address

_____

_____

_____

_____

_____

_____

_____

_____

_____

CAST AND CREW RELEASE

I accept all of the conditions and provisions of the following release form covering my work on the production which is tentatively titled

_____

and which is being produced by [PRODUCTION CO.].

Ownership
I assign to [PRODUCTION CO.] the ownership and all rights to use, exhibit, distribute, assign, license, and otherwise exploit the products of my work on the production. I also waive any and all claims to copyright, patent, or other ownership of my work products on the production.

I agree to keep confidential all written, creative, technical and financial details of the production unless requested by [PRODUCTION CO.] to disclose such information.

I agree to participate in publicity for the production.

Liability
I indemnify [PRODUCTION CO.], the owners of any locations used, and the owners of any uninsured rental equipment against any claims and demands of personal injury, damage to property, and death resulting from my work on the production.

I understand that I am responsible for all necessary personal injury, death, and liability insurances, and am responsible for any damage caused by my actions and by my personal property used during my work on the production.

I accept full responsibility for all personal risks during my work on the production.

Compensation
I am volunteering my services for the production. I understand that I will receive credit under the following name in the screen credits of the completed production:

Name for Screen Credits _____

Signatures

_____

Name [print]   Signature   Date

_____

Address

Social Security # _____ - _____ - _____

LOCATION RELEASE

I hereby grant permission to [PRODUCTION CO.] to enter and use my property located at

_____

for the purpose of photographing and recording scenes (interior and exterior) to be used in the motion picture tentatively titled

_____

Use of Property
I give permission for [PRODUCTION CO.] to bring personnel, equipment, props, temporary sets, and any other necessary materials and supplies onto this property for this purpose.

Ownership Rights
I give [PRODUCTION CO.] or any person or company it licenses, the right to use, exhibit, distribute, advertise or otherwise exploit worldwide forever any scenes photographed and recorded on this property in connection with this motion picture.

Care of Property
[PRODUCTION CO.] agrees to use reasonable care to prevent damage to this property and to remove any and all materials placed on the property in connection with this production. The property will be restored as nearly as possible to its original condition, excepting ordinary wear and tear.

Liability
During the photographing and recording on this property, [PRODUCTION CO.] agrees to indemnify and hold the property owner harmless from any claims and demands of any members of the cast or crew of the production arising from personal injuries or death suffered while working on this property.

Authority to Enter Agreement
I hereby state that I have full right and authority to enter into this agreement concerning the property described above and that the permission of no other person, company or corporation is necessary in order for [PRODUCTION CO.] to enjoy full rights to use this property. I also indemnify and hold harmless [PRODUCTION CO.] from all losses, costs, liability, damages, or other claims that arise out of any false statements or representations made by me in this agreement.

Signatures
Approved and accepted by,

_____

Printed name of property owner or authorized representative

_____

Signature of property owner or authorized representativee
Date _____

268

ARTWORK RELEASE

I, the undersigned artist, assign all rights to [PRODUCTION CO.] to use images of my original artwork in the movie tentatively titled [MOVIE TITLE]. I give all ownership of these images of my artwork, including all rights to use, exhibit, distribute, assign, license, and otherwise exploit these images of my artwork used in the movie tentatively titled [MOVIE TITLE]. I also waive any and all claims to copyright, patent, or other ownership of the images of my artwork used in the movie tentatively titled [MOVIE TITLE].

In exchange for screen credit under the following name,

_____

I waive all rights to further compensation for the use of my artwork in the movie tentatively titled [MOVIE TITLE].

Signatures

_____

Artist Name [print]   Signature   Date

_____

Address

Social Security # _____ - _____ - _____

SHOT LOG

Page _____ of _____

Tape # _____   Date _____

Project _____   Videographer _____

Locations _____

Time Code	Scene	Take	Description / Remarks / Sound

Equipment Rental List

Camera
- 3-CCD DV camcorder*
- Camcorder batteries and charger*
- Tripod with fluid head*

Sound
- Sound mixer
- Batteries for mixer
- Headphones*
- Shotgun microphone*
- Batteries for microphone*
- Windscreen*
- Shock mount*
- Boom pole*
- 100' and 20' mike cable*

Lighting
- 4 - 1000-watt lights with barndoors (Arriflex or Lowel DP)
- 4 - Light stands
- 4 - extra lamps
- 38" Flexfill reflector (white/silver)
- 2 - 1000-watt halogen construction lights on tripods*
- 2 - Westcott 2012 photo umbrellas*
- 4 - extra halogen lamps*

Expendable Supplies to Purchase
- 3 - 2" roll gaffer tape (white, grey, black)*
- 4 - 20" x 24" spun (105 Roscolux tough spun - 1 stop)*
- 4 - 20" x 24" 3200 K to daylight correction gel (3202 Rosco Full Blue CTB)*

Postproduction
- Desktop microphone for sound effects, foley, and dialogue looping
- DV record deck that uses full-size DV tapes

* We recommend purchasing these items, but renting may work better for you.

We fed a production company that ranged in size from 12 to 20 cast and crew for $125 each weekend of shooting, which included six meals and a snack. We fed everyone well for less than $1.50 per meal by purchasing supplies on sale and at bulk food and warehouse stores whenever possible. We bought very little prepared food, and we had the help of friends and relatives preparing and serving it. Our menus were planned around the foods that we could purchase within our budget.

Below are sample menus for two weekends of production.

Friday Evening
Snack
- Cucumber sandwiches on cocktail-bread slices
- Peanut-butter cookies
- Pink lemonade, soft drinks

Saturday
Breakfast
- Lemon bread and banana bread with butter
- Apple juice, coffee, milk, hot cocoa

Lunch
- Hamburger chili over sliced baked potato
- Raw vegetables (carrots, broccoli, cauliflower) and dill dip
- Chocolate-chip cookies
- Soft drinks, milk

Dinner
- Grilled bratwurst on buns
- Potato chips
- Lettuce salad and dressing
- Apples
- Brownies
- Soft drinks, milk

Sunday
Breakfast
- Egg-and-sausage baked casserole
- Orange juice, coffee, milk, hot cocoa

Lunch
- Submarine sandwich on French loaf (Swiss and cheddar cheese, turkey, ham, pastrami, lettuce, onion, tomato, mayonnaise)
- Oranges
- Cranberry juice, soft drinks, milk

Dinner
- Lasagna
- French bread with garlic butter
- Raw vegetables (green pepper, radish, celery, mushroom)
- Ice cream
- Apple cider, soft drinks, milk

Friday Evening
Snack
- Corn chips and onion dip
- Snickerdoodle cookies
- Soft drinks, lemonade

Saturday
Breakfast
- Coffee cake
- Orange juice, coffee, milk, hot cocoa

Lunch
- Ham-and-Swiss-cheese sandwiches
- Raw vegetables (carrot, celery)
- Red and green grapes
- Chocolate-chip bars
- Soft drinks, milk

Dinner
- Tacos (flour tortillas, hamburger, cheese, onion, lettuce, tomato)
- Tortilla chips
- Pineapple and apple slices
- Oatmeal cookies
- Ice cream
- Apple cider, soft drinks, milk

Sunday
Breakfast
- Muffins
- Apple juice, coffee, milk, hot cocoa

Lunch
- Chicken, broccoli, and rice casserole
- Green salad and dressing
- Rice-cereal bars
- Soft drinks, milk

Dinner
- Sloppy-Joe hamburger barbecues on buns
- Pickles
- Marinated pasta and vegetable salad
- Marble cake with chocolate frosting
- Soft drinks, milk

Condiments and Supplies for Meals
- Catsup
- Mustard
- Salt
- Pepper
- Instant cocoa
- Tea bags
- Coffee bags
- Sugar
- Instant creamer
- Paper plates
- Paper cups or borrowed ceramic mugs
- Utensils
- Paper towels
- Coffee urn for hot water

Press Kit: Sample Synopsis

"Resident Alien" — The Story

Resident Alien, a new science fiction-comedy feature film from Granite Productions, Ltd., is the story of a UFO crash that changes the lives of two down-on-their-luck people in a small Midwestern town.

Cal Gilbert (PATRICK COYLE), a former Ph.D. candidate in astrophysics, now runs a motel as a low-rent apartment building. He spends his evenings on the roof, scanning the night skies for a discovery that will re-establish his credibility within the scientific community.

His only tenant, Leslie Winter (NESBA CRENSHAW) is newly divorced, out of work, and at the end of her rope. Her dreams of world travel have gotten her out of Fargo, North Dakota and dumped her — without hope or cash — in Stillwater, Minnesota.

One night, after Leslie has climbed up on the roof to harangue Cal about her apartment's plumbing problems, they both witness — and are nearly incinerated by — a crashing UFO.

With this too-close encounter, Cal and Leslie embark on a journey of mystery and adventure, during which they become entangled with an enigmatic, but friendly, stranger (MARK PATRICK GLEASON); a wily, small-town sheriff (JOHN MUNGER); an unscrupulous UFO investigator (RICHARD GIBBONS); an Air Force cover-up; and an eye-opening rendezvous on a dark country road.

Resident Alien mixes comedy, science fiction and romance to create a memorable story about the dangers and complications that occur when you wish on a star — and your dreams come true.

"Resident Alien" — Credit List

CAST

Patrick Coyle... Cal Gilbert
Nesba Crenshaw... Leslie Winter
Mark Patrick Gleason.. Allen
Richard Gibbons.. Professor Davis
John Munger.. Sheriff Jack Martin
Janet Mitchko.. Joyce (social worker)
Nancy Gormley.. Leslie's Mother
Michael Paul Levin.. Deputy Gary Ort
Craig McNamara.. Bunsen
Tom Monn.. Verner
Amelia Barnes... Tish
Eve Black.. Noam
Marvel Newton.. Addie Wagner

CREW

Dale Newton.. Writer-Producer
John Gaspard... Director
Kathy Erickson.. Production Manager
Scott Lee Dose.. Director of Photography
Steve Knudsen.. Assistant Camera
Bryan Carey.. Sound Mixer
Rick Selin.. Sound Mixer
Dan Martinson.. Sound Mixer
Paul David... Lighting Gaffer
Debbie Simmons... Clothing Designer
Minnefex... Special Effects Design & Production
(Mike Berglund and Dave Weiberg)
Dale Newton... Second Unit Director
Dave Reynolds... Music
John Gaspard.. Editor
Kathleen Laughlin.. Consulting Editor
Kelly Kersting.. Editing Assistance
Kathy Hedberg.. Editing Assistance
Jeff Vlaming... Special Effects Art Direction

"Reach for a Star"(Theme from "Resident Alien")
Written & Produced by Dave Reynolds
Sung by Ruth MacKenzie

Press Kit: Sample Production Notes

"Resident Alien" — Production Notes

Making a low-budget movie is like riding a roller coaster without a seat belt — it's loaded with fun, excitement, terror, and you're never sure if you can hold on until the end. At least that's the way director John Gaspard and writer-producer Dale Newton describe their experience shooting *Resident Alien,* a science fiction-comedy feature film.

"There were many points when the work behind us and ahead of us looked overwhelming, and we asked ourselves, 'Why do we want to do this?'" Gaspard said. "And then we'd grin ear-to-ear because the answer was obvious: We were having the time of our lives."

The production was full of new challenges for the pair from Minnesota who founded Granite Productions, Ltd. to make feature films in the Midwest. But by combining their skills, they were able to guide the project to a smooth completion.

"We both had experience in different parts of the process," Gaspard said. "I had directed or produced five other feature-length projects on Super 8mm and video, while Dale was experienced with special effects and the technical considerations of 16mm. Plus we're both screenwriters, so we started with a strong screenplay and collaborated to turn it into a film."

The film chronicles how a UFO crash changes the lives of Cal (Patrick Coyle) and Leslie (Nesba Crenshaw), two down-on-their-luck residents of a small, Midwestern town. Comedy, romance and intrigue are provided by an enigmatic stranger (Mark Patrick Gleason); an unscrupulous UFO investigator (Richard Gibbons); a wily, small-town sheriff (John Munger); and other characters (Amelia Barnes, Eve Black, Nancy Gormley, Michael Paul Levin, Craig McNamara, Janet Mitchko, Tom Monn, Marvel Newton) who help and hinder Cal and Leslie's pursuit of their dreams.

"It's appropriate that the film's main characters are striving to achieve impossible goals. That pretty much describes the making of this movie," Newton said.

277

Other Resources

The following lists are not comprehensive; they are only a starting point in your search for the services and supplies that you need. These listings do not imply any endorsement by the authors. Buyer beware.

Independent Feature Project Offices

IFP/New York
104 West 29th Street, 12th Floor
New York, NY 10001-5310
(212) 465-8200
Fax: (212) 465-8525
E-mail: *newyorkmembership@ifp.org*
www.ifp.org

IFP/Chicago
1104 S. Wabash, Ste. 403
Chicago, IL 60605
(312) 235-0161
Fax: (312) 235-0162
E-mail: *Chicago@ifp.org*
www.ifp.org

IFP/Minnesota
2446 University Ave. W., Suite 100
Saint Paul, MN 55114
(651) 644-1912
Fax: (651) 644-5708
E-mail: *word@ifpmn.org*
www.ifp.org

IFP/Seattle
1001 Lenora Street
Seattle, WA 98121
(206) 860-8490
E-mail: *seattle@ifp.org*
www.ifp.org

278

Websites

(Please note that this list only scratches the surface and that it was out-of-date the instant we typed it.)

<u>Features and Shorts</u>

Always Independent Films
www.alwaysif.com

AtomFilms
www.atomfilms.com

Ifilm
www.ifilm.com

WireBreak Entertainment
www.wirebreak.com

Pop.com
www.pop.com

Bijou Cafe
www.bijoucafe.com

Undergroundfilm.com
www.undergroundfilm.com

<u>Educational Sites</u>

Cinema
www.learner.org/exhibits/cinema

The Complete Eejits Guide to Filmmaking
www.exposure.co.uk/eejit

The Film Maker's Home Pages
www.filmmaker.com

Film Secrets
www.rivalquest.com

MicroFilmmaker
www.microfilmmaker.com

Moviemaker magazine
http://www.moviemaker.com/filmeducation.html

Next Wave Films
www.nextwavefilms.com

Film Festival Resources

www.filmfestivals.com

http://www.moviemaker.com/festivals.html

www.eurofilmfest.org

www.filmland.com/festivals/
index.html

dir.yahoo.com/entertainment/movies_and_film/film_festivals

www.insidefilm.com

www.withoutabox.com

Film Commissions

http://www.moviemaker.com/
filmoffices.html

http://www.filmcommissionhq.com/

Movie Scripts On-Line

www.dailyscript.com

www.script-o-rama.com

www.movie-page.com/movie_scripts.htm

Educational Resources

American Film Institute
2021 N. Western Avenue
Los Angeles, CA 90027-1657
(323) 856.7600
www.afi.com

Association of Independent Video and Filmmakers
304 Hudson Street
New York, NY z10013
(212) 807-1400
Fax: (212) 463-8519
E-mail: info@aivf.org
www.aivf.org

Film Arts Foundation
145 Ninth Street
San Francisco, CA 94103
(415) 552-8760
Fax: (415) 552-0882
E-mail: *info@filmarts.org*
www.filmarts.org

Dov S-S Simens
Hollywood Film Institute
(310) 399-6699
E-mail: *info@webfilmschool.com*
www.hollywoodu.com

Sundance Institute
225 Santa Monica Boulevard
8th Floor
Santa Monica, CA 90401
(310) 394-4662
Fax: (310) 394-8353
www.sundance.org

Tape-to-Film Transfers

(There are many vendors supplying this service. This one is included because its website offers a lot of good preproduction information if you are planning to make a film print of your digital movie.)

DVFilm
2819 Foster Lane, Suite F150
Austin, TX 78757
Voice and Fax: (512) 459-0502
Cell: (512) 497-2271
www.dvfilm.com

DVD and Tape Duplication

Disc Makers
Plant & Main Office
7905 N. Route 130
Pennsauken, NJ 08110
(800) 237-6666
(856) 663-9030
Fax: (856) 661-3450
www.discmakers.com

Videotape, CD, DVD Suppliers

New Tape, CD, DVD

Disc Makers
Plant & Main Office
7905 N. Route 130
Pennsauken, NJ 08110
(800) 237-6666
(856) 663-9030
Fax: (856) 661-3450
www.discmakers.com

The Tape Company
Corporate Headquarters
325-A West Lake Street
Elmhurst, IL 60126
(800) 851-3113
www.thetapecompany.com
www.cheaptape.com

Recycled Videotape

Coarc Video
P.O. Box 2]
Route 217
Mellenville, NY 12544
(800) 888-4451
www.coarcvideo.visualnet.com/

Evaluated Videotape

Carpel Video
429 E. Patrick Street
Frederick, MD 21701
(800) 238-4300
Fax: (301) 694-9510
www.carpelvideo.com

Equipment Retailers

B&H Photo-Video-Pro Audio
420 Ninth Avenue
New York, NY 10001
(800) 947-9910 (video)
(800) 947-1183 (pro audio)
Fax: (212) 239-7770
www.bhphotovideo.com

Discount Video Warehouse
P.O. Box 36
Mt. Prospect, IL 60056
(800) 323-8148
Fax: (847) 299-4206
www.dvwonline.com

MegaWatts Computers, LLC
4131 S. Sheridan Rd.
Tulsa, OK 74145
(918) 664-6342
Fax: (918) 663-6340
E-mail: *sales@MegaMacs.com*
www.MegaWatts.com
www.MegaMacs.com

Other World Computing
1004 Courtaulds Drive
Woodstock, IL 60098
(800) 275-4576
Fax: (815) 338-4332
www.macsales.com

Where to Buy Movie Scripts

Script City
8033 Sunset Boulevard
Suite 1500
Hollywood, CA 90046
(800) 676-2522
E-mail: *info@scriptcity.com*
www.scriptcity.com

Hollywood Book City
8913 Lankershim Blvd.
Sun Valley, California 91352
(818) 767-5194
E-mail: *hwdbookcity@earthlink.net*
www.hollywoodbookcity.com

Publications

The Hollywood Reporter
5055 Wilshire Boulevard
Los Angeles, CA 90036
(323) 525-2000
www.hollywoodreporter.com

Variety
5700 Wilshire Boulevard, Suite 120
Los Angeles, CA 90036
(323) 857-6600
www.variety.com

Magazines
(Some of these are FREE for production professionals. Remember, you're a producer now.)

DV Magazine
P.O. Box 1212
Skokie, IL 60076-8212
(888) 776-7002
E-mail: *dv@halldata.com*
www.dv.com/

Millimeter
www.millimeter.com

Moviemaker
121 Fulton Street, Fifth Floor
New York, NY 10038
(212) 766-4100
www.moviemaker.com

Res
RES Media Group
76 Ninth Avenue, 11th Fl.
New York, NY 10011
(888) 732-3737
www.res.com

Studio Monthly
www.studiomonthly.com

Video Systems
www.videosystems.com

Videography
CMP Entertainment Media Inc.
460 Park Avenue, South, 9th Floor
New York, NY 10016
www.videography.com

Copyright and Script Registration

U.S. Copyright Office
Library of Congress
101 Independence Ave. S.E.
Washington, D.C. 20559-6000
(202) 707-5959
Hours: 8:30am to 5:00pm
Eastern Time, Monday to Friday
www.copyright.gov

Writers Guild of America, West
Registration Department
7000 West Third St.
Los Angeles, CA 90048
(323) 951-4000
(800) 548-4532
www.wga.org

Photo Processing

PhotoWorks
www.PhotoWorks.com

Shutterfly
www.shutterfly.com

Skrudland Photo
www.skrudlandphotoservice.com

Walgreen's Photo Centers
www.walgreens.com
(In blind tests judged by professional photographers, their photo processing ranked better than that of many high-priced professional labs.)

Business Information

Small Business Administration
www.sba.gov

Free Business Training

www.myownbusiness.org

Business Law Links by State

www.smallbusiness.findlaw.com

Corporate-Stock Rules

Security and Exchange Commission
(See "Small Business Information")
www.sec.gov

Business Tax Forms

Internal Revenue Service
www.irs.treas.gov

(Business and nonprofit forms and publications along with some wacky IRS humor)

Bibliography

While we don't recommend blowing your budget on a new library, we also recognize that this one book is by no means the final word. Most of the following books can be found at the library or can be read while standing in the stacks at your favorite bookstore.

Abbott, L. B. *Special Effects: Wire, Tape and Rubber Band Style*. Hollywood: The ASC Press, 1984.

Anderson, John. *Sundancing: Hanging Out and Listening In at America's Most Important Film Festival*. New York: Avon Books, 2000.

Aronofsky, Darren. π - *The Guerilla Diaries*. New York: Faber and Faber, 1998.

Bayer, William. *Breaking Through, Selling Out, Dropping Dead and Other Notes on Filmmaking*. New York: Limelight Editions, 1971.

Beacham, Frank. *American Cinematographer Video Manual — 2nd Edition*. Hollywood: The ASC Press, 1994.

Blake, Larry. *Film Sound Today: An Anthology of Articles from Recording Engineers and Producers*. City Reveille Press, 1984.

Bobker, Lee R. *Elements of Film*. New York: Harcourt Brace Jovanovich, 1974.

Brady, John. *The Craft of the Screenwriter*. New York: Simon and Schuster, 1981.

Buchanan, Mark A., and David John Thomas. *Simplified Business Incorporation: A Self-Help Manual — Minnesota Procedure*. St. Cloud, Minn.: Small Business Development Center, St. Cloud State University.

Chamness, Danford. *The Hollywood Guide to Film Budgeting and Script Breakdown for Low Budget Features*. Los Angeles: The Stanley J. Brooks Company, 1988.

Clark, Frank P. *Special Effects in Motion Pictures*. Hollywood: Society of Motion Picture and Television Engineers.

Corman, Roger, with Jim Jerome. *How I Made a Hundred Movies in Hollywood and Never Lost a Dime*. New York: Random House, 1990.

Detmers, Fred H., ed. *American Cinematographers Manual*. Hollywood: The ASC Press, 1986.

Eisen, Peter J. *Accounting*. New York: Barron's Educational Series, 1985.

Engel, Joel. *Screenwriters on Screenwriting*. New York: Hyperion, 1995.

Favreau, Jon. *Swingers Screenplay*. New York: Hyperion, 1996.

Field, Syd. *Screenplay: The Foundations of Screenwriting*. New York: Dell Publishing, 1979.

Field, Syd. *The Screenwriter's Workbook*. New York: Dell Publishing, 1984.

Froug, William. *The New Screenwriter Looks at the New Screenwriter*. Los Angeles: Silman-James Press, 1992.

Gaspard, John. *Fast, Cheap and Under Control: Lessons Learned from the Greatest Low-Budget Movies of All Time*. Los Angeles: Michael Wiese Productions, 2006.

Gaspard, John, and Dale Newton. *Persistence of Vision: An Impractical Guide to Producing a Feature Film for Under $30,000*. Los Angeles: Michael Wiese Productions, 1996.

Gelmis, Joseph. *The Film Director as Superstar*. New York: Doubleday, 1970.

Glimcher, Sumner, and Warren Johnson. *Movie Making: A Guide to Film Production*. New York: Simon & Schuster, 1975.

Goldman, William. *Adventures in the Screen Trade*. New York: Warner Books, 1983.

Goldman, William. *William Goldman: Five Screenplays*. New York: Applause Books, 1994.

Goldner, Orville, and George E. Turner. *The Making of King Kong*. New York: Ballantine Books, 1976.

Goodell, Gregory. *Independent Feature Film Production*. New York: St. Martin's Press, 1982.

Gore, Chris. *The Ultimate Film Festival Survival Guide*. 3rd edition. Lone Eagle Publishing Company, 2004.

Gore, Chris, and Paul J. Salamoff. *The Complete DVD Book: Designing, Producing and Marketing Your Independent Film on DVD*. Los Angeles: Michael Wiese Productions, 2005.

Grodin, Charles. *It Would Be So Nice If You Weren't Here*. New York: City Vintage Books, 1989.

Hamilton, Peter, and David Rosen. *Off-Hollywood: The Making and Marketing of Independent Films*. New York: Grove Weidenfeld, 1990.

Hunter, Lew. *Lew Hunter's Screenwriting 434*. New York: Perigee Books, 1993.

288

Hurst, Walter E., and William Storm Hale. *Motion Picture Distribution (Business and/or Racket?)*. Hollywood: Seven Arts Press, 1975.

Jarecki, Nicholas. *Breaking In*. New York: Broadway Books, 2001.

Kael, Pauline, Herman J. Mankiewicz, and Orson Welles. *The Citizen Kane Book*. New York: Bantam Books, 1971.

Karlin, Fred. *Listening to Movies — The Film Lover's Guide to Film Music*. Schirmer Books, 1994.

Karlin, Fred, and Rayburn Wright. *On the Track — A Guide to Contemporary Film Scoring*. Schirmer Books, 1990.

Katz, Steven D. *Film Directing Shot by Shot*. Los Angeles: Michael Wiese Productions, 1991.

Katz, Steven D. *Film Directing Cinematic Motion*. Los Angeles: Michael Wiese Productions, 1998.

Linklater, Richard. *Slacker*. New York: St. Martin's Press, 1992.

Litwak, Mark. *Deal Making in the Film and Television Industry*. Los Angeles: Silman-James Press, 1994.

Litwak, Mark. *Contracts in the Film and Television Industry*. Los Angeles: Silman-James Press, 1995.

Lowenstein, Stephen. *My First Movie: 20 Celebrated Directors Talk About Their First Film*. New York: Penguin Books, 2000.

Lumet, Sidney. *Making Movies*. New York: Alfred A. Knopf, 1995.

Lyons, Donald. *Independent Visions*. New York: Ballantine Books, 1994.

Muir, John Kenneth. *An Askew View*. New York: Applause Theatre & Cinema, 2002.

Pierson, John. *Spike, Mike, Slackers & Dykes*. New York: Hyperion, 1995.

Pintoff, Ernest. *Directing 101*. Los Angeles: Michael Wiese Productions, 1999.

Pope, Thomas. *Good Scripts, Bad Scripts: Learning the Craft of Screenwriting Through 25 of the Best and Worst Films in History*. New York: Three Rivers Press, 1998.

Rodriguez, Robert. *Rebel Without a Crew*. New York: Plume, 1996.

Rosen, David, with Pete Hamilton. *Off-Hollywood*. New York: Grove Weidenfeld, 1987

Rosenblum, Ralph, and Robert Karen. *When the Shooting Stops, the Cutting Begins.* New York: Penguin Books, 1979.

Sautter, Carl. *How to Sell Your Screenplay: The Real Rules of Film and Television.* New York: New Chapter Press, 1988.

Schanzer, Karl, and Thomas Lee Wright. *American Screenwriters: The Insiders' Look at the Art, the Craft, and the Business of Writing Movies.* New York: Avon Books, 1993.

Schmidt, Rick. *Feature Filmmaking at Used Car Prices.* New York: Penguin Books, 1988.

Sherman, Eric. *Directing the Film: Film Directors on Their Art.* Boston: Little, Brown & Co., 1976.

Seger, Linda. *Making A Good Script Great.* New York: Dodd, Mead & Co., 1987.

Soderbergh, Steven. *sex, lies and videotape.* New York: Harper & Row, 1990.

Vogler, Christopher. *The Writer's Journey.* Los Angeles: Michael Wiese Productions, 1993.

Warshawski, Morrie. *Shaking the Money Tree.* Los Angeles: Michael Wiese Productions, 1992.

Weston, Judith. *Directing Actors — Creating Memorable Performances for Film and Television.* Los Angeles: Michael Wiese Productions, 1996.

Wiese, Michael. *Film & Video Financing.* Los Angeles: Michael Wiese Productions, 1989.

Wiese, Michael. *Film & Video Marketing.* Los Angeles: Michael Wiese Productions, 1988.

Wiese, Michael. *The Independent Film & Videomakers Guide.* Revised edition. Los Angeles: Michael Wiese Productions, 1990.

Wiese, Michael. *Producer to Producer.* Los Angeles: Michael Wiese Productions, 1993.

Wiese, Michael, and Deke Simon. *Film & Video Budgets. 4th revised edition.* Los Angeles: Michael Wiese Productions, 2006.

Wolff, Jurgen, and Kerry Cox. *Top Secrets: Screenwriting.* Los Angeles: Lone Eagle Publishing Company,

About the Authors

When it comes to producing successful movies on a shoestring, John Gaspard and Dale Newton know of what they speak.

Together they created the digital feature, *Grown Men*, as well as *Resident Alien* and *Beyond Bob*, two critically-acclaimed, ultra-low-budget feature films.

DALE NEWTON wrote and produced *Resident Alien*, produced *Beyond Bob*, and was executive producer on *Grown Men*. He's an award-winning writer of numerous screenplays and scripts. He's also received awards for his work producing and directing films, videos, and audiovisual projects, which he has done for more than 20 years. An early goal in life was to avoid working as an accountant or business manager. Sadly, producing three feature movies has dashed both those dreams.

Besides *Grown Men*, *Resident Alien*, and *Beyond Bob*, JOHN GASPARD has also directed, written, or produced four other features. His other writing credits include the book *Fast, Cheap and Under Control: Lessons Learned From the Greatest Low-Budget Movies of All Time*, also published by Michael Wiese Productions. John has also written for American Public Radio's *Good Evening* and *First House On the Right* programs, along with episodes of the popular European comic-western television series *Lucky Luke*, starring Terence Hill.

Authors Dale Newton (left) and John Gaspard looking for even more ways to save money on the set of their digital movie, Grown Men. *(Photo courtesy of Granite Productions, Unlimited)*

You've Read the Book... *Now See the Movies!*

To find out more about our three ultra-low-budget features, *Resident Alien*, *Beyond Bob*, and our digital feature, *Grown Men*, please visit our web site at: *www.graniteproductions.org*

Each feature was produced using techniques outlined in this book.

RESIDENT ALIEN mixes comedy, science fiction, and romance to create a memorable story about the dangers and complications that occur when you wish on a star — and your dreams come true.

BEYOND BOB is an award-winning comedy from the other side. It's a story of love and friendship, of passion from beyond the grave, and of a love that was made in heaven... and was just too darned important to stay there.

GROWN MEN is an award-winning comic-drama with five interlocking stories that are funny, sexy, sad, bizarre and uplifting, revealing what it means to be a grown man... and demonstrating how far the average male has to go to become one.

Granite Productions, Unlimited
P.O. Box 852
Stillwater, MN 55082
www.graniteproductions.org

FAST, CHEAP & UNDER CONTROL

LESSONS LEARNED FROM THE GREATEST LOW-BUDGET MOVIES OF ALL TIME

JOHN GASPARD

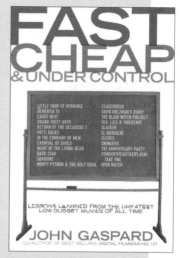

Other filmmakers — with as little money, as little time, and just as many pressures as you'll be facing — have achieved remarkable feats in low-budget filmmaking. They overcame the same problems, and some that you could never have imagined. And now their lessons are available to you, thanks to low-budget guru John Gaspard.

Each of the nearly three dozen low-budget classics examined in this book offer a handful of indispensable how-to's, from stretching your production dollars and making your movie stand out from the pack to developing a unique story, from getting great performances out of your actors when you have limited time and money to establishing your reputation as an indie filmmaker.

Includes revealing new interviews with such low-budget mavericks as Steven Soderbergh (*Sex, Lies, and Videotape*), Roger Corman (*The Little Shop of Horrors*), Jon Favreau (*Swingers*), Henry Jaglom (*Festival in Cannes*), Daniel Myrick (*The Blair Witch Project*), Bob Odenkirk (*Melvin Goes to Dinner*), Barbara Steele (*Caged Heat*), L. M. Kit Carson (*David Holzman's Diary*), Alan Cumming (*The Anniversary Party*), and more.

"*I wish I'd read this book before I made* Re-Animator."
— Stuart Gordon, Director, *Re-Animator*

"*John Gaspard has brought it all together, extracting lessons learned the hard way by successful indie filmmakers. This book is an indispensable manual for those about to go into the trenches.*"
— William Bayer, Author
*Breaking Through, Selling Out, Dropping Dead
and Other Notes on Filmmaking*

JOHN GASPARD co-authored the best-selling *Digital Filmmaking 101: An Essential Guide to Producing Low-Budget Movies* (see page 40). He has directed and/or produced six low-budget features, including the award-winning *Grown Men* and *Beyond Bob*.

$26.95 · 275 PAGES · ORDER NUMBER 59RLS · ISBN: 1-932907-15-7

FAST, CHEAP & WRITTEN THAT WAY

TOP SCREENWRITERS ON WRITING FOR LOW-BUDGET MOVIES

JOHN GASPARD

Hollywood's top screenwriters look back at their early low-budget efforts and provide valuable tips, tricks, and advice on how to create a solid screenplay for a low-budget movie.

Includes in-depth interviews with 23 top screenwriters, including Academy Award®-nominated films *You Can Count on Me*, *Metropolitan*, and *Capote* plus such classics as *Living in Oblivion*, *Repo Man*, *Martin*, *Re-Animator*, *subUrbia*, *Love Letters*, *Personal Velocity*, *Roger Dodger*, *Hester Street*, and *Venice/Venice*. Writers and screenwriters will learn from the pros how to write a low-budget movie, including these "tricks of the trade":

1. Re-write. Then re-write again. Repeat.

2. Never over-explain.

3. Listen to your script being read out-loud — either by actors sitting around a table or by yourself.

4. Write parts actors will want to play.

"Gaspard is the undisputed champ of straight talk when it comes to moviemaking."
— Timothy Rhys, Publisher and Editor
MovieMaker Magazine and *MovieMaker.com*

"Indie filmmakers at all levels would benefit greatly by reading this incredible collection of filmmaker war stories."
— Chris Gore, Founder of *FILMTHREAT* Magazine
and Author of *The Complete DVD Book*

JOHN GASPARD wrote the companion book to this one, *Fast, Cheap, and Under Control: Lessons Learned from the Greatest Low-Budget Movies of All Time*. He also co-authored, with Dale Newton, the books *Digital Filmmaking 101: An Essential Guide to Producing Low-Budget Movies, 1st and 2nd Editions*. He has directed and/or produced six low-budget features, including the digital feature, *Grown Men*, which premiered at the Ashland International Film Festival and won the "Best of Fest/Best Screenplay" award at the Black Point Film Festival.

$26.95 · 320 PAGES · ORDER NUMBER 70RLS · ISBN: 1-932907-30-0

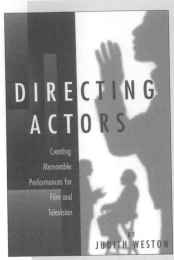

THE WRITER'S JOURNEY
2ND EDITION
MYTHIC STRUCTURE FOR WRITERS

CHRISTOPHER VOGLER

BEST SELLER
OVER 116,500 UNITS SOLD!

See why this book has become an international bestseller and a true classic. *The Writer's Journey* explores the powerful relationship between mythology and storytelling in a clear, concise style that's made it required reading for movie executives, screenwriters, playwrights, scholars, and fans of pop culture all over the world.

Both fiction and nonfiction writers will discover a set of useful myth-inspired storytelling paradigms (i.e., "The Hero's Journey") and step-by-step guidelines to plot and character development. Based on the work of Joseph Campbell, *The Writer's Journey* is a must for all writers interested in further developing their craft.

The updated and revised second edition provides new insights and observations from Vogler's ongoing work on mythology's influence on stories, movies, and man himself.

"This book is like having the smartest person in the story meeting come home with you and whisper what to do In your ear as you write a screenplay. Insight for insight, step for step, Chris Vogler takes us through the process of connecting theme to story and making a script come alive."

> — *Lynda Obst, Producer*
> Sleepless in Seattle, How to Lose a Guy in 10 Days
> *Author*, Hello, He Lied

"This is a book about the stories we write, and perhaps more importantly, the stories we live. It is the most influential work I have yet encountered on the art, nature, and the very purpose of storytelling."

> — *Bruce Joel Rubin, Screenwriter*
> Stuart Little 2, Deep Impact, Ghost, Jacob's Ladder

CHRISTOPHER VOGLER, a top Hollywood story consultant and development executive, has worked on such high-grossing feature films as *The Lion King, The Thin Red Line, Fight Club,* and *Beauty and the Beast.* He conducts writing workshops around the globe.

$24.95 | 325 PAGES | ORDER # 98RLS | ISBN: 0-941188-70-1

SETTING UP YOUR SHOTS
GREAT CAMERA MOVES
EVERY FILMMAKER
SHOULD KNOW

JEREMY VINEYARD

BEST SELLER
OVER 27,300 UNITS SOLD!

Written in straightforward, non-technical language and laid out in a nonlinear format with self-contained chapters for quick, on-the-set reference, *Setting Up Your Shots* is like a Swiss army knife for filmmakers! Using examples from over 140 popular films, this book provides detailed descriptions of more than 100 camera setups, angles, and techniques — in an easy-to-use horizontal "wide-screen" format.

Setting Up Your Shots is an excellent primer for beginning filmmakers and students of film theory, as well as a handy guide for working filmmakers. If you are a director, a storyboard artist, or an animator, use this book. It is the culmination of hundreds of hours of research.

Contains 150 references to the great shots from your favorite films, including *2001: A Space Odyssey*, *Blue Velvet*, *The Matrix*, *The Usual Suspects*, and *Vertigo*.

"Perfect for any film enthusiast looking for the secrets behind creating film. Because of its simplicity of design and straightforward storyboards, Setting Up Your Shots *is destined to be mandatory reading at film schools throughout the world."*
— Ross Otterman, Directed By Magazine

*"*Setting Up Your Shots *is a great book for defining the shots of today. The storyboard examples on every page make it a valuable reference book for directors and DPs alike! This great learning tool should be a boon for writers who want to choose the most effective shot and clearly show it in their boards for the maximum impact."*
— Paul Clatworthy, Creator, StoryBoard Artist and StoryBoard Quick Software

"This book is for both beginning and experienced filmmakers. It's a great reference tool, a quick reminder of the most commonly used shots by the greatest filmmakers of all time."
— Cory Williams, President, Alternative Productions

JEREMY VINEYARD is a filmmaker, internationally published author, and screenwriter. He is currently assembling a cast and crew for a crime feature to be shot in 2005.

$19.95 | 132 PAGES | ORDER # 8RLS | ISBN: 0-941188-73-6

I'LL BE IN MY TRAILER!

THE CREATIVE WARS BETWEEN DIRECTORS & ACTORS

JOHN BADHAM AND CRAIG MODDERNO

What do you do when actors won't do what you tell them to? Remembering his own awkwardness and terror as a beginning director working with actors who always had their own ideas, director John Badham (*Saturday Night Fever*, *WarGames*, *Stakeout*, *The Shield*) has a bookload of knowledge to pass along in this inspired and insightful must-read for directors at all levels of their craft.

Here are no-holds-barred out-of-school tales culled from celebrated top directors and actors like Sydney Pollack, Michael Mann, John Frankenheimer, Mel Gibson, James Woods, Anne Bancroft, Jenna Elfman, Roger Corman and many more that reveal:

- · The 10 worst things and the 10 best things you can say to an actor
- · The nature of an actor's temperament and the true nature of his contributions
- · The nature of creativity and its many pitfalls
- · The processes of casting and rehearsal
- · What happens in an actor's mind during a performance
- · What directors do that alienates actors
- · And much more

"Most young directors are afraid of actors. They come from film school with a heavy technical background, but they don't know how to deal with an actor. Even many experienced directors barely talk to their actors."
— Oliver Stone, Director, JFK, Platoon, Wall Street, Born on the Fourth of July

"Directors have needed a book like this since D.W. Griffith invented the close-up. We directors have to pass along to other directors our hard-learned lessons about actors. Maybe then they won't have to start from total ignorance like I did, like you did, like we all did."
— John Frankenheimer, Director, The Manchurian Candidate, Grand Prix, Seconds

JOHN BADHAM is the award-winning director of such classic films as *Saturday Night Fever*, *Stake Out*, and *WarGames*. Badham currently is the DeMille Professor of Film and Media at Chapman University.

CRAIG MODDERNO is a contributing writer to the *New York Times*.

$26.95 · 243 PAGES · ORDER NUMBER 58RLS · ISBN: 1-932907-14-9

Since 1981, Michael Wiese Productions has been dedicated to providing both novice and seasoned filmmakers with vital information on all aspects of filmmaking. We have published more than 70 books, used in over 500 film schools and countless universities, and by hundreds of thousands of filmmakers worldwide.

Our authors are successful industry professionals who spend innumerable hours writing about the hard stuff: budgeting, financing, directing, marketing, and distribution. They believe that if they share their knowledge and experience with others, more high quality films will be produced.

And that has been our mission, now complemented through our new web-based resources. We invite all readers to visit www.mwp.com to receive free tipsheets and sample chapters, participate in forum discussions, obtain product discounts — and even get the opportunity to receive free books, project consulting, and other services offered by our company.

Our goal is, quite simply, to help you reach your goals. That's why we give our readers the most complete portal for filmmaking knowledge available — in the most convenient manner.

We truly hope that our books and web-based resources will empower you to create enduring films that will last for generations to come.

Let us hear from you at anytime.

Sincerely,
Michael Wiese
Publisher, Filmmaker

www.mwp.com

Cinematic Storytelling: *The 100 Most Powerful Film Conventions Every Filmmaker Must Know* / Jennifer Van Sijll / $24.95

Complete DVD Book, The: *Designing, Producing, and Marketing Your Independent Film on DVD* / Chris Gore and Paul J. Salamoff / $26.95

Complete Independent Movie Marketing Handbook, The: *Promote, Distribute & Sell Your Film or Video* / Mark Steven Bosko / $39.95

Costume Design 101: *The Business and Art of Creating Costumes for Film and Television* / Richard La Motte / $19.95

Could It Be a Movie?: *How to Get Your Ideas Out of Your Head and Up on the Screen* / Christina Hamlett / $26.95

Creating Characters: *Let Them Whisper Their Secrets* Marisa D'Vari / $26.95

Crime Writer's Reference Guide, The: *1001 Tips for Writing the Perfect Crime* Martin Roth / $20.95

Cut by Cut: *Editing Your Film or Video* Gael Chandler / $35.95

Digital Filmmaking 101, 2nd Edition: *An Essential Guide to Producing Low-Budget Movies* / Dale Newton and John Gaspard / $24.95

Digital Moviemaking, 2nd Edition: *All the Skills, Techniques, and Moxie You'll Need to Turn Your Passion into a Career* / Scott Billups / $26.95

Directing Actors: *Creating Memorable Performances for Film and Television* Judith Weston / $26.95

Directing Feature Films: *The Creative Collaboration Between Directors, Writers, and Actors* / Mark Travis / $26.95

Eye is Quicker, The: *Film Editing; Making a Good Film Better* Richard D. Pepperman / $27.95

Fast, Cheap & Under Control: *Lessons Learned from the Greatest Low-Budget Movies of All Time* / John Gaspard / $26.95

Film & Video Budgets, 4th Updated Edition Deke Simon and Michael Wiese / $26.95

Film Directing: Cinematic Motion, 2nd Edition Steven D. Katz / $27.95

Film Directing: Shot by Shot, *Visualizing from Concept to Screen* Steven D. Katz / $27.95

Film Director's Intuition, The: *Script Analysis and Rehearsal Techniques* Judith Weston / $26.95

Film Production Management 101: *The Ultimate Guide for Film and Television Production Management and Coordination* / Deborah S. Patz / $39.95

Filmmaking for Teens: *Pulling Off Your Shorts* Troy Lanier and Clay Nichols / $18.95

First Time Director: *How to Make Your Breakthrough Movie* Gil Bettman / $27.95

From Word to Image: *Storyboarding and the Filmmaking Process* Marcie Begleiter / $26.95

Hitting Your Mark, 2nd Edition: *Making a Life – and a Living – as a Film Director* Steve Carlson / $22.95

Hollywood Standard, The: *The Complete and Authoritative Guide to Script Format and Style* / Christopher Riley / $18.95

I Could've Written a Better Movie Than That!: *How to Make Six Figures as a Script Consultant even if You're not a Screenwriter* / Derek Rydall / $26.95

Independent Film Distribution: *How to Make a Successful End Run Around the Big Guys* / Phil Hall / $26.95

Independent Film and Videomakers Guide – 2nd Edition, The: *Expanded and Updated* / Michael Wiese / $29.95

Inner Drives: *How to Write and Create Characters Using the Eight Classic Centers of Motivation* / Pamela Jaye Smith / $26.95

I'll Be in My Trailer!: *The Creative Wars Between Directors & Actors* John Badham and Craig Modderno / $26.95

Moral Premise, The: *Harnessing Virtue & Vice for Box Office Success* Stanley D. Williams, Ph.D. / $24.95

Myth and the Movies: *Discovering the Mythic Structure of 50 Unforgettable Films* / Stuart Voytilla / $26.95

On the Edge of a Dream: *Magic and Madness in Bali* Michael Wiese / $16.95

Perfect Pitch, The: *How to Sell Yourself and Your Movie Idea to Hollywood* Ken Rotcop / $16.95

Power of Film, The Howard Suber / $27.95

Psychology for Screenwriters: *Building Conflict in your Script* William Indick, Ph.D. / $26.95

Save the Cat!: *The Last Book on Screenwriting You'll Ever Need* Blake Snyder / $19.95

Screenwriting 101: *The Essential Craft of Feature Film Writing* Neill D. Hicks / $16.95

Screenwriting for Teens: *The 100 Principles of Screenwriting Every Budding Writer Must Know* / Christina Hamlett / $18.95

Script-Selling Game, The: *A Hollywood Insider's Look at Getting Your Script Sold and Produced* / Kathie Fong Yoneda / $16.95

Selling Your Story in 60 Seconds: *The Guaranteed Way to get Your Screenplay or Novel Read* / Michael Hauge / $12.95

Setting Up Your Scenes: *The Inner Workings of Great Films* Richard D. Pepperman / $24.95

Setting Up Your Shots: *Great Camera Moves Every Filmmaker Should Know* Jeremy Vineyard / $19.95

Shaking the Money Tree, 2nd Edition: *The Art of Getting Grants and Donations for Film and Video Projects* / Morrie Warshawski / $26.95

Sound Design: *The Expressive Power of Music, Voice, and Sound Effects in Cinema* / David Sonnenschein / $19.95

Stealing Fire From the Gods, 2nd Edition: *The Complete Guide to Story for Writers & Filmmakers* / James Bonnet / $26.95

Storyboarding 101: *A Crash Course in Professional Storyboarding* James Fraioli / $19.95

Ultimate Filmmaker's Guide to Short Films, The: *Making It Big in Shorts* Kim Adelman / $16.95

What Are You Laughing At?: *How to Write Funny Screenplays, Stories, and More* / Brad Schreiber / $19.95

Working Director, The: *How to Arrive, Thrive & Survive in the Director's Chair* Charles Wilkinson / $22.95

Writer's Journey, – 2nd Edition, The: *Mythic Structure for Writers* Christopher Vogler / $24.95

Writer's Partner, The: *1001 Breakthrough Ideas to Stimulate Your Imagination* Martin Roth / $24.95

Writing the Action Adventure: *The Moment of Truth* Neill D. Hicks / $14.95

Writing the Comedy Film: *Make 'Em Laugh* Stuart Voytilla and Scott Petri / $14.95

Writing the Killer Treatment: *Selling Your Story Without a Script* Michael Halperin / $14.95

Writing the Second Act: *Building Conflict and Tension in Your Film Script* Michael Halperin / $19.95

Writing the Thriller Film: *The Terror Within* Neill D. Hicks / $14.95

Writing the TV Drama Series: *How to Succeed as a Professional Writer in TV* Pamela Douglas / $24.95

DVD & VIDEOS

Field of Fish: *VHS Video* Directed by Steve Tanner and Michael Wiese, Written by Annamaria Murphy / $9.95

Hardware Wars: *DVD* / Written and Directed by Ernie Fosselius / $14.95

Sacred Sites of the Dalai Lamas – DVD, The: *A Pilgrimage to Oracle Lake* A Documentary by Michael Wiese / $22.95